AF412673

Politics and the Criteria of Truth

Politics and the Criteria of Truth

Alireza Shomali

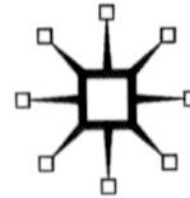

First published 2010 by
PALGRAVE MACMILLAN

Palgrave Macmillan in the UK is an imprint of Macmillan Publishers Limited, registered in England, company number 785998, of Houndmills, Basingstoke, Hampshire RG21 6XS.

Palgrave Macmillan in the US is a division of St Martin's Press LLC, 175 Fifth Avenue, New York, NY 10010.

Palgrave Macmillan is the global academic imprint of the above companies and has companies and representatives throughout the world.

Palgrave® and Macmillan® are registered trademarks in the United States, the United Kingdom, Europe and other countries.

ISBN: 978–0–230–23767–4 hardback

This book is printed on paper suitable for recycling and made from fully managed and sustained forest sources. Logging, pulping and manufacturing processes are expected to conform to the environmental regulations of the country of origin.

A catalogue record for this book is available from the British Library.

A catalog record for this book is available from the Library of Congress.

10 9 8 7 6 5 4 3 2 1
19 18 17 16 15 14 13 12 11 10

Printed and bound in Great Britain by
CPI Antony Rowe, Chippenham and Eastbourne

To my father and mother
for their love beyond language
and
to my siblings
for their support and sacrifices

Contents

Acknowledgments

The genesis of this book is in my doctoral dissertation, completed at Syracuse University's Maxwell School of Citizenship and Public Affairs. In the process of its formation, I received intellectual loans and insightful suggestions from Fred M. Frohock, Mehrzad Boroujerdi, Mark E. Rupert, Elizabeth F. Cohen, Reza Lahroodi, and Martha J. Reineke, and also from anonymous reviewers. For that I am grateful. My most special thanks go to Linda Martín Alcoff, who supervised this study from beginning to the end and kindly allowed me to use the expression *political epistemology*, which she has coined, for the approach utilized in this volume. I thank Jacquie Meyer, Candy Brooks, and Ruth Homrighaus for their support, and I am grateful to all the staff of Palgrave-Macmillan—in particular to executive editor Priyanka Gibbons—for their careful and coordinated efforts in the publishing of this book. Finally, I am grateful to Wheaton College (Massachusetts) for providing me with a serene atmosphere in which I could carry out the final revision of the manuscript.

Introduction

In the tumult of modern times, Hannah Arendt complains, philosophy, the search for truth, has become "a solitary business" (Canovan 1992, p. 254). Great philosophers have a taste for "rational tyranny" (Sluga 2008, p. 92), and Plato, the father of Western political thought, is hostile to democracy. Political philosophy is shallow and in its triviality contributes to the "banality of evil." Moreover, the philosopher thinks—or wishes to think—in solitude and disdains the authentically political experience of acting in the polis and among others. *Apolitia*, the "indifference and contempt for the world of the city," she continues, characterizes all post-Platonic philosophy (1990, p. 91). Eternal truth, according to such philosophers, is achievable only if the philosopher turns away from the ever-changing polis, the world of "becoming," and seeks the essential of "being." As Plato states, "The organ of knowledge must be turned around from the world of becoming together with the entire soul...until the soul is able to endure the contemplation of essence and the brightest region of being, that is to say, that which we call the good" (1994, p. 518d). Understanding the truth, in other words, requires a purified form of reasoning that withdraws from human opinions and passions in the polis and from entanglement in politics. Through this purified reasoning, an apolitical truth/*episteme*—with a transhistorical content that transcends the ever-changing particulars of everyday life and its constituent *doxa*—discloses itself to the philosopher who has withdrawn from society.

As a result, and possessing the eternal truth, the post-Platonic philosopher does not need to intellectually persuade the masses. As a philosopher-king, he subordinates politics to the universal truth of philosophy. Using a more professional form of intellectual coercion, he "leads" the masses through the pathway of deductive, and not dialogical, reasoning and, quite frequently indeed, victimizes "living human beings on the altars of abstractions" (Berlin 1991, p. 16).

Arendt believes that the execution of Socrates in the Athenian polis had a traumatic effect on Plato and partially caused the subsequent divorce between thinking/finding truth and interacting in the polis (see Dolan 2000, pp. 263–4). She also offers a philosophical account of this divorce. This account helps me clarify an introductory understanding of the relationship between knowledge and its constitutive sociopolitical context—an understanding which, I hope, will become clearer as this volume unfolds.

According to Arendt, post-Platonic philosophical thought cannot incorporate politics, since its area of concern is "the man"—or "the subject," in its more modern versions—as a universal concept. In the view of the universal concept of man all particular men are basically the same. They are repetitions/cases of the same universal essence of the individual. Accordingly, the subject-centered view implies, there is something political in man that belongs to its essence. Arendt, however, states that this "simply is not so; *man* [as either a species or an individual, i.e., a repetition of the same essence] is apolitical," because "politics arises *between men,* and so quite *outside* of [the so-called essence/concept of] *man.*" Politics, Arendt insists, rests on the "fact of human plurality" (2005, pp. 93–5), on human differentiation, on *different* men's coexistence and associations. Politics is based on men's equal right to be different—and, in Jean-Paul Sartre's terms, on man's having concrete sociopolitical and material *existence* that precedes his *essence.* In Arendt's view, post-Platonic philosophy cannot account for politics, since it does not go beyond the concept/essence of man. Philosophy pays dearly—indeed, as greatly as the cost of democracy in Plato's case—for its infatuation with the abstract concept, the universal individual, or the "subject" of the modern time.

Plurality—the fact that "nobody is ever the same as anyone else"—is a condition of human life and action (Arendt 1998, p. 8). Men live, act, and interact in the polis as political animals, and the principal medium of their human affair is speech. Human being, Aristotle states, has a political way of life. *Bios politikos* is the sphere of human action needed to maintain the polis. The polis, in its turn, is where excellence creates beautiful deeds (Aristotle 1996, pp. 184–7). According to Arendt, politics underlines the very togetherness, the living-together, of the people who apply praxis (action) and lexis (speech), as the premier of all human capacities. Lexis and praxis "belong" to one another (1998, p. 25). They comprise each other. Action and speech are, in words that

I will frequently use throughout this study, *mutually constitutive*. They mediate through one another so much so that each one is the condition for the possibility of the other. Speech and action, Arendt writes, are "coeval and coequal, of the same rank and the same kind" (p. 26). And "thought," including meaning and truth content, is "secondary to speech" (p. 25). In other words—and this is the way I tend to understand Arendt—the ensemble of lexis/praxis, the very living-together of the people in the polis, must be seen as that which makes meaning and truth content possible in the first place. Meaning and truth content are "secondary" to the lexis/praxis ensemble not because they come after it in a temporal sequence, not because they are reducible to the latter, but in the sense that one should not abstract them from the togetherness of the people in the city. They are secondary to speech/action because the knowledge of meaning and truth content cannot emerge without attendance to the contextual reality of political life that harbors them.

In a sense, the present study seeks to elaborate on this point. Together, speech and praxis preserve the polis, constitute its politics, and create a people as *zoon politikon.* To be political, to live in the polis, demands that the ensemble of praxis/lexis continuously reproduce itself. Consequently, speech—its meaning and its truth claims—cannot be understood as detached from praxis. Since politics is but the continuous happening of the praxis/lexis ensemble, we may conclude that for Arendt's Aristotle, the meaning and truth of speech cannot be detached from politics without harming the very humanity of man. Indeed, what Arendt articulates as the modern man's "thoughtlessness" signifies the detachment of truth/speech from (totalitarian) politics (2006b; also see Bernstein 1996, chapters 7–8).

As we have seen, the truth-holder philosopher does not engage in dialogue with the people's doxa. He uses violent force, and, as Arendt states, "violence is mute" (1998, p. 26). It is speechless and accordingly lacks truth content or justification. The post-Platonic philosopher is opposite to Arendt's Socrates. Socrates knows that he does not know any final truth (if any). He approaches his fellow citizens as a friend, respects the inequality of people, and trusts the exchange of opinions in "friendship" to equalize himself and his fellow citizens as "equal partners in a common world" (Arendt 1990, p. 83). Freedom of the partners in dialogue and their openness toward one another's views—both integrated in the Aristotelian notion of friendship—are necessary preconditions for the disclosure of the partial truth of doxa within the dialogue.

Arendt's politics, and, accordingly, meaning and truth content (as constituents of the speech/action ensemble, the polis) reside in the in-between, the intersubjective public life. It is here that "worldly reality truly and reliably appears" (Arendt 1998, p. 57); it is this space that the "inter-subjective individual" (Habermas 1991, p. 138), the *social individual*, inhabits. The abstract man or the autonomous subject is neither the locus of politics nor the holder of truth and meaning. Following this line of thought, the present study situates the truth and meaning of lexis in its constitutive relationship with praxis. This study, in other words, is a call for seeing truth and meaning *in* their sociopolitical context, in their mutually constitutive relationship with the "material" reality of communal life. It is a call for paying attention to the political makeup of knowledge and to the fact that meaning and truth content are constituents of politics, of the very togetherness of the people who apply praxis and lexis.

Perhaps the same cause that fails post-Platonic philosophy in integrating genuine politics—that is, infatuation with the *abstract* man/subject— also accounts for this philosophy's identification of knowledge with *abstract* and universal truth that is available only to the abstract knower. (Accordingly, knowledge is achieved when the abstract knower, the out-of-cave/city self, is mythically—in Theodor Adorno's terms—united with the universal concept/idea.) The present-day "fall" of the abstract subject (see Honneth 1998) and the "exhaustion of the cogito" (see Canguilhem 2005), however, has been detrimental to the subject-centered understanding of knowledge. The fall decentralizes the allegedly self-sufficient subject, underlines the latter's social constructedness and materiality, and undermines the associating idea of normativity. In so doing, it leaves us with "nihilism," in Arendt's words (2005, p. 103), or "critical barbarity," in Bruno Latour's terms (2004, p. 240).

In our time, Latour writes, scientific, ethical, and political criticisms have run out of steam. Criticism has lost its "sure ground" (2004, p. 227); that is, a critic can no longer base his or her claim on "facts" without being accused of naïveté, of not taking seriously the fact that facts, including the fact of the knower/subject, are but social constructions, laden with theories and prejudgments, formed by power relations and interests. At present, Latour continues, explanations based on genesis—for example, those based on power relations, society, and discourse—have left no room for justifications based on epistemic validity. Reality, "the object," is no longer the "stubborn" thing (p. 237) that used to settle our disputes, and the knowers are no longer an abstract subject of pure reasoning unpolluted by materiality. Claims to objectivity are weakened, and science's solid realism is substituted for by constructivism.

We are left, Latour states, with a method of criticism that disqualifies general norms and universal claims of truth as fetishes of the falling subjects who are blind to forces that take away their freedom and act on them. These forces include "economic infrastructures, fields of discourse, social domination, race, class and gender," and so forth (2004, p. 238). What makes this method of criticism barbaric is that when it comes to these forces, the critic takes them as unmediated and purely accessible realities. It is as if a selective use of "solid causality of objectivity" (p. 239), or a positivistic realism, enables the critic to disqualify the positions under critique (as constructed fetishes caused by a chain of forces) and simultaneously to regard these forces as facts accessible to the critic himself! In other words, an element of arbitrariness resides in the current method of criticism: While the theory, person, or action being critiqued is seen as materially constituted and caused, the critic's position is not. The latter's access to the constructing and causal forces is conceived as unmediated by the same forces. Those forces, moreover, are seen as objective/given causes, unmediated by the mind, life, and language of the critic! As Latour states, "Antifetishists debunk objects they don't believe in by showing the productive and projective forces of people; then, without ever making the connection, they use objects they do believe in to resort to the causalist or mechanist explanation and debunk conscious capacities of people whose behavior they don't approve of" (p. 241).

It seems that we are left with a dilemma. One choice is to close our eyes to the arbitrariness and inconsistency of barbaric criticism, and the other is to apply the materialist logic of causality to the critic's position too and, therefore, embrace epistemic relativism. Yet the dilemma appears so only to those who bet epistemic normativity wholly on the abstract subject and universalism.

Rather than repeatedly pointing to the problems with truth concepts, Latour calls for a reconstructive moment in the evaluation of science and of truth. After all, political criticism and Enlightenment imply demythologization, and accordingly, political emancipatory activity must proceed in the name of truth: Epistemic relativism and epistemic absolutism are equally dangerous and irrational. In the postpositivist era, in which Cartesian ontology and epistemology must be overcome (see Taylor 1995) and ahistorical metaphysics should be abandoned, we require a normative criterion of truth. Without it, the rationality of our beliefs and the justifiability of our political acts are both in question: For epistemic as well as political reasons, then, we need a normative criterion of truth.

Whereas nostalgic yearning for the resurrection of the prefall subject and its abstract universals is not a proper reaction, is there any other way to secure epistemic normativity and make real critique possible? Dialectical materialism—and not the sheer materialism of antifetishists—might open the horizon for a positive answer, for the proposal that perhaps a normative coherence theory of knowledge is in principle defensible. This volume suggests that it is possible to be attentive to the political makeup of knowledge and simultaneously to secure normativity and reject epistemic relativism. It is this modest suggestion that introduces *the project of political epistemology*, not as an already developed model of normativity but as a nascent research program. This program benefits from the views of a variety of thinkers who might seem strangers at first, from Karl Marx to Hans-Georg Gadamer and from Theodor Adorno to Jacques Derrida.

As Thomas Kuhn resourcefully argues, when the dominant paradigm (the foundationalist epistemology, in our case) is weakening and the new paradigm has not yet emerged, a diversity of voices will be raised, and ideas that used to be deemed irrelevant under the dominant paradigm come to the fore. Following Kuhn's model of explanation, I envision the project of political epistemology as an emerging research program that signals dissatisfaction with the dominant but failing epistemological paradigm. The project of political epistemology hopes for a future *hybrid paradigm* that is open to the voices of the "other," to Marx, to Derrida, and to Adorno, the thinkers who are considered irrelevant under the foundationalist epistemological paradigm. I situate the *project* of political epistemology—and not "political epistemology" as a systematic, well-articulated model in a full-fledged paradigm—in the turmoil of the Kuhnian era of crisis. In this context, I learn from each thinker's diverse contestations and reconstructions of the traditional ontology of truth. I witness that they have political understandings of knowledge and investigate how they indirectly juxtapose the political nature of knowledge with its epistemic normativity.

Political epistemology is a research project that investigates how politics frames questions of knowledge. As a strategic activity to make the production of truth meaningful, ethically valuable, and politically emancipatory, it promotes a new understanding of the theory–practice relationship, a new understanding of the connection between political engagement and epistemic normativity. The project of political epistemology seeks an epistemological criterion of truth that is attentive to the sociopolitical conditions that determine meaning. This research project presupposes recognition of the roles that interests, social contexts, moral commitments, political involvements, and the historicity of the knower play in the formation of knowledge.

The project of political epistemology conceives of a normative criterion of truth, *new coherence*, as the relation of mutual support among the superstructural and the structural elements of reality. *New coherence* is new because it transcends the traditional coherence theory of truth that defines truth as logical consistency among propositions. The concept of new coherence and the epistemological new coherentist theory of truth were first introduced by Linda Martín Alcoff in *Real Knowing: New Versions of the Coherence Theory* (1996). The present study theoretically builds on the arguments and articulations of the new coherentist theory of truth as developed in Alcoff's work. This volume's contribution to Alcoff's articulation of new coherence is to argue that the criterion of new coherence is *also* new because it ties the disclosure of truth to the alteration of the present contradictory reality. New coherence has to do with openness toward the possibilities of reality being otherwise than it is in the present. In other words, new coherence harbors the notion of praxis, the actual change of the present reality in the name of doing justice to the other. And this is what I hear from Derrida among others: As a version of the project in the era of Kuhnian crisis, the project of political epistemology can be seen as deconstructive, inasmuch as it changes the present in order to open a site for the incoming of the different.

The chapters that follow argue that despite the important differences in the ways that Marx, Adorno, Gadamer, and Derrida look at the subject/knower, give centrality to it in the ontology of meaning (Gadamer), disseminate it into the other and the other others (Derrida), and consider it as a social individual with aspirations of self-fulfillment (Adorno and Marx), they nonetheless share a political understanding of knowledge, of epistemic normativity, and of the way politics frames the question of knowledge. As indicated above, this study does not develop a system or a new epistemological model. It proposes nothing more than a sketchy comment on how the task of finding new accounts of normativity might proceed. At the time of crisis, even little proposals like this might come in handy.

One last point before the introduction of the following chapters: In addition to the above-mentioned Arendtian interpretation, the term *political* in the present study indicates whatever changes, solidifies, resists, weakens, or strengthens a specific pattern of differential forces and power relationships. The third, correlated meaning of the term *political* as it is applied in the expression *political epistemology* follows

Karl Marx's logic in conceptualizing the notion of *political economy*. (The rationale for this designation is discussed in the Chapter 1.)

Indeed, Marx and his dialectical materialism frame the intellectual sphere in which the present investigation of the lexis–praxis relationship proceeds. It is worth mentioning that by "dialectical materialism," I do not mean a metaphysical system akin to the transhistorical universals of post-Platonic philosophy. Such a system gains universality and consistency at the cost of abstraction from the *material* reality, the becoming, and the non-identical-to-itself. As Simon Jarvis accurately states, "A seamlessly noncontradictory system could never be [dialectical] 'materialist,' because what makes such a system a system is the reduction of the different and the variable to unchanging identity" (2004, p. 80). Dialectical materialism is not primarily a metaphysical doctrine but a "practice of thinking" that seeks, "the end of suffering" (p. 84). It has an "empirical substance," the experience of "the resistance which otherness offers to identity" (Adorno 1973, pp. 160–1). There is, therefore, an ethical justification for the application of dialectical materialism. As Theodor Adorno states, it is the feeling of "all pains and all negativity" of the oppressed other, the damaged life, which is one of the "moving forces of dialectical thinking" (1973, p. 202). Ethical and epistemic justifications, this volume argues, are mutually implicative.

While wishing to respect their differences, and through dialectical materialist readings of their works, I explore in each chapter the contribution of a particular thinker to the project of political epistemology. Chapter 1 begins by justifying my choice to use a dialectical materialist perspective throughout the study. The chapter introduces Karl Marx's transcendental analysis, applied in his critique of political economy, and explores Marx's idea of the historicity and social situatedness of concepts. Marx presents sociopolitical reality as a transcendental condition of meaning and truth, and in so doing he helps us conceptualize and justify new coherence as the best criterion of truth. The chapter defines the concept of "new coherence" and also explains why the project of political epistemology is designated as such—why it is a project and how it is aware of its own sociopolitical function, motivation, and embeddedness.

The project of political epistemology presents strong similarities to critical theory. To verify this claim, the second chapter examines those similarities and studies the lessons that participants in the project of political epistemology learn from the Frankfurt School thinkers, especially Theodor Adorno and his idea of *negative dialectic*. Negative dialectic is in fact a perpetual alteration of the concept into its opposites—to what the concept can be but is not. This observation, the chapter argues, suggests a new understanding of the theory–practice relationship. According to this understanding, a truthful critical theory can project normative goals, politically change reality, and forge its truth through a practice of making the truth actually happen. For historical, political, and philosophical reasons, critical theoreticians needed a new, nonpositivist epistemology, though they did not finally articulate one. Addressing this need, the chapter offers a political epistemological reading of critical theory, arguing that critical theory opens up a space for offering new coherence as the normative criterion of truth.

Chapter 3 asks whether the project of political epistemology and the strong program in the sociology of knowledge are basically the same. If yes, why bother to (re)articulate political epistemology? And if no, then what are the differences between them? Does the project of political epistemology suffer from the same sort of relativism that dogs the sociology of knowledge? Does political epistemology, in order to be normative, offer a response to the allegation of relativism? In order to underline the differences between the two, the chapter looks into the nature of understanding and provides a materialist dialectic reading of Hans-Georg Gadamer's ontology of understanding. According to this reading, Gadamer's hermeneutic philosophy contributes to the project of political epistemology by showing the interactive and social nature of understanding. This investigation provides us with sufficient reasons to prove the falsity of the epistemic neutrality thesis, the crux of the strong program. The third chapter, therefore, highlights the relativist nature of the strong thesis. It also examines the way in which the project of political epistemology rejects the strong program's nonevaluative fiat and thus remains normative and nonrelativist.

In order to understand the politics of cognitive change in cognitive/material reality, to see how the alteration of the superstructure affects the superstructure/structure reality, Chapter 4 inquires into the nature of contingency. The notion of contingency of language, consciousness, and reality extends a site for studying the relationships between political act, ethics, and epistemic normativity. Within this site, I believe, Jacques Derrida's ideas of *différance* and deconstruction can help us envision a pattern of the relation of mutual implication between epistemic normativity as new coherence, radical ethical normativity as openness, and political activity in the name of doing justice to the other and other others. Far from saying that political epistemology as such (let's assume that such an expression has meaning!) is deconstructive, the chapter suggests that perhaps *one* version of political epistemology can be deconstructive in its method. Therefore, if the reader disagrees with my reading of Derrida, I nonetheless hope that this disagreement does not negatively affect the arguments offered in the previous chapters. In this last chapter, I do not claim that Derrida is an epistemologist with an articulate ontology of truth. Rather, the modest claim advanced is that Derrida's teachings open a site for a political understanding of normativity.

Accordingly, the chapter reconstructs/reinterprets Derrida's notion of *différance* as a play of forces. Through a dialectical materialist reading, it argues that Derrida's *différance* should not be understood as a mere semiological phenomenon abstract from other constituents of cognitive/ material reality. The chapter explores the way in which Derrida's notion of deconstruction might account for coexistence between political strategic acts, ethical responsibility, and epistemic normativity. Here, the final observation is that political activity in search of justice, an ethical mode of relating to the other, and the epistemic pursuit of truth cannot be abstracted from one another.

1
The Project of Political Epistemology: Its Grounds and Method

In order to provide a theoretical justification for initiating the project of political epistemology, I begin this chapter with a critique of the commonsensical and traditional ontology of truth. According to the traditional ontology, consciousness and reality are two separate "things." Thus, truth as the representation of independent reality transcends human beings' sociopolitical involvements. Empiricists and rationalists have historically promoted the traditional ontology of truth and ignored the constitutive role of the social and political involvement of the subject/knower with reality and in the processes of meaning making and truth formation. In the first section of this chapter, I explore G. W. F. Hegel's immanent critique of empiricism and rationalism. Against empiricism, Hegel contends that any sensory experience is already for-us; that is, our point of view, interests, projects, sociopolitical positions, and so forth are constitutive of it. Contrary to rationalism, Hegel argues that we cannot abstract reason or logic from nature and objective reality. Reason is concrete, and rationality is intersubjective, social, and interactive.

Hegel's immanent critiques are also determinate. He substitutes a dialectical ontology for the traditional one. In the second section of the current chapter, I investigate Hegel's dialectical account of the in-itself-for-us and argue that a valid epistemological grasp of truth and consciousness must necessarily attend to the relation of reciprocal constitutiveness between cognition and reality. The dialectal view implies that reality, the in-itself-for-us, is contradictory. Hegel offers this position in his discussion of the "inverted world." In the third section, I consider how Hegel's notion of the inverted world contributes a new understanding of contradiction to the project of political epistemology. This new concept of contradiction demands that participants in the project also articulate a new idea of consistency as the normative criterion of truth.

How can we reconcile a dialectical ontology that endorses the contradictory nature of cognitive/material reality with an epistemological criterion that promotes coherence? To address this question, I shall explore Hegel's concept of coherence in the next section. Here, I argue that only a new conceptualization of consistency, that is, *new coherence*, can successfully accomplish the above compromise.

Through a comparison between Marx's and Hegel's notions of dialectic, the following section clarifies why Marx's dialectical materialism provides the project of political epistemology with better articulations of new coherence. This section explains that Hegel's would-be epistemology is essentialist about truth and as such harbors universality claims of a metaphysical kind that forget their own situatedness. Marx's dialectical materialism, on the other hand, helps us retrieve a tacit theory of meaning and truth in Marx's thought. Marx presents sociopolitical reality as a transcendental condition of meaning and truth and in so doing helps us conceptualize and justify new coherence as the best criterion of truth. To better understand transcendental analysis, I examine three examples of its application: Marx's treatment of Feuerbach; his analysis of the social, political, and psychological *a priories* of private property; and, finally, his critique of ideology. I then investigate the meaning of transcendental analysis in Kant and show how it is different from a dialectical materialist understanding of transcendental analysis. While Kant's transcendental argument is ahistorical, Marx's investigation of the sociopolitical conditions of possibility of meaning is empirical and historical. This section also explains the reasons why the project of political epistemology is designated as such, why it is a project, and how it is aware of its own sociopolitical function, motivation, and embeddedness.

The concluding section inquires into the features of a new epistemology that would allow us to overcome the traditional epistemology. The new epistemology must harbor a dialectical-materialist ontology of truth. It should be normative and should take new coherence as its criterion of truth. It should be aware of its political motivation and function. This observation alludes to similarities between the project of political epistemology and critical theory.

Hegel's critique of empiricist and rationalist ontologies of truth

It might seem rather commonsensical and intuitive that consciousness (experience, knowledge, and cognition) is one thing and reality is something else. The epistemological question that follows this specific ontology is how consciousness ever moves from within-us, to the beyond, to reach the thing-in-itself. In the commonsensical view, consciousness is either a tool for the active seizure of the thing-in-itself or a mirror for the rather passive representation of reality. In both cases, there remains the threat of distortion when the tool or the mirror strives to re-present something that is "the very opposite of its own end" (Hegel 1974a, p. 44). As Hegel describes the commonsensical ontology, "the Absolute [the reality] stands on one side and...knowledge on the other side, by itself and cut off from the Absolute." This knowledge, by being outside the reality, "is certainly outside truth." It nevertheless aspires to be true, though it is seemingly doomed to be different and cut off from the Absolute/true, since "the Absolute alone is true" (p. 45). The inherent possibility of distortion Hegel describes has prompted some (Descartes and Locke, among others) to pursue a method of securing a foundation for knowledge—a set of rules and cautionary principles independent of and prior to the sought-for knowledge.

The idea of a self-enclosed realm of experience, then, leads to belief in a subject/mind separate and distinct from the object/reality and the demand for a methodology that secures the movement from the former to the latter. Both concepts are problematic. Hegel argues that if experience is *in* the mind and the thing-in-itself is outside, one cannot be sure that methodology will ever prevent skepticism. In other words, if what we immediately know is our experience, we can only hope for a correspondence between the knowledge in the subject and the thing-in-itself. Hence, the correspondence theory of truth seems incapable of providing the certainty that Cartesian epistemology promises us.

In *Phenomenology of Spirit*, Hegel's immanent critique of traditional epistemology is associated with a determinate critique of traditional ontology. Hegel reveals, first, how traditional epistemology ends in skepticism and, as such, fails to fulfill its own promise to secure the truth of knowledge. Then—and far from giving up the notion of truth and knowledge—he offers his completely original solution in synthesizing sensory experience, nature, and reason, as well as uncovering the connections between them all.

An empiricist in pursuit of the *immediate* maintains that the justified starting point in the deductive method of argumentation is sense-certainty. Sense-certainty, as an epistemological theory, views the "truest" knowledge as an immediate, that is, as unmediated by concepts (Hegel 1974a, p. 54). Sense-certainty as an ontological theory, moreover, regards the particular objects as the most real reality. Though Kant criticizes this position by pointing out that any sensory experience is always for-us, Hegel underlines Kant's failure to take the next crucial step to realize that the realm of the immediate is *already* a synthesis of idea and nature, subject and object. While the sense-certainty argument regards consciousness as capable of identifying particular objects without the mediation of universal concepts, Hegel reminds us that even an inarticulate pointing requires the definition of a context and the identification of the particular thing through its name and properties. While for sense-certainty the object is given, for Hegel nothing is simply given.

According to Hegel, "by saying 'this Here,' 'this Now,' 'an individual thing,' I say all Thises, Heres, Nows, or Individuals" (p. 58). In other words, indexicals (e.g., "this," "that," "I") are in fact universals. They can refer to infinite things or referents, and we cannot distinguish one referent from the other just by pointing at it and saying, "that."[1] By definition, a universal property, concept, or proposition can be defined independently from all particular instances of it. As such, the designation of a particular presupposes a context in which the act of referencing (e.g., pointing, saying "this," or asserting more articulate sentences) is defined. This context provides some prior understanding of what kind of thing is being pointed to. Thus, the ontological claim that the world consists of atomic facts that correspond to, and are manifest in, atomic statements or data loses its justification. This is because the atomic data and statements are necessarily in part constituted by universal concepts and properties, by something more than what an empiricist allows.

Indeed, what refers to a particular is not an atomic proposition. It is people, engaged in intersubjective and social acts, who assert propositions against determinate contexts and apply the entire conceptual apparatus of language at their disposal (Hegel 1974a, p. 55). In Hegel's view, people's communication through universal concepts is the precondition of reciprocal recognition, confirmation, and, therefore, certainty about sensory experiences. Hegel insists that we do know the particular object, and our knowledge has its basis in the sensory experience, but that our identification of a particular object *presupposes* our knowledge of universals as well as our use of language and concepts. Hence, there is no uninterpreted experience or sense data. Universals are necessary conditions that make the experience of a particular object possible: The object, for its very being an object, is mediated through concepts. The particular-universal dialectic means that the universal/concept is constitutive of the particular object.[2]

We may ask, however, how a set of diverse properties and conceptualizations can refer to one and the same substance. How can the thing we designate as "cold" and "white" (e.g., ice cream) be the same thing that we call "sweet" and "inexpensive"? Why don't universal concepts like cold, white, sweet, and inexpensive denote four different particular objects? Indeed, players in different language games of interpretation (chemistry, physiology, economics, and so forth) would designate different entities as the referents of "white color" (eyes that receive a particular wave length), "cold" (molecules with a low movement energy), "sweet" (the glucose combination's effect on the tongue), or "expensive" (a specific demand–supply contrast in the market). These language games might even remain untranslatable and irreducible. Therefore, according to Hegel's analysis, it seems that at each level of interpretation, and on the basis of each context, "we" (not exactly the transcendent self/knower of Kant) constitute the particular object by assuming the same substance as the unique referent for diverse universals. This is a part of our contribution to the particular-making process.

This interpretation might identify Hegel as a follower of Kant, for Hegel does not believe that the particular object is nothing, but rather that it is the sum total of properties. For him, properties are always properties *of* something real.[3] But we cannot take the next step and interpret Hegel as if he believes that this "something real" is the Kantian thing-in-itself beyond the reach of our understanding and that the by-us-imposed substance is only a for-us phenomenon. Assuming an in-itself noumenon is diametrically opposite to Hegelian thought (see Hegel 1977, p. 88). For Hegel, the very idea and assumption of a substance distinct from properties is an unjustified abstraction. What really exists, according to the Hegelian dialectical ontology, is the synthesis of these two opposites (i.e., substance and universal that are not independent unless by abstraction). The quest for substance and the inquiry into its birthplace (in the Kantian transcendent self rather than in the Kantian world-in-itself) are pointless, because they presuppose a dichotomy between thing-in-itself and for-us, as well as a dualism between the subjective self and the objective world. Therefore, the aforementioned Kantian interpretation of Hegel's idea of substance stems from nondialectical assumptions.

Hegel's critique of empiricists is that any sensory experience is already for-us: Our point of view, interests, projects, sociopolitical positions, and so forth are constitutive of it. The realm of the immediate is already a synthesis of the idea and the nature, the subject and the object. Therefore, knowing the truth demands our being critical of experience, as Descartes and rationalists were, since there is no foundation of simple sense-certainty for true knowledge. Likewise, Hegel criticizes rationalists and points out that we cannot abstract reason or logic from nature and objective reality. Reason is concrete through and through.

The basic mistake of rationalism, Hegel argues, is found in its separating reason from context, while rationality is intersubjective, social, and interactive. This dialectical description, I will argue, leads to a specific coherentist idea of truth and rationality.

Hegel's dialectical ontology and the interdependence of cognition and reality

According to Hegel, "everything that surrounds us may be viewed as an instance of Dialectic." He explains:

> We are aware that everything finite, instead of being stable and ultimate, is rather changeable and transient; and this is exactly what we mean by that Dialectic of the finite, by which the finite, as implicitly other than what it is, is forced beyond its own immediate or natural being to turn suddenly into its opposite. (1974c, p. 97)

For Hegel, dialectic describes the nature of reality. According to this ontological view, there is concrete unity and necessary connections between the subjective and the objective. That is, appearance shows nothing that is not in the essence, and in the essence there is nothing but what manifests, because the patterns and categories of thought are never purely subjective: They reflect objective reality. Accordingly, consciousness is a part of reality in dynamic relationship with the other parts and with reality as a whole. Appearance is the transient shape this permanent dynamism takes.

Dialectical ontology regards the existence of things as not outside of or prior to the processes or relations that create, sustain, or undermine them. In other words, becoming is the essence of each being, and therefore, we should ask of an entity or event: "Through what processes was it constituted?" and "How is it sustained?" Dialectic has an epistemological corollary according to which dialectical enquiry is a process of producing theories and institutionalized structures of knowledge that stand to be supported or undermined by a continuing process of inquiry. Reaching (partial) truth is thereby possible through the repeated overthrow of less adequate conceptions, beginning with the skeptical overthrow of our original naïve and "natural" certainty. Hegel provides several examples in order to justify the value of a dialectical approach in understanding (p. 98). Indeed, he takes all of history—or, better, his (dialectical) interpretation of history—as proof of the priority of the dialectical approach.

Hegel offers a more theoretical argument, moreover, to demonstrate the kernel of dialectical ontology: the belief in the contradictory nature of the world. In the Hegelian world, internally related processes are simultaneously supporting and undermining one another. In the Kantian system of thought, pairs of contradictory principles could be validly derived whenever we try to ascertain the nature of the thing-in-itself. For Hegel, however, the world we experience is but the in-itself. Therefore, antinomies are not nonsense arguments, but conceptualizations of the world, the in-itself-for-us. They emerge from our diverse and contradictory experiences in the world. And because our experience is a part of the world, Hegel concludes that contradictions are in the world, in the in-itself-for-us.

We may imagine each moment of our persistently changing relationship with other human beings or with the world as a whole to be a contingent moment in which we live our social, political, cultural, and economic lives. It is out of our experiences against these backgrounds—and based on the specific dynamism of our consciousness in them—that we establish our conceptual systems and form our understandings and truth claims. These conceptual systems may be incompatible with the system we could make out of our experience in another contingent moment. In other words, those Kantian antinomies manifest the contradictory nature of the world and of us as parts of it.

According to this interpretation, the world as a whole is an ensemble of potentially infinite, transient, and (partly) interwoven patterns of relationships that are not necessarily reducible or translatable into each other. Multiplicity and heterogeneity are inscribed in the essence of the in-itself-for-us, the cognitive/material reality, or, in Hegel's terms, the "appearance." Indeed, Hegel traces the contradiction among the Kantian antinomies back into the very nature of what Kant calls the "noumenon," the in-itself. In so doing, Hegel finds the dialectical description of such a contradictory world inevitable. As a result, antinomies testify to the transitory movements of consciousness from one contingent mode of involvement in the sociopolitical context to the other and, as such, illustrate a permanent state of flux and becoming as the phenomenological structure of being-in-the-world.

Hegel's critique of Kant follows this insight and introduces historicity to the Kantian categories of understanding. Contrary to Kant, Hegel believes that categories are not given or fixed: Far from dwelling in the Kantian "transcendent self," categories are intersubjective, social, and historical, and as such they do not establish an independent domain of "knowledge for its sake." In Hegel's view, Kant fails to grasp that the nature of our own thought, and that of the in-itself reality to which Kant always contrasts the understanding through categories, are indeed one and the same (see Ameriks 1985; Guyer 1993).

Hegel's dialectical account of the in-itself-for-us indicates that a valid epistemological grasp of truth and consciousness must necessarily attend to the relation of *reciprocal constitutiveness* between cognition and reality. It also needs to offer its normative criterion of truthfulness in agreement with the relation of *interdependence* between the subject and the object. The crucial point—that it is the very cognitive/material reality, and not just concepts and propositions *about* reality, that is contradictory—needs further investigation. I must inquire into the nature of this contradiction and underline how it is different from logical inconsistencies among concepts, theories, and propositions. For this purpose, Hegel's discussion of the "inverted world" is particularly important.

Contradiction and change as immanent to cognitive/material reality

According to Plato's parable, the "real" supersensible world of forms is a static and unchanging realm above and beyond the world of appearance (see Hegel 1977, pp. 87–8). The supersensible world is said to be the true world because it—its universal law(s)—is what remains throughout the continuous change and disappearance of everything in the appearing world. Hegel follows Aristotle, however, in believing in "the absoluteness of change, i.e. the principle of alteration" (Gadamer 1976, p. 44). According to this view, the static world of Plato that lacks the ability of incorporating and explaining change in appearance cannot be considered the true world. As Gadamer points out, "a world which contains the *arche kineseos*, and as such is the true world, is an inversion of Plato's world in which motion and alteration were supposed to be naught.... It is a world in which everything moves because everything contains the origin of change in itself" (pp. 44–5; see also Hegel 1977, p. 97).

Indeed, Hegel maintains that Plato's static world is "topsy-turvy" and "perverse," and that there are no eternal forms in the real world.[4] "We have to think pure change," he writes (1977, p. 99). The world of appearance, the real world, is changing. There is no way it *is*, for, as we change our concepts we change the laws and the cognitive/material reality. In other words, the reality of appearance, the in-itself-for-us, is more than the static laws of appearance. Appearance/reality is *becoming*: It is always already more than, and nonidentical to, itself. Appearance is simultaneously "the law and the perversion of the law" (Gadamer 1976, p. 46). Hence, it is contradictory.

Hegel's appearance, his inverted world of reality, harbors a concept of law in which difference, change, and alteration are all internal (see Hegel 1977, p. 92). Appearance—cognitive/material reality, Hegel's *only* reality—is heterogeneous and changing, fragmentary, and always opposite to itself. Contradiction, thus, is not simply within Quine's web of propositions or beliefs *about* reality. In Hegel's view, contradiction is constitutive of the real world.[5] Hegel does not have a logical contradiction in mind when he proposes that appearance/reality is contradictory. For him, contradiction is inscribed in dialectical interactions in which consciousness and the in-itself are permanently engaged. (Again, an in-itself appears so only through abstracting—and reifying—it from the dialectical-interactive context.) Thus, contradiction has to do with change that is essential to the in-itself-for-us reality. It is as though the *becoming*, the cognitive/material reality, has a tendency to always differ from itself and be rather than, or opposite to, what it momentarily is. This tendency, or *existential contradiction*, amounts to the facticity and finitude of consciousness, in particular, and to cognitive/material reality, in general.

Logical inconsistencies among theories, beliefs, and propositions do take place—not always, but in some moments of becoming. At such moments, logical inconsistency becomes constitutive of (and constituted by) the transient cognitive/material reality. In other words, logical inconsistencies are situated. They obtain their meaning, relevance, and resolutions against their transitory real-world contexts—so much so that their resolution contributes to the very process of alteration in the in-itself-for-us. Therefore, even the logical consistency among theories and beliefs cannot be abstractly separated from the sociopolitical context that situates the logical inconsistency, gives meaning to it, and opens possibilities for its resolution. The resolution involves change in the sociopolitical context of inconsistency. In other words, politics, among other things, is involved in reaching logical consistency, the hallmark of truth.

Hence, we need to think of a new concept of coherence as the normative criterion of truth: a *new coherence* that cannot be reduced to mere logical consistency among propositions in a web of belief. Hegel's dialectical view signifies that "in the alteration of the knowledge, the object itself alters for it too, for the knowledge that was present was essentially a knowledge of the object: as the knowledge changes, so too does the object, for it essentially belonged to this knowledge" (1977, p. 54).

This is why, from both Hegelian and Marxian perspectives, "interpreting" the world is "changing" it at the same time: The dialectical view implies that the resolution of contradictions, and rectification of errors, requires a transformation of the cognitive/material reality (not "ideas" alone). To be an adequate criterion of truth, the idea of new coherence must incorporate these observations.

Hegel and new coherence

Hegel's discussion of coherence as the normative criterion of truth can be found in his introduction to *Phenomenology of Spirit*, sections 80–7. As we have seen, his immanent critiques of empiricism and rationalism stress the inadequacy of these systems as accounts of knowledge. Hegel scorns empiricism and rationalism for their failure according to their own internal standards, since both begin by promising to secure our sense-certainty and perception and end up in skepticism. They are untrue theories about consciousness: They are incoherent, Hegel concludes.

For Hegel, coherence is not a logical consistency of judgment, but self-satisfaction in reaching goals and fulfilling criteria. Goals, laws, and criteria change, however. Indeed, appearance/reality and its laws are constantly becoming, changing, and contradicting themselves. Hence, "two moments" of consciousness "do not correspond to one another" (Hegel 1977, p. 54). In Hegel's view, moreover, "consciousness provides its own criterion from within itself, so that the investigation becomes a comparison of consciousness with itself" (p. 53). Due to the everlasting alteration of the in-itself-for-us reality and its constituent, consciousness, a multiplicity of internal criteria exist.

Hegel's idea of coherence, the internal self-satisfaction of consciousness, is, therefore, compatible with his belief in the contradictory nature of cognitive/material reality. The Hegelian coherence is recognized as the criterion of truth because dialectical contradiction forever reigns over the cognitive/material realm of reality. Due to the permanent changeability of reality, Hegel's criterion of truth is not context free and universal, but internal to moments of the in-itself-for-us. The contradictory dialectic of reality is the condition of possibility for an internal Hegelian coherence: The former is the transcendental condition of the latter. The idea of coherence as self-satisfaction, then, does not (logically) contradict the doctrine of (dialectical) contradiction in reality, but rests on it—or, at least, they are not necessarily inconsistent with each other.

Yes, the idea of coherence as self-satisfaction and the doctrine of dialectical contradiction in reality logically contradict when a contingent consciousness' internal standard implies that the cognitive/material reality must be static and contradiction free. For such a consciousness, truth claims must be eternal and universal and must correspond with a static (nondialectical) reality. In other words, there might be—and indeed there actually are—moments of dialectic between consciousness and in-itself at which an (alienated) consciousness fantasizes its internal criterion as not internal, but universal. Having universal claims, either a universal criterion or a knowledge that must accord with the context-free criterion, is obviously incompatible with believing in dialectical fluidity of the in-itself-for-us.

Such a consciousness is fetishized, however, since it, in order to fulfill its (Hegelian internal) criterion, strives to mummify the in-itself-for-us; ignores reality's dialectical fluidity and contradiction; and simultaneously forgets the very reciprocally constitutive relationship of itself (as a contingent, though fetishized, consciousness) with the (always-contradictory-but-momentarily-seen-as-static) reality. Marx calls such a reifying consciousness a fetishized ideology (see Korsch 1970, p. 83). Metaphysics, with its search for *arche,* essence, and structure, is fetishized too. Fetishism thus is the sign of untruth of consciousness, for it implies a static reality, a *per se,* an in-itself, that is not dialectically changing. As a *theoria,* such a consciousness aspires to still the flux, arrest the movement, and resolve the dialectical contradictions in the in-itself-for-us once and forever. Thus, Hegel's notion of coherence as self-satisfaction, his pluralism of criteria, has a proviso. This proviso lodges in Hegel's own metaphysics and amounts to the assertion that no internal criterion can claim universality.[6] The crucial point here is that Hegel's coherence, that is, self-satisfaction, happens to consciousness while consciousness is in a reciprocally constitutive relationship with the in-itself. Coherence thus takes place when, at a moment of dialectic, there is a relationship of constitutiveness, mutual support, and implication among different constituents of reality. In order to distinguish this idea from a mere logical consistency of propositions, we shall call it *new coherence.*

The dialectical perspective also indicates that consciousness is a living, internal engagement in the world, such that the knower cannot be conceived of as a spectator from nowhere. Thus, the dualism of subject-object as radically dissimilar entities should be substituted for, by "a process of converting, so to speak, the object *into* the subject (or showing that the patterns and relations of objectivity are isomorphic with the patterns and relations of subjectivity)" (Zimmerman 1982, p. 343). The subject and the object are indeed modes and moments of the same dialectical event. They are identical in difference and united in opposition.[7] They are mutually constitutive.

Kant thought that the transcendent self has no "knowledge," no "rational" understanding about the thing-in-itself and that it is only through the faithful practices and moral actions of human beings-in-the-world that the in-itself becomes "intelligible" to us. Hegel's "determinate negation" of the thing-in-itself amounts to the idea that consciousness includes both the (Kantian) practical mode of contact with the thing-in-itself (faith, morality, and will) and knowledge through concepts and categories. Indeed, action and knowledge are dialectically intertwined with each other and with the in-itself. Therefore, for Hegel, the moment of consciousness (understanding) has moral and practical/political dimensions. It has a moral dimension because the implementation of categories is an act contingent upon moral decisions. Simultaneously, the moment of understanding has a political dimension since, through this practice of implementing contingent categories, the in-itself-for-us, the practico-inert, emerges. Hence, an adequate normative account of knowledge must attend to the interaction of these dimensions.

Hegel's dialectic

According to Hegel's idea of dialectic, each society is a unique whole with elements that cannot be disconnected from each other. The religion, art, tradition, constitution, sociopolitical institutions, language, manners, cultural etiquette, and ethics of a people, among other characteristics, establish a systematic and organic unity in which detachment or alteration of an element affects the whole and other parts. Hegel calls this organic whole the spirit of a nation (Beiser 1993, p. 274). The spirit is the way a nation thinks about and involves itself in the world. Nature is not a dualistically related deformation of the spirit but a dialectically related concretization of it. The spirit thus is constitutive of a historic bloc and immanent to the world (Hegel 1982, pp. 30–5). Therefore, the spirit, apart from the sociopolitical reality of the era, is a void and abstract universal that is reified while given an ontological status independent Zent of the so-called material reality. Through this reification, the spirit emerges as the mere mechanical effect of the "structural base," as the *superstructure* of orthodox Marxism.

Like Marx, Hegel believes that philosophy, religion, and literature are products of social and political conditions. Unlike Marx, he believes that social, economic, and political institutions are, in the final analysis, concretizations of the absolute idea. Nevertheless, in Hegel's view, as Frederick Beiser argues, "the idea realizes itself *only through* the workings of these social, political and economic factors" (1993, p. 278). In other words, for Hegel, ideas are existentially in the same order as socio-politico-economic factors, because ideas and socio-politico-economic factors are mutually and dialectically constitutive. Thus, Hegel's view is compatible with Marx's materialism, though Hegel believes that ideas are first in the order of explanation. The healthy affinity between this Hegelian position and what is presently known as cultural Marxism is evident. Marx and Hegel both believe that the structure and the superstructure existentially presuppose each other. While historical materialism gives the explanatory priority to the former, Hegel prefers the latter for explicatory purposes.

Surely the above interpretation of Hegel deploys a set of select elements of his thought rescued in Marx's dialectical materialism. It is important to underline, however, what we have also abandoned in Hegel's system in order to reach this agreement between Hegel's idealism and Marx's dialectical materialism. Hegel's epistemological discussion in *Phenomenology of Spirit* convenes a combination of "immanent criticism" and "determinate negation." Through an immanent criticism, Hegel argues, a particular form of consciousness—a Lockean or a Cartesian one—realizes that the thought–object dualism it holds impedes a genuine and truthful grasp of consciousness' own relationship with the world. Consciousness, therefore, becomes self-conscious about the "alienating" character of its dualistic view. A "negation" of the dualistic scheme, which is now, thanks to the immanent criticism, proved inadequate, accompanies an appreciation of the situatedness of the dualistic view within certain background assumptions relative to the scheme. In Hegel's view, the latter appreciation of the limited and partial truth of dualism makes rejection of dualism a "determinate negation." This observation reveals the historical character of truth, according to which consciousness at its "absolute standpoint" realizes its dialectical interaction with the world and also the fact that historical systems are partially true relative to their contexts.

Hegel's idea of knowledge is historicist *and* essentialist, however: When he says that all historical systems are partially true, he believes in a progressive and teleological movement of consciousness toward an all-encompassing final form. For him, all historical systems are partially true because they all partially participate in, and approximate toward, a final *telos*. It is retrospectively, at the end of this historical movement, that the overall rationality of these approximations will be made clear. Indeed, Hegel believes that the endpoint is implicitly and indeterminately present in every step of movement. This presence ensures the partial truth of each system of consciousness: a "teleological necessity,"[8] an "immanent telos of history" (Horkheimer 1993a, p. 115), and an intrinsic guidance organize the dialectic of consciousness-reality. This is the metaphysical closet essentialism of Hegel (Horkheimer 1972a, p. 27). Consequently, as Max Horkheimer states, "the dialectic is closed" (1993d, p. 239): A historical essentialism impedes the multiplicity, heterogeneity, and contingency of historical dialectic.

We like to embrace the historicism of Hegel's philosophy and concurrently discard its essentialism. Nonetheless, it is Hegel's teleological necessity that, so far, has given meaning and justification to the claim of partial truthfulness of contextual consciousness. How should we reunderstand contextuality and partial truthfulness in the absence of historical essentialism? Does dialectical materialism open a horizon of possibility for new understandings of epistemology that attend to the historicity of consciousness and its contextuality in the web of social, political, economic, and similar relations? Can we still normatively evaluate the (partial) truthfulness of a consciousness that is dialectical through and through? While giving up the essentialist elements in Hegel's epistemology, can we rearticulate the dialectical relationship between knowledge and sociopolitical context in a nonrelativist way? Can we couple the historicity and sociopolitical contextuality of truth claims with criteria of epistemological normativity? We accompanied Hegel in leaving Locke and Descartes; perhaps the time has come to also part from Hegel and think of a new normative epistemology for which reality is cognitive/material, contradictory, and dialectical—an epistemology with new coherence as its criterion of truth, and an epistemology that attends to the political and ethical nature of consciousness/ knowledge, as well as the sociopolitical function of itself qua epistemology. We shall call such an epistemology-to-come *political epistemology*.

Marx's dialectical materialism

In a dialectical view, the subject and the object are opposites in unity (Marx 1972d, p. 138). That is, the mental and the physical are existentially reciprocal: We need to learn how not to reduce the mental to the physical or to take them as identical. We also need to learn how to transcend the naïve realist dogma according to which opposites/ differents independently exist. The real subjectivity of human beings, in this view, is in dynamic union with the objective material. They interact and constantly transform into each other. They are moments of the process of permanent change in cognitive/material reality (see Ollman 1993, p. 11). Their difference-in-identity and opposition-in-unity, their contradictory and fragmentary nature, seem absurd only to the reifying eyes that abstract the subjectivity or the objectivity from their dynamism, ontologize each, and, in so doing, aspire in vain to find their unchanging essences. In other words, the linguistic application of the indexical "they" should not mislead us into the metaphysician's fly bottle, in which lives have been spent investigating supposedly independent substances as the referents of the "they." What "is" is relations among the relata, period.

Dialectic, therefore, amounts to the position that relations form the final level of ontological analysis: The secret of dialectic is that there is no secret of substance, for relations are not external to the nature or the essence of things. Things "shine forth" and unconceal what they are through the ways in which they relate to other things (see Sayers 1985, p. 37). Thus, what is determinate is so only within the nets of epistemic, social, political, economic, aesthetic, psychological, and other relationships with other things, with what it is *not*, with what is other than it. As such, the thing, the self, the same is always already mediated through and by the other. Relationship with the other gives the thing its identity and, concurrently, makes the thing transgress that identity, simply because there are also, from the very beginning, the other others in relationships with the thing/becoming. Society and politics mediate the very "thingness" of the thing. Marx's dialectical materialism brings together these considerations and argues that the sensible activity of human beings determines as it transforms cognitive/material reality in light of historically conditioned needs, impetuses, hopes, and desires that are grounded in humans' material existence.

According to dialectical materialism, the subject matter of philosophy is the scope of contingent cognitive/material reality. This is why, for Marx, without economics and social sciences that investigate the realm of the possible, one cannot advance a truly philosophical understanding of reality. Hegel argued that philosophy is the history of philosophy; that is, the subject matter of philosophical thinking is not independent from the very act of thinking. From a dialectical materialist perspective, Hegel's point also indicates that philosophy, as well as the social and economic sciences that study the realm of the possible, simultaneously intervene in it because matter is imbued by consciousness. Hence, philosophy, sociology, and economics are at once strategic and scientific. They can and should make normative arguments to choose—or, better, to contribute to and partially constitute—the morally justified possible world of cognitive/material reality. For Marx, then, philosophy, sociology, and economics are political, inasmuch as they reproduce, affirm, legitimize, negate, disconfirm, conserve, revolutionize, support, disqualify, and transform cognitive/material reality. They are forms of praxis. Marx's own philosophy, as well, is, as Antonio Gramsci calls it, a "philosophy of praxis." Indeed, what is dialectical in the teachings of Marx is the awareness of the political interaction between his theoretical activity and the ongoing social process. Marx understood his own theoretical activities to be engaged in such an interaction.[9]

To summarize the above points, dialectical materialism indicates that things, structures, ideas, and theories do not have a substance prior to the processes and relations that produce, endure, or alter them. Accordingly, things are always "internally heterogeneous" and contradictory "at every level" (Levins and Lewontin 1985, p. 272) because they internalize a multiplicity of contextual processes and relations (Ollman 1971, p. 63). Having no hidden substratum, things and meanings are indeed crossing points of multiple relations (social, political, cultural, semiological, aesthetic, phonic, and so forth) that simultaneously support, undermine, confirm, and weaken one another: Things and meanings are fragmentary and contradictory (Ollman 1990, p. 49). To put it differently, dialectical materialism amounts to the idea that processes and relations at once "unify and differentiate" things and meanings (Harvey 1996, p. 58). Concepts, theories, and ideas find their very meaning and epistemic value only within the web of dialectical relationships between the structure and the superstructure.

It is based on this understanding of dialectical materialism that Marx criticizes the ideas and concepts developed by liberal political economy: He investigates the constitutive share of political, economic, historical, and social/psychological contexts in forming the very content and meaning of capitalist concepts and theories. This explains why, for him, capital is not a static thing but a process, a relation, which assumes the form of money in some sociopolitical contexts and the form of commodity or productive activity in others (Marx 1972a, p. 231). Marx argues that it is the specific historical mode of appropriating the labor process and the mental, physical, and cooperative powers of the laborer that makes a phenomenon like capital possible. This specific historical *a priori* is the condition of possibility that simultaneously gives meaning and reality to an in-itself-for-us, *the* capital.[10]

Marx presents a transcendental analysis of the meaning/reality of capital. This analysis signifies that, abstract from the social, political, and economic processes and relations in which a phenomenon emerges, endures, and functions *as* capital, the proper meaning/reality of capital remains unknown. For Marx, ideology is epistemologically false and politically dangerous due to its harboring such an abstraction.

Before further clarifying the meaning of *transcendental analysis*, let us consider a few more examples in which Marx applies his implicit theory of meaning.

Marx on Feuerbach

In Marx's view, Feuerbach understands religious ontology in isolation as a pure, though false, thought and consequently attempts to rectify the untrue ontology by showing the "correct" alternative: materialism. From a materialist perspective, Feuerbach maintains, the religious metaphysical world and its inhabitants are not transcendent entities. Rather, "theology is anthropology." Metaphysical and theological entities, Feuerbach believes, are products of "the reflection of religion upon itself": "I by no means say…God is nothing, the trinity is nothing, the World of God is nothing." Feuerbach writes:

> I only show that they are not that which the illusions of theology make them,—not foreign, but native mysteries, the mysteries of human nature, I show that religion takes the apparent, the superficial in Nature and humanity, for the essential, and hence conceives their true essence as a separate, special existence…religion…only defines or makes objective the true nature of the human world. (1855, pp. 11–14)

For Feuerbach, then, religious enigmatic entities are internal to human discourse, though they are "absurdly" conceived as transcendent entities. Feuerbach rejects the dualism that pits the secular world against the metaphysical world. Nevertheless, he believes in a binary between the world of objects and the realm of thought. Feuerbach traces religious alienation to what he recognizes as the "nature" or "essence" of human being, that is, something in-itself, abstract and independent from the contextual world in which human beings are involved. He views his philosophy as a criticism that takes place in the realm of thought.

Marx's Feuerbach believes that rectification of religious thought can be accomplished through speculative discussion. Feuerbach does not feel, in other words, that anything in what he calls "the objective world" needs to be rectified.[11] It is as though if we show the cause of religious ontology, it will immediately lose its epistemological justification and attraction, just like a psychic problem that is cured once the patient notices its rootedness in his or her life complex. This interpretation is not dialectical enough, since it harbors a nonreciprocal understanding of the causal relationship.

A Marxist evaluation of Feuerbach's belief might tentatively indulge the materialist presupposition of one-sided cause–effect relationships, ignore the dualistic assumption, and still criticize Feuerbach's materialism based on its conservative function because Feuerbach's position implies that, without changing or removing the cause, the particular form of the material world—the effect, religious ontology—is curable. It thus leaves the social reality untouched. This understanding of Marx's critique holds that there are some deeply rooted contradictions in the cause (i.e., the social life and material world, or what Marx and Feuerbach call "secular basis") that would reproduce the effect, and Feuerbach's mistake is in his ignorance of this fact. Following a permissive interpretation, Feuerbach's goal of removing religious alienation cannot be achieved through his speculative, merely theoretical attempt: The solution lies in a practical removal of contradictions in the "real" factual, as opposed to mental, world. This is how an orthodox Marxist view understands Marx's statement: "The fact that secular basis detaches itself from itself and establishes itself in the clouds as an independent realm can only be explained by the cleavage and self-contradictions within this secular basis" (1972e, p. 109).

A permissive interpretation of Marx's critique, however, ignores the dialectical, and not dualistic, relationship between the material world and the realm of thought. For Marx, materialism's fault follows Feuerbach's failure to recognize material reality as human sensuous activity. Feuerbach forgets that religious sentiment as a constituent of social reality contributes meaning to a human being's practice and life and in so doing shapes his or her interactions with other parts of reality. Thus, religious ontology is not an abstract system of ahistorical beliefs that may, or may not, "correspond" to Feuerbach's "real"/"material" world: Religious thought is as real as the material world. They are mutually mediated. Hence, Marx's evaluation of religious ontology is not directed at its illusory and abstract "truth-value." Rather, it takes into consideration the political role and the social relevance of religious thought in constituting the capitalist practico-inert. This role, Marx maintains, has so far been advancing the hegemony of a capitalist mode of domination. For a dialectical understanding of reality as an in-itself-for-us, the sociopolitical function of religion is not alien to the very epistemic content of religion: The epistemic content and meaning emerge from within, and reciprocally affect, the sociopolitical context. Therefore, an adequate epistemic evaluation of religion must add sensitivity to the sociopolitical context to its normative evaluations.

Marx on private property

Yet another example of this sensitivity can be seen in Marx's analysis of the concept of private property. Private property, Marx maintains, is "the product, the result, the necessary consequence of alienated labor, of the external relations of the worker to nature and to himself" (1972d, p. 65). Marx explains why the relationship between alienated labor and private property is a necessary one. Before Marx, Hegel reserved a principal role for desire and understood it (and, particularly, second-order desire) as the demarcation criterion between the animal and the species lives of human being. Following Hegel, Marx considers labor to be the factual manifestation of desire and gives an absolutely important position to humans' work in making humans' being. Desire implies "negating" and transforming the present. Marx includes negation and transformation in the concept of human activity.

In Marx's account, human beings transform the real world to satisfy their needs. They put their productive activity into the object, and therefore, the product of labor becomes the objectification of humans' work and life. Hegel believed that through this transforming activity human beings establish and enhance their self-consciousness and freedom.[12] Marx, however, finds productive activity in the capitalist epoch incapable of performing such functions. Accordingly, he offers a structural analysis of human activity in the capitalist period that cannot be reduced to a merely individualistic and psychological argument.

For Marx, those things with which human being is closely related but over which he or she has no control are in fact controlling him or her. The capitalist mode of work, in which the object, the product, and the machine have regulating power over the worker, and not vice versa, makes a strong case for Marx's analysis. In the capitalist mode of production, the worker has no control over the process or the result of his or her activity. Therefore, Marx argues, the worker gets no satisfaction during work. Workers deny themselves in their labor and, in so doing, become mere machines. The worker's activity, his or her essential being, becomes a stranger over which he or she has no command. Marx describes this alienated labor as follows:

> First, the fact that labor is external to the worker, i.e., it does not belong to his essential being; that in his work, therefore, he does not affirm himself but denies himself, does not feel content but unhappy[,] does not develop freely his physical and mental energy but mortifies his body and ruins his mind. The worker therefore only feels himself outside his work and his work feels outside himself. He is at home when he is not working and when he is working he is not at home. His labor is, therefore, not voluntary, but coerced: it is *forced labor*. It is not, therefore, the satisfaction of a need, it is merely a *means* to satisfy needs external to it. (1972d, p. 60)

For such a worker, work is not a matter of passion and interest. The work, the negating and transforming activity, ceases to be the goal of labor. Marx argues that when the forces of production, the products of past labor, appear as a world-in-itself independent from the worker, the worker labors to satisfy needs external to his or her work. Production thus becomes independent and external to the worker. It becomes the property of another. The worker cannot use it or recognize it as his or hers because only by spending the wage can he or she possess the product. Hence, in Marx's view, private property is private, for the alienated workers, no longer feeling as freely active, have no influence on its destiny. Private property is the lives of the workers objectified. In other words, alienated labor results in the production of an alien product, and vice versa. The alienated labor belongs to an alien other, that is, the capitalist who has private control over it: It is the private property of the other.

Marx's analysis underlines the political, economic, and social/psychological context in which an entity that has become *this* entity by being conceptualized as private property rolls out. In other words, the meaning and content of private property is dialectically intertwined with social, political, economic, and other factors in a capitalist mode of life. Beyond this specific context, private property means something else. It is within the momentary mode of dynamism in the practico-inert that private property constitutes, and gets partially constituted by, its sociopolitical context.[13]

Marx on ideology

In Marx's view, ideology is a socially significant system of beliefs, presuppositions, or sentiments that harbor a false perception of reality.

The pervasiveness of such systems, Marx believes, is the result of truth-distorting sociopolitical relations that contextualize a specific ideology. For Marx, the ruling class's control over idea-producing institutions is not the whole story of ideology. Subordinate classes may tend to have false beliefs on account of truth-distorting factors in their own ways of making a living (see Marx 1972b, p. 462; Marx and Engels 1972, p. 355). Ideology, therefore, is not just a cognitive error in the abstract realm of ideas-*about*-reality. Intertwined with other sociopolitical elements, ideology is a constituent of a way of life. It provides the mass with tools of subsistence in it. Therefore, according to Marx, abstract and speculative analyses are incapable of grasping, changing, or abolishing an ideology. Such analyses, Marx argues, are indeed ideological. They reproduce the capitalist mode of sociopolitical life.

Ideology serves the functions of concealing class antagonisms and presenting the interests of the ruling class as universal human interests—as if there is but one class in the society and there is no class opposition (Schmitt 1987, p. 55), as if the "universal" truth claims of the ruling class are *really* universal, that is, context free and independent from sociopolitical reality. Ideology obscures relations that do not appear on the surface but are embedded in production, where the exploitation of wage labor takes place. Ideology, the "universal truth" of market relations, masks the exploitation of surplus value (Hall 1983, p. 70). According to this Smithean "truth," market relations are not contingent processes (or becoming-in-flux) but things-in-themselves independent of the laborer's mind and activity. Ideology, therefore, involves reification in arresting the dynamism of becoming, and it also involves fetishism in universalizing a contingent moment of history and illusion in naturalizing the world as it is. This truth-distorting epistemic function of ideology, the dialectical view indicates, cannot be separated from ideology's political function unless by producing another ideology. Such a separation is epistemologically false, politically dangerous, and morally wrong.

Let me elaborate on this point by investigating Marx's diverse applications of the word *ideology*. Though in his writings Marx applies the term *ideology* in at least three different senses (Wood 1981, pp. 117–22), his critique of the reifying and fetishized "nature" of ideology is present in each specific instance of application. In "The German Ideology," "ideology" connotes primarily a philosophical belief in the domination of thought, the thesis that ideas and concepts are the ultimate determining factors. This "idealist" ideology,[14] as Marx's critique of Feuerbach shows, prioritizes the essentialist element of Hegel's system at the cost of a dialectical analysis. For Marx, ideology in this sense is epistemically false for its failure as a philosophical attempt: It is inconsistent with the truth of dialectical philosophy. In other words, in Marx's view, if ideas cannot themselves determine or explain historical development, it is because they have no separable existence in themselves. They are "organically related" to peoples' productive activities and materialistic connections (Marx 1973, p. 88). There is no cause–effect relationship between social relations as material base and ideas as superstructure. As Alasdair MacIntyre states, "The economic basis of a society is not its tools, but the people cooperating using those particular tools in the manner necessary to their use. And the superstructure consists in the social consciousness molded by the shape of this co-operation.... Creating the basis, you create the superstructure. These are not two activities but one" (MacIntyre 1995, p. 39).

There is also another aspect to Marx's epistemic evaluation of ideology. According to Marx, ideological belief forgets its own embeddedness in a social, political, and economic context. Ideology, in this second sense, is a consciousness that is ignorant of its own real social and historical significance—a kind of illusion is associated with ideology. In Marx's account, mass mentality is politically functional: It reproduces the dominant mode of production. This political function partially accounts for the belief system's social prevalence. People tend to think, however, that the belief system is so widespread because it is justified, intuitive, universal, and uniquely rational. However, as Marx describes,

> each new class which puts itself in the place of one ruling before it, is compelled, merely in order to carry through its aim, to represent its interests as the common interests of all the members of society, that is, expressed in ideal forms; it has to give its ideas the form of universality, and represent them as the only rational, universally valid ones. (Marx 1972c, p. 138)

Ideology as illusion, therefore, implies an attempt to "universalize and give ideal form" to situated, class-bound ideas and interests (Miliband 1977, p. 32). In other words, ideology reifies and abstracts its otherwise historical and provisional content (See Bienenstock 1993). It is epistemically false and illusive because it is universal and fetishized. Marx calls this misleading function of ideology "the *externalization* of relations which are in fact historically specific; and the *naturalization* effect— treating what are the product of a specific historical development as if universally valid, and arising not through historical processes but, as it were, from Nature itself" (Hall 1983, p. 68). Ideological one-sided abstractions that are partial, part-for-the-whole types of explanation, allow their followers only to abstract one element out (the market, for example) and explain things, which are inadequate precisely on those grounds. For this reason as well, ideology can be considered epistemically false. Marx demonstrates how individualist liberalism, an ideology that abstracts the individual from his historical context, social relations, and natural world, is instantiated in and reproduced by the appearance of market relations. Individualist liberalism abstracts politics from the economy and obscures the relations of class/power embodied in the social organizations of capitalist production.

Ideology is used by Marx, finally, to present a materialist explication of effective and "ruling ideas" on a social scale. Socially influential forms of consciousness can be explained by showing how they support and indeed partially constitute the social, political, cultural, and emotional relations of the present mode of production. Ideology operates politically in the interests of a dominant class and in so doing constructs its own meaning through this process. According to Marx's dialectical materialist analysis, then, the political function of ideology is constitutive of its very meaning, and the very meaning and content of ideology facilitates its political function. Hence, ideology mediates through the relations of production, and vice versa. According to Marx, in the capitalist historic period jurisprudence, art, religion, politics, philosophy, and morality are all ideological in this sense (1972c, p. 125). Indeed, ideology in this third sense is the very cognitive/material reality of the capitalist mode of life *expressed as ruling ideas*, while the structural elements of production are the very same cognitive/material reality of the capitalist mode of life *expressed as material forces*. Ideology and structure are opposite faces of the same Janus (Marx 1973c, pp. 136–7).

Therefore, ideology partially constitutes cognitive/material reality. It is not *about* reality. It is not a false *representation* that does not *correspond* with reality. It *is* (a part of) reality. Not only ideology but, in a broader sense, Marx's "superstructure" is indeed the ideal form in which the totality of material relations that makes up the "base" itself is manifested to consciousness: Superstructure is not a substantially separable order of reality at all. Consequently, in a capitalist mode of social relationships, mass consciousness—and ideology in all its discussed senses—is not secondary, epiphenomenal, subordinate, or a kind of senseless hallucination (Sayer 1987, p. 42). For Marx, superstructure interacts with, and reproduces, the very social relationships it "describes." Take Adam Smith's idea of the hidden hand of the market: It is a fetishized theory that partially constitutes and is in part constituted by a fetishized mode of practice. They are two moments of the same dynamism. Therefore, we may conclude, Adam Smith's theory somehow "corresponds" with "reality."

According to Marx, however, it is equally fetishistic to think that Smith's ideas are independent from the very "reality" they "describe." As he states,

> The categories of bourgeois economy consist of such like forms. They are forms of thought expressing with social validity the conditions and relations of a definite, historically determined mode of production. The whole mystery of commodities…vanishes therefore, as soon as we come to other forms of production. (1967, p. 76)

In other words, according to dialectical materialism, the categories of bourgeois economy, including Adam Smith's ideas, *do have (partial) correctness*: Inasmuch as they constitute cognitive/material reality, they "correspond" with it. Marx's dialectical materialism, or "dialectical ontology" (Ollman 1971, pt. 1), demonstrates that the social versus rational dichotomy is misleading. Therefore, for Marx, to the extent that the epistemic criteria stem from a dualistic ontology, so far as the positivist sense of socially transcendent truth is concerned, one cannot meaningfully talk about the truth or falsity of Adam Smith's theory. But Marx believes that Adam Smith's theory and the liberal individualism behind it are positively false and that his own socialist theory is definitely true. How does he justify this position? Marx argues that their falsity arises once they forget their dialectical situatedness and claim universality. This is why, as stated above, "the whole mystery of commodities…vanishes…as soon as we come to other forms of production" (1967, p. 76).

Marx's truth and the project of political epistemology

It seems that a peculiar idea of truth and correspondence is emerging here. What does Marx really mean by "truth" if other worlds, "other forms of production," are possible? What happens to our understanding of truth if categories of understanding—Adam Smith's economics for one—and reality are both contingent? Based on which epistemic justification, if any, could we accept or reject Adam Smith? Positivist epistemology, in order to preserve the objectivity of knowledge, draws a sharp distinction between justifying a theory's truth and explaining its genesis, between the context of discovery and that of justification (see Hanson 1958). The strong program in the sociology of knowledge accepts this distinction as a precondition of objectivity and shows that, in practice, all justification processes and their truth standards are genetically social. The strong program thus concludes that the demanded objectivity is unavailable and, as such, the universally objective truth should be relativized in favor of local claims of understanding (Longino 2002, pp. 15–17). Does dialectical materialism follow the strong program and forsake the epistemic normativity of its judgments and criticisms of the capitalist mode of cognitive/material reality? In other words, is Marx's dialectical materialism promoting a sort of epistemic relativism? Does historicizing the categories of consciousness mean that truth has history and is contingent? Can modern epistemology stand this "blasphemy"?

After all, what does Marx mean by judging *ideology qua reality* as false consciousness? Granted, reality can be ethically, as well as politically, judged and given negative value. Nonetheless, how could reality be ever judged as *epistemically false*? Does Marx not commit a category mistake here? This is a serious issue. Should dialectical materialism discard epistemic judgment about the *falsity* of ideology qua reality and, in so doing, limit the scope of dialectical criticism to the ethical and the political? This path, if taken, would have the result of rendering the dialectical approach epistemologically relativist. As such, dialectical materialism would cease to claim veracity for its own criticisms. This move would exile epistemic truth beyond the realms of the ethical and the political.

Contrary to this path, should dialectical materialism retain the notion of epistemic normativity and launch its critique of ideology, also and among other things, upon the latter's epistemic falsity? A positive response obligates us to develop a normative epistemology. Furthermore, the dialectical view demands that such a positive response also clarify the *unity in opposition* of the epistemological, the political, and the moral critiques of cognitive/material reality. An adequate positive response must show how, from a dialectical perspective, the epistemological, political, and moral evaluations mutually imply one another without surrendering their differences. These obligations and demands motivate my study. Accordingly, the project of political epistemology is an inchoate step in addressing the above questions.

Still, why should we ever give a positive response to the last question? Giving a positive response to that question and saying yes to the demands that follow it are a moral choice and a political/strategic intervention. These two motivate, contextualize, and situate my participation in the project of political epistemology. Political epistemology, far from being a systematic theory of knowledge with universality claims, is a situated project of inquiry. It is a project initiated, and constructed, to serve as the epistemology of the excluded *differend*, the ignored other. And it is exactly here, inscribed in this political and ethical function, that the project of political epistemology also claims its own truthfulness: It partially seeks its justification through its political as well as ethical attempt to open the horizon of the present for the truth and justice to come.

The project of political epistemology is called so because, qua epistemology, it *is* political. It is political because the conditions of production of epistemology, like the conditions of production of other discourses (law, science, philosophy, and so forth) are political; that is, relations of power are operative in deciding who gets to partake in, and who is excluded from, the performative practices of debate. It is political because the socially and politically constructed identities of the participants affect their communication and its outcome. And it is also political because "epistemologies have political effects insofar as they are discursive interventions in specific discursive and political spaces" (Alcoff 1993b, p. 66). Epistemology legitimates or delegitimates different discourses in society and in so doing mediates the hierarchies of relationships of power and affects the way these relationships are maintained, remade, changed, or challenged.[15] Marx's dialectical materialism highlights the political function of a positivist idea of knowledge: It reifies knowledge as absolute and unchanging truth that is incarnated in the capitalist economic system. It promotes an "unchangeable" human nature and a "natural" division of labor. It produces fatalism about "reality" as an inert, an in-itself. From a dialectical materialist perspective, all these operations are political.

Though epistemology has a specific and privileged relationship with other discourses/constituents of cognitive/material reality (after all, it establishes the standards of truth and evaluates other constituents' truthfulness), having a political function is not unique to epistemology.[16] Indeed, there is also another reason that accounts for the designation of political epistemology. This reason is embedded in Marx's implicit theory of meaning, in his transcendental analysis of the ideas and concepts of liberal political economy. Let us now further delve into the meaning and concept of transcendental analysis.

Transcendental analysis

The idea of transcendental analysis is generally associated with Immanuel Kant's philosophy. For Kant, criticism should locate the conditions of possibility and impossibility and thereby the "origin…, extent and limits of the idea" (see Guyer and Wood 1998, pp. 6–14). Transcendental analysis interrogates a phenomenon, an experience, a concept, and an idea with regard to its conditions of possibility and meaningfulness. It asks about what a phenomenon, or a concept, necessarily presupposes to be this specific phenomenon, this particular concept. Kantian transcendental deduction starts from the insight that we must be able to distinguish within experience an objective order of things from a merely subjective order, for otherwise we would not have an experience *of* something, such as an object. In order to experience an object as an object coherently—that is, in order to have experience at all—we must accept the necessary applicability of certain categories to the world of experience. We do have experience, Kant's argument goes; therefore, we can be a priori certain that categories apply (see Chisholm 1978, pp. 19–22).

Nonetheless, Kant's transcendental criticism is ahistorical, since Kant's philosophy is undialectical: He believes in a thing-in-itself, beyond the realm of historicity and knowledge. Kant's transcendental deduction infers the timeless, universal *a priories* of understanding for a transcendent and abstract subject/knower. As such, he fetishizes a dualism between the noumenal and the phenomenal world (see Schott 1988, pp. 137–48). As Charles Taylor points out, however, Martin Heidegger and Maurice Merleau-Ponty, contrary to Kant, apply transcendental arguments to disclose the very fact that a subject/knower is in, and engaged with, the world. "The claim," Taylor states, "is that our perception as an experience is such that it could only be that of an embodied agent with the world" (1979, p. 154). In other words, according to Heidegger—and, indeed, Hegel and Marx before him—being-in-the-world, involvement in activity and embeddedness in the web of sociopolitical relationships, is the necessary precondition of knowledge.

As the above examples of Marx's examination of meaning demonstrate, Marx's transcendental analysis pinpoints the political, economic, social/psychological, cultural, and other conditions that dialectically coexist and mediate concepts, theories, and ideas in the capitalist mode of cognitive/material reality. In other words, his implicit theory of knowledge investigates the conditions of possibility of cognition on the one hand and cognition of meaning on the other in the capitalist mode of sociopolitical reality (Arndt 1987, p. 44). He analyzes the essential relations that must exist if the world as experienced in the capitalist era is to be possible (and also changeable).

In Marx's view, the capitalist mode of social relations is a contingent, historical, and transient practico-inert. This means that the specific dialectical relations of mutual constitution between structural and superstructural elements are not established out of necessity. Dialectical interdependence is a process of becoming, Marx would add, and every moment of it is contingent.[17] Therefore, for Marx, marking the possibility conditions of an idea is an empirical/inductive research act akin to genealogy (Foucault 1984a; Wolf 2000).[18] Hence, Marx's empirical/transcendental analysis is different from the Kantian transcendental method. Kant, as an atomist, denies the priority of society as the locus of the individual's identity: His subject is not communal. He starts from a metaphysical analysis of the knower's mind that is assumed to be categorically separate from the world to be known. Thus, "intentionality" and its conditions of possibility become the main point of concentration for Kant. Using conceptual analyses, he determines what the necessary conditions of intentionality have to be. This analysis is not empirical. Its outcomes, the schemas of understanding and intuition, are supposedly universal and timeless, since the knower, the transcendent subject, is abstracted away from any specificity, contextuality, and locatedness. Following Hegel, Marx finds Kantian assumptions fetishized. As such, he historicizes and materializes Kantian categories and looks into the social, political, and economic relations and realities with which categories dialectically interact.

By way of his transcendental analysis, Marx shows how the historical attributes of a phenomenon like the capitalist mode of life are falsely universalized. Marx is aware of the political, as well as the epistemic, outcome of his transcendental analysis. He writes:

> This relationship, however, is regarded by the Ricardian school as given, as a natural law, on which the production process itself is based.... But from the moment that the bourgeois mode of production and the conditions of production and distribution which correspond to it are recognized as *historical*, the delusion of regarding them as natural laws of production vanishes and the prospect opens up of a new society, [a new] economic social formation, to which capitalism is only the transition. (1971, p. 429)

Using this transcendental method, Marx demonstrates how the particular social division of labor mediates the ideology of individualism and constitutes individuals as allegedly autonomous, free-contracting subjects who own either the means of production or the labor power.

Therefore, according to Marx's method,[19] concepts like civil society, political state, capital, commodity, surplus value, exchange value, freedom, equality, public and private domains, property, money, profit, and so forth—together with the theories that produce them—are all subject to transcendental study in order to be seen as specific, contingent, and changeable social relations (Sayer and Frisby 1986, p. 102). Marx believes that empirical/transcendental analysis is the real task of political economy.

The second reason for the designation *political epistemology* becomes clear at this point. Political epistemology is called so because, following Marx's idea of political economy, it promotes analyses of meaning by situating a concept within its sociopolitical context (and offers normative criteria for judging the truthfulness of meaning). Rejecting subject–object dualism, political epistemology explores the sociopolitical contextual elements that are in reciprocally constitutive relationships with meaning and truthfulness of ideas, concepts, and theories.

Toward a normative, dialectical epistemology

Dialectical materialism implies that adequate articulations of epistemology—what the project of political epistemology strives for—should include both political and epistemic considerations and reflect the awareness that normative epistemology is politically involved and sociohistorically embedded. Separating sociopolitical considerations and relegating them to the realm of the sociology of knowledge is epistemically wrong and politically dangerous: It is epistemically wrong since it ignores the political content of epistemology, meaning, and truth claims. It is politically dangerous because it hides the political effect of epistemology, meaning, and truth.

Modern epistemology that believes in the separation of epistemology from social, historical, and political context, as Charles Taylor portrays it, rests on a specific ontology of the disengaged subject. Its model of rationality is instrumental rationality. It embraces an atomistic interpretation of society, moreover, as constituted by, and explainable in terms of, individuals. Also, for modern epistemology, knowledge is representation. Taylor suggests that a dislike of the moral and spiritual consequences of epistemology has initiated metaphysical criticisms against it, and what he calls "overcoming epistemology" signifies an awareness that emerges once we recognize the being-in-the-worldhood of the knower. Accordingly, that which epistemology underlines as representation of the world within our theories, concepts, and sentences is rather a certain grasp of the world that we as agents in it possess. "This shows the whole epistemological construal to be a mistake," Taylor writes (1995, p. 12). This "reflection," according to Taylor, leads to the negation of Cartesian duality between subject and object: There is no sharp line between the subject's *dealing* with the object and that object. It also entails conceiving reason differently. Instrumental reason and its correlated morality, that is, utilitarianism, should both be discarded, Taylor believes.

The "denunciation of (instrumental) reason" as a determinate negation, however, must offer new articulations of reason that surpass subject–object and fact–value dichotomies.[20] Overcoming epistemology means indeed overcoming *an* epistemology that is oblivious of its historicity. *Overcoming epistemology* thus is a call to rectify a mistake. For moral, metaphysical, and political reasons, however, and because a critical standpoint on society must be able to claim truth, we still need criteria to recognize truth. We still need a *normative* epistemology that will reflect a dialectical ontology, embrace new (noninstrumental) notions of reason, and recognize the relevance of moral values for truth. This epistemology should also acknowledge its historical, political, and social embeddedness.

Epistemology has historically assumed a descriptive role in explaining how concepts like knowledge, belief, understanding, and truth are used in practice. It has also taken a normative position in offering criteria for meaning and truth and, in so doing, giving standards for comparing rival systems. Different epistemologies have defined truth differently. Among diverse definitions of truth, the most famous are truth as correspondence to an independent object, as a state of subjective certitude, as coherence between beliefs (or between beliefs and reality), and, finally, as pragmatic success. Dialectics rejects the two first definitions based on their false dualism between an independent, in-itself reality and an abstract subject. The idea of pragmatic success as the criterion of truth is also problematic, since it has politically dangerous functions—as the next chapter will show. The coherence theory of truth, however, is potentially compatible with dialectical ontology. According to coherence theory, a belief is justified "to the extent to which the belief-set of which it is a member is coherent" (Dancy 1985, p. 127; see Dancy and Sosa 1992, pp. 67–70).

The dialectical ontology of truth starts with a knower, who already has a set of beliefs and is always-in-the-world, engaged in practical activities and encumbered with commitments. In other words, from a dialectical perspective, the knower is constitutively linked in various complex ways to that about which he or she seeks knowledge. Accordingly, knowledge is considered immanent to human belief systems and practices, social organizations, and lived reality. Therefore, human existence need not be transcended in order to reach an "extrinsic world." Justification, too, is an immanent feature of beliefs' interrelationships, rather than their relationship with an external reality. In fact, truth appears out of a final coherence between beliefs, practices, and lived reality.

Content, justification, and truth, therefore, are all situated in a context of heterogeneous elements and relations, a heterogeneous process of mutual constitutive relations in the cognitive/material reality. Consistency, broadly speaking, is the relation of mutual support between theory and other elements in the context. While context is not reducible to a set of statements, the relations between theory and other elements are not limited to logical consistency or entailments. Succession, dispersion, unity, derivation, exclusion, mutual alteration, mutual support, intersection, displacement, and subjugation are other possible relations that situate theory within the context (Alcoff 1993a, p. 104). These elements signify the ontological dimension of truth: Truth claims, according to dialectical ontology, refer to, intervene with, and represent reality.

The organic relationship between a truth claim and its context discloses an "immanent realism": "Contexts are not mind-made versions of the world, but portions or locations of the world that are historically and socially specific" (Alcoff 1996, p. 218). Context is indeed an entire set of political, social, and historically situated human praxis—that is, thought and action in combination. Truth thus is an emergent property of all the elements involved in the context, including but not limited to theory. This holistic view decentralizes the subject/knower.

The affinity between the dialectical versions of coherence theory and the empirical/transcendental method of Marx and other thinkers seems clear now. Empirical/transcendental analysis looks into the context (the sociopolitical relations that interact with, and give meaning, justification, and truth to, the theory) in order to see whether it is coherent (i.e., whether the theory and sociopolitical relations mutually support each other). In other words, empirical/transcendental analysis investigates the new coherence among constitutive elements of cognitive/material reality. The project of political epistemology, therefore, appoints new coherence as its criterion of truth.

Contrary to Quine's web of beliefs, in which an ahistorical proviso of logical consistency embodies the criterion of coherence, for the project of political epistemology it is cognitive/material reality that is *new coherent* or *new incoherent*. Furthermore, and as a dialectical process, cognitive/material reality always harbors *new contradictions*—contradictions that are not reducible to logical inconsistencies. It is the project of political epistemology's task to negate those contradictions in a *determinate* way and, in so doing, strive for an upper level of new coherence at the next moment of the cognitive/material process. This "determinate negation" is an epistemic move in search of truth, since truth is inscribed in the upper level of new coherence. Moreover, it is a political act, actually changing the present cognitive/material reality so that an upper new coherence can emerge. The project of political epistemology, therefore, consciously involves politics in the name of truth. These considerations call to our attention the affinity between the project of political epistemology and critical theory, which is the subject of the next chapter.

2

Critical Theory, Negative Dialectics, and the Project of Political Epistemology

As Chapter 1 suggests, the project of political epistemology presents profound similarities to critical theory. The present chapter examines these similarities and explores the lessons that participants in the project of political epistemology learn from the Frankfurt School thinkers, especially Max Horkheimer and Theodor Adorno. The first section of the chapter compares critical to traditional thinking. Traditional theory is not dialectical. It forgets the constitutive role of human interests, social activities, and also of itself qua theory in the makeup of the object. Consequently, traditional thinking takes the actual as a given. Critical theory, on the contrary, problematizes the "given" objective reality as antagonistic and changeable. The problematization of the object proceeds through uncovering its antagonistic nature. This first section, therefore, studies Georg Lukacs's dialectical materialist account of reification and contradiction. Here, the point is that theoretical contradictions of bourgeois thought cannot be resolved theoretically. In other words, there is a constitutive relationship between societal and theoretical contradictions: Contradiction is indeed a cognitive/material reality, *new incoherence*.

Based on the idea of contradiction as a cognitive/material reality, a social fact, Adorno argues that positivist sciences that stay silent before sociopolitical contradictions and ignore their own constitutive part in reality are irrational and untrue. The second section asks, however, whether it is meaningful to talk about a *true*—not just ethically good or politically just but also an *epistemically* true—cognitive/material reality. A proper response must link the idea of epistemic truth to the notion of a dialectical unity of logical and practical critiques. Highlighting

Adorno's idea of *objective abstraction*, the section suggests that while the "correctness" of positivist social sciences and epistemology is due to their constitutive role in the exchange system, the present objective abstraction as a capitalist state of affairs is not "truthful." It is antagonistic and new incoherent. Positivist social sciences' untruth resides in their fetishistic fixation of the present state of affairs through universal claims. As a remedy for this fetishism, critical theory applies *negative dialectics* to the contradictions of social reality and brings social antagonisms to the level of mass consciousness. Negative dialectics is in fact a perpetual alteration of the concept into its opposites—to what the concept can be but is not. This observation, the second section argues, suggests a new understanding of the theory–practice relationship. According to this understanding, a truthful critical theory can project normative goals, politically change reality, and forge its truth through a practice of making the truth actually happen.

The third section investigates the fact that critical theory regards its own understanding of society as partially conditioned by the present situation. Hence, without a clear epistemological theory that could justify critical theory's claim of truthfulness, a dialectical materialist understanding of consciousness would remain incapable of distinguishing itself from the sociology of knowledge. As such, critical theory would cease to escape a self-referential relativism. Furthermore, there is a political aspect to this need for a new normative epistemology. Since political criticism in the name of justice cannot proceed without a claim of truthfulness, unless Horkheimer and Adorno provide normative epistemic justifications for their critical theoretical positions, the apparently relativistic nature of the dialectical materialist approach cripples their political criticisms. Addressing this need, the third section offers a political epistemological reading of critical theory. Here, the idea is that critical theory opens a space for offering new coherence as the normative criterion of truth.

How do Adorno and Horkheimer philosophize the sociopolitical context of their own thought, however? How do they actually locate critical theory in its context of meaning and truthfulness? The fifth section studies Adorno's and Horkheimer's *dialectic of Enlightenment*, an untrue cognitive/material reality. Here, I argue that, for Adorno, negative dialectics is a strategic intervention, truthful and politically apt vis-à-vis the sociopolitical context of 1930s and 1940s Enlightenment. It is within this context that the truth of negative dialectic, as the way of philosophizing "after Auschwitz," parallels its strategic intervention in the present.

For the reified Enlightenment subject, the pure thinking, nature becomes an alien other that must be tamed and dominated. Looking into the epistemic content of this domination makes clear how abstraction, the universal concept's domination over the particular/singular, and the subject–object identity signify the cognitive constituent of modernity's iron cage. In the following sections, I explore *why*, according to Adorno's and Horkheimer's philosophical/psychoanalytical study, subjective reason purports domination and also *how*, epistemically speaking, this domination proceeds. Here, Adorno's transcendental analysis of meaning and truth claims manifests its close affinity to the project of political epistemology: To transgress the hegemony of instrumental rationality, Adorno points out that the *concept* is empty without the *nonconceptual*. In political epistemological language, Adorno says that the nonconcept is indeed the transcendental precondition of the concept's very meaning. The nonconcept signifies society: the "lived a priori" of concept, of meaning, in Adorno's terms. This section also explores how Adorno, underlining the cognitive/material nature of society, attempts to break identity thinking, the secret of subjective reason's domination. Here, the idea is that uncovering the transcendental preconditions of meaning, the sociopolitical constituents of the concept, brings dialectic back into the reified Enlightenment reasoning and loosens the rigidity of modernity's iron cage. Openness, it is argued, is a precondition of knowing the truth.

The next section, which constitutes the most important contribution of the chapter, argues that openness is not a matter of immediate access to the object-in-itself. Rather, openness demands more human modes of mediation between the concept and the nonconcept. Mediation is a social interaction, and the morality of mediation is a transcendental condition of truth. Openness, in other words, refers to a mode of sociopolitical interaction that is ethical and of epistemic value. Accordingly, *new contradictions* signify a "wrong" state of affairs foreclosed on the nonidentical, the possibility of being otherwise. Sociopolitical closure, therefore, is politically dangerous—partly because it is epistemically disastrous.

The following section points out that Adorno's and Horkheimer's dialectic of Enlightenment embodies a reifying process that has historically ended in the birth of the transcendent subject and the objective world. The positivist epistemology that accompanies this ontology holds that in order to discover the truth of the objective world, the knower should not intervene in the world. Thus, through separating the subject from the world, identity thinking separates truth and politics. In this section,

I argue that the sociopolitical possibility of being otherwise is an epistemic value, and, inasmuch as openness as a cognitive/material possibility awaits realization, politics, the art of the possible, cannot be alien to epistemic truth and normativity. I end the chapter by summarizing my political epistemological reading of Adorno's negative dialectics.

Critical versus traditional thinking

Traditional theory of society (e.g., rationalist idealism and reductive materialism)[1] sees the whole perceptible world as "the sum-total of given 'facts': it is there and must be accepted" (Horkheimer 1972d, p. 199). Traditional theory overlooks the mediation of the factual through the activity of society and forgets that the world of objects is produced through activity that is partially determined by the very idea that helps the individual to recognize that world and grasp it conceptually. This activity need not be productive (i.e., a money-making enterprise). It can belong to the existing order and help make it possible, as is the case with specialized sciences that take the industrial and technological accomplishments of the bourgeois era as their own proof of justification, value, and truthfulness (Althusser 1971, p. 142; Horkheimer 1972d, p. 205). A specialized science becomes a force of production when its norms and canons are effectively generalized to encompass commonsense practices. Traditional theories' unawareness of mediation facilitates the subjugation of the traditional social theories to society.

As Jurgen Habermas argues, human interests mediate the very object of knowledge. The subject/knower, far from being abstractly separate from the object of knowledge, enacts the process of "objectivation." Knowledge-constitutive interests thus are a priori to human understanding: They are the possibility conditions of the very object of knowledge (1973, p. 25). Habermas emphasizes the fact that knowledge-constitutive interests take form in the medium of work, language, and power (1968, p. 313). Hence, they are historical transcendental conditions in dialectical relationship with knowledge, and they should be investigated empirically. Traditional theory, including positivist epistemologies, forgets the constitutive role of human interests and of itself as a theory in the makeup of the object. Accordingly, it ignores its political and moral obligations toward the object, the cognitive/material reality, which it mediates.

Traditional theory harbors universalistic, nonhistorical claims joined with an instrumental conception of reason. For Horkheimer, positivist science, with its universalistic applications across historical confines, is also a form of traditional theory: Positivist science is indeed the economic form of capitalism constitutive of and expressed in bourgeois consciousness. As a traditional theory, it ignores its relation of reciprocal constitutiveness with specific forms of human social, political, economic, and cultural organization, and it thereby advances reification (see Horkheimer 1972d, p. 194). (According to the dialectical view, this reification is itself a process enacted by human activity. As Adorno points out, "the autonomy of social processes is itself not an 'in-itself,' but rather it is grounded in reification; even the processes estranged from human beings remain human" [1976b, p. 119].) Thereafter, a historically and culturally specific collective, which is the transcendental constituent of science's "universal truths," gets fetishized as the only alternative to disorder and disorganization (Wilson 1983). The fetishism in its turn sustains the illusion of the neutral observer "outside" the social structure. Indeed, the organic interaction between traditional theory and bourgeois social relationships "ontologizes" the abstract subject/knower (Taylor 1993, p. 322). The abstract subject/knower can only "explain" the supposedly independent world by yielding its reason to scientific, technological, and organizational-bureaucratic conceptions of (instrumental) "rationality." For such an ontologized subject, theories have a subordinate instrumental role as testable and falsifiable hypotheses that must finally bow to unchangeable reality. "If we think of the object of the theory in separation from the theory," Horkheimer states, "we falsify it and fall into quietism or conformism" (1972d, p. 229; see also Adorno 1968, pp. 338–70). Positivism cannot go beyond the "given." Positivism is defeatism, Adorno states.

Positivist epistemologies, therefore, cease to assign a genuinely critical nature to social and natural sciences. Withdrawing the dialectical significance of objectivation qua a social activity, critical rationalism, a variant of positivist epistemologies, is only critical *within* science, that is, among scientific statements *about* the allegedly independent, and as such reified, "reality."[2] Critical rationalism, as reflected in Karl Popper's epistemological attitude, seeks logical coherence among theoretical and experimental propositions and limits the scope of criticism to logical consistency within the web of statements. The dialectical view indicates, however, that logical contradictions are not mere maladjustments of thought related to an independent reality. Accordingly, they can resolve only through an alteration in cognitive/material reality. Whereas for a positivist epistemology the problem is located in the incoherent web of knowledge, for critical theory the problem is at the same time practical: It is in the very thing that a positivist takes as the object of knowledge, and "in the last instance, even [in] the problematic condition of the world" (Frisby 1972, p. 111; see also Adorno 1976b, p. 109). Criticism, then, cannot be limited to contradictory statements. To reach the truth, society and its sociopolitical contradictions must also be criticized and changed accordingly.

There is a relation of mutual implication between epistemic truth, epistemology, and political engagement. As Adorno points out (new) contradictions in cognitive/material reality are mediated by knowledge. Hence, logical and practical critiques "are moments of the same movement of the concept" (1976a, p. 25). Adorno understands this movement as the unity of scientific and metascientific critique. From a political epistemological perspective, the goal of such a movement is upper levels of new coherence.

Adorno and Horkheimer follow Lukacs in seeing contradiction and reification as social realities. In his book *History and Class Consciousness*, Georg Lukacs offers a metacriticism of bourgeois intellectual efforts and underlines the necessary limits of all truth claims within the general framework of the bourgeois mode of social relationship. His *negative critique* is indeed a social critique of the bourgeois consciousness. Lukacs's *Ideologiekritik* is based on the notion that "ideological and economic problems lose their exclusiveness and merge into each other" (1971, p. 34). Far from taking a simplistic reductionist position, Lukacs maintains that the nature of economic conditions of bourgeois production is expressed in intellectual phenomena and vice versa. Also, to borrow Adorno's term, the bourgeois mode of social relationships is the "concretion" of the intellectual phenomena.

To justify this position, Lukacs analyzes the tradition of bourgeois philosophy and shows that its antinomies have the same structure as the contradictions in the bourgeois mode of social and economic relations. Just as commodities get reified in the societal mode and become fetishes cut-off from production processes; for example, the theoretical fetish, that is, the fixed "object," emerges. The reified object appears as a constant given, independent from the historical process through which it has come into intellectual and actual existence. Hence, the limit to bourgeois thought is "objective"; Lukacs writes: "It is the class situation itself" (1971, p. 83). Lukacs concludes that the theoretical contradictions of bourgeois thought cannot be resolved theoretically—that there is a constitutive relationship between the societal and the theoretical contradictions. In political epistemological language, contradiction is cognitive/material contradiction, new incoherence.

Reification, accordingly, is an entity of a peculiar cognitive/material nature. It is a mode of social relationship expressed in thought and, at the same time, a mode of thought concretized in a specific societal reality. Reification highlights the juncture at which contradictions in social reality and inconsistencies in thought entwine and make it impossible, practically as well as theoretically, to separate them without committing more reification. It seems that the traditional epistemological doctrine that seeks coherence and looks for the resolution of inconsistency merely within the web of propositions commits this further reification. Hence, the obstacles of irrationality and inconsistency in bourgeois thought cannot be overcome without being removed from the society. No doubt, dialectical materialist understandings of contradiction as a cognitive/material reality pose critical epistemological questions for critical theoreticians. Let us investigate the nature of these questions.

Contradiction and truth

Highly influenced by Lukacs's nonorthodox version of Marxism,[3] Adorno argues that a science that remains silent before the sociopolitical contradictions of the cognitive/material world is "irrational" and untrue (1976a, p. 26), since it displaces "the real import" (Frisby 1972, p. 113). As a result, the project of political epistemology learns from Adorno that "the idea of scientific truth cannot be split off from that of a true society" (Adorno 1976a, 27). How can we meaningfully talk about a *true*—not just ethically good or politically just but also *epistemically* true—cognitive/material reality, however? A proper response must link the idea of epistemic truth to the notion of the unity of logical and practical critiques. I shall argue that Adorno's critique of positivism and Horkheimer's idea of critical theory tie the truthfulness of science to new coherence.

Positivist epistemology does not see the constraints posed by the operation of critical rationalism as "a socially institutionalized regulatory system."[4] It ceases to criticize the sociopolitical constituents of theories *epistemically*, politically, as well as ethically. In other words, and from a political epistemological perspective, positivist epistemologies, including critical rationalism, are not dialectically critical, inasmuch as they aspire to leave cognitive/material reality intact (they do not, however, leave the "independent" reality intact, ignoring their engagement in the cognitive/material reality, positivist knowledge, and epistemology help reifying it). The dialectical view implies that "the critique of the relationship of scientific statements to that to which they refer is...inevitably compelled towards a critique of reality" (1976a, p. 24). As Horkheimer and Adorno show in their critique of modern capitalist societies, this false idea of science contributes to the totality, the false whole,[5] of advanced industrial societies, and, together with the extension of norms of maximization, technical rationality and scientism effectively influence the entire structure of modern life.

From a dialectical perspective, positivist social sciences that aspire to comprehend society are indeed products, or, better, constituents, of the very processes of rationalization that are concretized and incarnated in the modern society, the subject of social science's comprehension. Therefore, positivist social sciences and their truth claims are forces of production that contribute to the present capitalist mode of social life. They are, in turn, sustained by the capitalist mode of power relationships. Positivist social sciences thus somehow correspond—not to an independent society but instead to the society they dialectically constitute. Oddly enough, then, and apparently despite all the above criticisms, the dialectical view seems to imply that positivist social sciences are "correct." This seemingly paradoxical situation expands when we remember that for Adorno and Horkheimer, the capitalist mode of sociopolitical life is a *false* whole. What do this falsity and that correctness mean? No doubt they are normative, epistemological terms with sociopolitical connotations and moral relevance. Can participants in the project of political epistemology learn lessons from critical theory's responses to these questions? Does critical theory offer a way out of the above paradox?

Adorno's analysis of *objective abstraction* offers a way of thinking about these questions. As he argues, the abstraction of exchange value is embodied in the real-world development of the exchange system. The exchange system, therefore, is the objective abstraction, the practical fetishization, of exchange value. "Exchange value, merely a mental configuration when compared with use value, dominates human needs and replaces them: illusion dominates reality," and Adorno adds, "At the same time, however, this illusion is what is most real, it is the formula used to bewitch the world" (1976c, p. 80). The exchange system, furthermore, is the sociopolitical context that makes positivist social sciences meaningful, possible, and "correct." Accordingly, "the abstraction of exchange value is a priori allied with the domination of the general over the particular, of society over its captive members....The domination of man over man is realized through the reduction of man to agents and bearers of commodity exchange" (Adorno 1976a, p. 14). Positivist social sciences are guilty of this reduction. Violent abstraction is, therefore, a theoretical move and a social practice at once. Adorno devotes a large part of his theoretical efforts, especially in *Negative Dialectics*, to resisting the domination of the general over the particular. It is based on his dialectical understanding of objective abstraction that Adorno regards the materialist understanding of the concept and meaning, the rejection of universals, and the denial of the subject–object dichotomy, as political activities against the dominance of the capitalist system. I will return to this point later in this chapter.

For Adorno, while the "correctness" of positivist social sciences and epistemology is due to their constitutive role in the exchange system, the objective abstraction, as a capitalist state of affairs, is not truthful. It is antagonistic and (new) contradictory.[6] "The separation of subject and object," Adorno states, "is real and illusory." He continues: "True, because in the cognitive realm, it expresses the real separation, the dichotomy of human condition, a coercive development. False, because the resulting separation must not be hypostasized, not magically transformed into an invariant. This contradiction in the separation of subject and object is imported into [positivist] epistemology" (2000c, p. 139). Metaphysics is indeed loaded by this contradiction; it is thus untrue.

The falsity of positivist knowledge also stems from the fact that it, for the sake of logical coherence, ignores the antagonistic moment of cognitive/material reality. This moment cannot be inaugurated in logical coherence. The systematic ignorance of both the antagonistic—new contradictory—moments of reality and of sciences' entanglement in social facts gives positivist science the illusion of ahistoricity and the fantasy of universal claims. The positivist view is oblivious to the fact that resolving contradictions in thought requires a historical development beyond which we cannot leap in thought: It requires changing social conditions (Horkheimer 1972c, p. 269).

The fetishism of universality is indeed a mark of epistemic falsity. In other words, for Adorno, logical coherence that hides the new contradictions of a cognitive/material reality contributes to the untruth of consciousness. Universality fetishism is also politically dangerous, since social antagonisms are breaking points at which social individuals can "feel" the resisting voices of the fellow oppressed. Universal theories and concepts doubly tyrannize the subjugated voices by further covering up the cognitive/material new contradictions under the seamless blanket of logical consistency among universal claims. Positivist social sciences' untruth, therefore, resides in their fetishism of universality, in their contribution to a local, historically situated, and class-dependent way of thinking that, although it "correctly" and partially constitutes the reality of the bourgeois class, aspires to generalize the local self-awareness of the bourgeoisie to all social classes.[7] Now that the critique of the traditional theory of society shows the "correctness" and, simultaneously, the untruth of traditional thinking, we shall study the affirmative side of a determinate negation of traditional theory.

Contrary to the traditional way of thinking, critical theory relativizes the detachment of the individual from society. It calls upon social individuals to see their interactions as constitutive of social reality and accordingly to refuse to take as given the limits prescribed for their activity. Critical theory also refuses to take values as nonscientific presuppositions about which one cannot offer rational criticism. Indeed, the insistence on neutrality is itself a value-laden move with political functions that are meant to be hidden under the pretext of neutrality. The claim of neutrality, therefore, has normative/political effects.

The critical mind recognizes the present economy and culture as products of human works and organizations. At the same time, however, as Horkheimer points out, "it experiences that the society is comparable to non-human processes, to pure mechanisms, because cultural forms which are supported by war and oppression are not creations of unified, self-conscious will." "That world is not their own," he concludes, "but the world of capital" (1972d, p. 208). The realization of this tension characterizes the critical way of thinking. Like Adorno, Horkheimer argues that the separation of fact from value and the disconnection of knowledge from its social function and context in traditional theory leave no room for the outburst of this tension. For critical theory, social facts are not natural accidents. They are partially constructed by human activity, and as such a *truthful* critical theory can project normative goals, politically change reality, and forge its truth through a practice of making the truth actually happen (see Horkheimer 1993c, pp. 191, 200). Such a strategic move indicates a new relationship between theory and practice.

Critical theory's agenda is to apply negative dialectics to the contradictions of social reality and bring social antagonisms to the level of mass consciousness. Critical theory valorizes the voice of the oppressed, covered up by the universal concepts of the bourgeois class (Horkheimer 1972d, 215). Negative dialectics amounts to "the transformation of the concepts which dominate the economy into their opposites; fair exchange into deepening of social injustice, a free economy into monopolistic control, productive work into rigid relationships which hinder production, the maintenance of society's life into the pauperization of the people" (Horkheimer 1972b, p. 247). Negative dialectic is in fact a perpetual alteration of the concept into its opposites—to what the concept can be but is not. The idea of negative dialectic indicates a rejection of the teleological or structural necessity of the present. Bringing social antagonisms (new contradictions) to the surface, critical theory dissolves the rigidity of the objective abstraction into "a field of tension of the possible and the real" (Adorno 1976c, p. 69). To some extent, this tension is between the way cognitive/material reality is and the ways it can possibly be. Dialectically speaking, the tension is indeed between consciousness and matter that unite in opposition. This is why negative dialectics is simultaneously a critique of cognition and matter, of the object, and the concept of the object.

Critical theory in its sociopolitical context

Critical theory and its negative dialectical content do not suggest a straightforward positive outline for political action (Horkheimer 1972d, p. 242). For Horkheimer, "true theory is more critical than affirmative" (p. 242). That Horkheimer and Adorno strategically choose negative dialectic over affirmative programs is partially based on a theoretical/experimental study of the logic of domination in the 1930s and 1940s. Investigating this point sheds light on the relationship between critical theory and its sociopolitical context.

In the 1930s and 1940s, the Frankfurt School thinkers were occupied with understanding the defeat of the German working-class movement by Fascists (see Dubiel 1985, pp. 69–119). Disappointed with Stalinist Marxism, they wondered why the consciousness of the proletariat was alienated from the emancipatory truth of Marxism. For critical theoreticians, in other words, philosophy and orthodox Marxism seemed to have lost their legitimacy in the sociopolitical turbulence of this period, when they relinquished material experience and took refuge in metaphysics—when philosophy thought that the search for truth and its criteria have nothing to do with political or revolutionary goals and when positivism prevailed over the commonsense and captivated the intellectual sphere.

Addressing this concern, critical theoreticians underlined the metamorphosis of free market capitalism into state capitalism and maintained that, due to this alteration in reality, the traditional Marxist critique of liberal political economy and the proletariat's consciousness had ceased to be effective (see Benhabib 1986, pp. 158–63). From a political epistemological perspective, this position implies that since cognitive/material reality is now different, the mass consciousness—constituted by, and constituting, the new reality—cannot be understood or criticized in a traditional way.

In critical theoreticians' view, state capitalism refuses the autonomy of the market and "politicizes" the distribution of wealth and power. In this new sociopolitical situation, normative ideas and ideologies of liberal capitalism lose their justification and, in turn, fail to justify each of the two newly emerged systems of state capitalism: "mass democracy" and "totalitarianism."[8] This is why, in *Dialectic of Enlightenment*, Horkheimer and Adorno substitute the traditional critiques of liberal political economy with a critique of instrumental rationality. Of course, Adorno and Horkheimer share the dialectical materialist view with Marx. Like Marx, they believe in the dialectical interdependence between the structure and the superstructure. Unlike him, however, they underscore cognition, instrumental reason, the culture industry, and the media—the superstructure—as the primary variants for explaining and criticizing the contemporary cognitive/material reality. From a political epistemological point of view, neither Marx nor critical theoreticians were wrong in their prioritizing one of the two opposites of matter and cognition, respectively. Rather, the very reality, the in-itself-for-us, had changed, and the new cognitive/material reality required a new philosophizing and conceptualization. As Horkheimer states, "The movement of reality is mirrored in the fluidity of concepts" (1993c, p. 209). As we will see, Adorno's and Horkheimer's philosophizing and criticisms of the new reality communicate important insights into the project of political epistemology.

According to Horkheimer's and Adorno's dialectical materialist view, while the proletariat's consciousness "represents" reality as a *camera obscura*, this representation is mediated, and mediation "is social and historical" (Adorno 1973, pp. 174–6). Moreover, any materialist theory is itself a moment of the historical totality. Adorno and Horkheimer are well aware that their own understanding of the present situation is partially conditioned by it. Hence, without a clear epistemological theory that could justify the claim of truthfulness,[9] their materialist understanding of the present proletarian consciousness would remain incapable of distinguishing itself from the sociology of knowledge and, in so doing, escaping the latter's self-referential epistemic relativism.

Furthermore, there is a political aspect to Horkheimer's and Adorno's need for a new normative epistemology. Adorno asserts: "Criticism implies demythologization. This, however, is no mere theoretical concept nor one of indiscriminate iconoclasm which, with the distinction between true and untrue, would also destroy the distinction between justice and injustice" (1976b, p. 121). Since political criticism in the name of justice cannot proceed without a claim of truthfulness, unless Horkheimer and Adorno provide normative epistemic justifications for their critical theoretical positions, the apparently relativistic nature of a dialectical materialist approach cripples their political criticisms. After all, the dialectical materialist view does not separate validity and genesis (Adorno 1976a, p. 22). The relativism that apparently comes next seems detrimental to the project of critical theory. At this historical stage of the Frankfurt School's intellectual development, there was a need for "rephilosophizing" the project of criticizing mass consciousness. Investigating the nature of this need, Seyla Benhabib argues that "only an epistemology carried out as social theory can provide the program of interdisciplinary materialist research with the reflexive legitimation that no specialized science can lend to it." She adds:

> The early program of interdisciplinary materialist research was naïve in this epistemological sense. For when a materialist theory of social life process explains the conditions of its own genesis as an aspect of the very process it investigates, it introduces the epistemological problem of genesis and validity, or in modern terms, of "context of discovery" and "context of justification." This problem cannot be resolved by the methods of the specialized sciences, but presupposes a meta-theory of the development and justification of human knowledge, and this remains a philosophical task. (Benhabib 1986, p. 377)

Again, the need for an epistemology that would properly reconcile epistemic validity with sociopolitical situatedness imposes itself on Adorno and Horkheimer.

Adorno traces the root of the genesis–validity dichotomy in Aristotle's metaphysics. Aristotle, Adorno states, does not believe in the Platonic opposition between the true being of the world of ideas and the nonbeing of the world of sensible diversity. Opposite to Plato's idea, Aristotle's "form" or "essence" (or shall I say meaning, the concept and the subject?) "does not lie outside the things whose essence it is, but is only in so far as it is in things themselves" (Adorno 2001, p. 26). The concept, in other words, has a "historical dimension," and "the essential is always historical" (pp. 5, 19). Therefore, Aristotle's metaphysics implies the "particular thing," that is, the world of sensible diversity, is the "substantial": The object really and truly exists. Aristotle thus is a "mediating thinker," though, as Adorno complains, his is a nondialectical notion of mediation.[10]

However, in a "Platonic moment," and despite his belief in the reality of the world of becoming and the ontological immanence of the concept/form in the object/matter, Aristotle locates truth in the eternally immutable, the higher, and the form (Adorno 2001, p. 56). As Adorno states, "The central contradiction—to return to the specific problematic of Aristotle's work—is that, on the one hand, the idea is supposed to be only immanent, only mediated, only something inhering in an existent and not transcendent with regard to it; yet, on the other, it is made into something which has being in itself" (p. 46). The contradiction in Aristotle's metaphysics resides in the point that the mediated concept realized in matter is simultaneously the *higher* reality.

Aristotle separates genesis from validity in order to address the above contradiction in his metaphysics: *For us*, the becoming thing, the object, is primarily given, but *in itself* the higher is the idea, the subject or the concept. So the truth content of the concept is distinct from the path toward knowledge. It is as if the moments of genesis and validity are separated by an "abyss of meaning" (Adorno 2001, p. 39). This results in an unresolved opposition between the two moments, and Aristotle makes no effort to reconcile this opposition. In this Platonic moment, Aristotle's object, the "primarily given," ceases to be for-us-in-itself. Abstracting knowledge from genesis, Aristotle ignores "the sedimented history contained in any piece of knowledge." Therefore, "a part of truth is also lost," and this is the root of metaphysics' falsity: through a process of abstraction, a "de-temporalization" that mediates the concept and takes place within time and history, metaphysical "truth" appears as transhistorical and disregards its temporal moment (pp. 44, 71).

According to Adorno, only a dialectical understanding can surpass the contradiction in Aristotle's metaphysics (2001, p. 100): "the genetic moments are…inherent in the character of validity itself," and "the moment of the origin or the temporal genesis of knowledge…is inherent in the character of truth" (p. 45). Truth has a "temporal core," a sociopolitical constituent. Consequently, the genesis of the genesis–validity dichotomy is constitutive of this dichotomy's very meaning. The genesis–validity dichotomy resides at the core of the sociology of knowledge's materialist, and not dialectical materialist, approach to knowledge—and also at the center of what Bruno Latour calls the "critical barbarity" of our time. In the chapter that follows, I shall address this point. At present, it suffices to mention that Adorno indicates an approach that might successfully reconcile epistemic validity with sociopolitical situatedness and, in so doing, contribute to the project of political epistemology.

Hegel believed that the end point, telos, is indeterminately and implicitly present in each historical form of consciousness. The idea of essential truth helped him to rescue the partial truths of nonfinal forms of consciousness. For Hegel, determinate negations uncover the indexical share of truth that each form of emerging consciousness holds. Since Horkheimer and Adorno reject Hegel's teleological essentialism,[11] however, they cannot follow Hegel's metaphysical path of saving the partial truth of indexical consciousness. Accordingly, they cannot reject epistemic relativism in a Hegelian way. Again, Horkheimer and Adorno seem obligated to provide a new, nonrelativist epistemology.

Critical theory's would-be normative theory of truth

Unfortunately, Horkheimer and Adorno gave up the project of new epistemology and did not pursue more articulated versions of a dialectical materialist, nonrelativistic normative theory of truth and meaning (see Rush 2004, pp. 26–7). I will study the idea of relativism in the next chapter and explain that the Frankfurt School's critiques of the sociology of knowledge broach important insights for understanding truth–practice relationships. These insights can be supplemented by a dialectical materialist reading of Hans-Georg Gadamer's ontology of meaning. The combination, I shall argue, shows the project of political epistemology a path for transcending the genesis–validity dichotomy. It also opens up the possibility of preserving a nonrelativist idea of partial truth for the situated consciousness.

Let me conclude my discussion so far by presenting (and, to some extent, repeating) a political epistemological reading of critical theory. This reading underlines critical theory's would-be contribution to the project of political epistemology. As we have seen, for critical theory, the subject/knower is neither an isolated individual nor a sum total of individuals. Rather, the subject is always already situated in the social context, and "his activity is the construction of social present" (Horkheimer 1972d, p. 211). Nevertheless, the subject's mode of engagement is different in different classes of society. Furthermore, contradictions among classes are organically interrelated to theoretical contradictions in the intellectual sphere of society. For that reason, when the categories with which the bourgeoisie identifies itself, such as harmony of interests, free exchange, and free competition, are applied to other social classes, the contradictions appear, and the untruth of the bourgeois social order manifests itself. This means that the coherence between the bourgeois social order and bourgeois self-awareness, which provides "correctness" to the bourgeois theory/life complex, is revealed to be a tentative and local one.

The normative idea of new coherence provides us with an epistemological understanding of this phenomenon. According to this understanding, bourgeois self-awareness has historically managed to establish a tentative consistency between a traditional theory, bourgeois social science, and a lived reality, the bourgeois form of life. As constitutive of the bourgeois reality, positivist social sciences are "correct" but only to the extent to which they respect their own situatedness within the bourgeois reality and refrain from stating universal claims about the whole society. The bourgeois mode of life is a cognitive/material complex—a tentative totality that lives within the neighborhood of invisible (new) contradictions. Critical theory, "dominated at every turn by a concern for reasonable conditions of life" (Horkheimer 1972d, p. 199), makes these contradictions visible and, in so doing, adds to the new contradictions of society with the hope of changing the cognitive/material reality into a less new contradictory one. At the moment of critique, the tentative coherence of the bourgeois totality vanishes, and the untruth of positivist consciousness and its universal claims come into sight. It is exactly from within this social, political, and epistemic context of new incoherence that the move toward an upper level of new coherence is initiated. This movement amounts to understanding, criticizing, and changing the reality all at once. In other words, a specific kind of determinate negation takes place when the critical theoretician attempts to resolve the tensions and abolish new contradictions.

Hegel's teleological dialectics suggests that determinate negation "passes over into affirmation" and "by being pushed far enough and by reflecting itself, is one with positivity" (Adorno 2001, p. 144). As mentioned above, this is how Hegel secures the partial truth of the emerging consciousness: the negation of the negative results in the positive, the indexical share of truth at the specific moment of dialectic. The unity of subject and object, therefore, happens at the very end. Adorno, on the contrary, finds this telic interpretation of determinate negation ideological, since it turns Hegel's teleological metaphysics into a philosophy of identity and makes the real change and the radically open future impossible. This ideology makes genuine and "autonomous" political activity by human beings, that is, the alteration of the present into something radically new, impossible (p. 92). As the positive, the not radically open future (the "present-future," in Jacques Derrida's term) dictated by the telic logic of history is already determined through the higher concept of the negation of the negation.

Openness, as the transcendental precondition of truth, implies the radical possibility of the future. Therefore, for participants in the project of political epistemology, there is always a multiplicity of new coherent cognitive/material reality on the horizon of possibility. The present reality is indeed the actuality of one possibility and at the same time the subjugation of others. The present cognitive/material reality's untruth stems from this subjugation, this concealment, which might be even doubled if the dominant actuality claims universality and denies the very existence of the subjugated possibilities. Therefore, the partial truthfulness, correctness, of a theory as a constituent of reality accompanies two levels of untruth. The first sort of untruth refers to the concealment of other voices and possibilities. This, as we saw, happens whenever an actuality emerges, and it has to do with the "facticity," the historicity, of us. The second sort of untruth carries greater political danger. It escalates subjugation by denying the very existence of other possibilities qua possibility. It is the voice of the subjugated that resonates in new contradictions. It is this voice that, in the name of truth, must be heard. It is this voice that, as Adorno insists, the logical consistency among dominant propositions strives to silence.

I will expand these thoughts in the final chapter of this study and argue that the more open to other possibilities a "societal relationship" is, the less (new) contradictory it becomes. In other words, I attempt to tie social, political, and cognitive openness in truth. For now, the brief discussion above should suffice to help us understand Adorno's normative statement, "Opinion should not be rejected with Platonic arrogance, but rather its untruth is to be derived from the truth: from the supporting societal relationship and ultimately from the latter's own untruth" (1976c, p. 86).

The emerging cognitive/material reality and its degree of new coherence—its *truthfulness* in political epistemological terms, or its *objective validity* in Adorno's language—are path dependent. "Objective validity," Adorno states, "preserves that moment of its emergence and this moment permanently affects it" (1976a, p. 21). This is why, according to the dialectical materialist view of critical theory, the critique is always a critique of cognition and matter, the object, and the concept of the object. The cognition/matter—the concept/object—is actual only because there are other possibilities that are not so. The critique that actualizes other possibilities, therefore, uncovers new truths simultaneously. When the new coherence is realized, the new truth appears. The idea of dialectics without essentialism—the rejection of teleology—however, means that (new) contradictions never end.[12] New coherence and new truths, then, are moments of dialectical processes that have no immanent logic, necessity, and emancipatory direction.[13] As such, there are always elements of hope, emotion, collective will, moral decision, responsibility, and strategic action engaged in the never-ending wars of position *and* maneuver (to evoke Antonio Gramsci's articulation of political practice) in the name of truth. The justness of these elements is not alien to the truth of the cognitive/material reality.

The dialectic of Enlightenment

As critical theoreticians, Horkheimer and Adorno seek a philosophical/ theoretical as well as experimental description of the defeatist consciousness of the proletariat—a description, or, better, self-liquidating critique, which must dialectically interact with its object and change it accordingly (Horkheimer 1993c, p. 205). This purpose, however, demands of Horkheimer and Adorno that they establish a new, non-positivist epistemology that secures the truth claims of critical theory's situated "descriptions." In other words, Adorno and Horkheimer look for a new philosophy and a new epistemology, since the very world, the object of philosophizing, is now changed. Now that the philosophies of Hegel, Marx, Nietzsche, and other philosophers have played their own historic roles in partially transforming cognitive/material reality—now that the promises of the Enlightenment are not fulfilled—what, they ask, is the philosophy of our time?

Horkheimer and Adorno embrace Hegel's notion that philosophy is one's own time expressed in thought.[14] In order to understand their own time, they ask why, after decades of struggle, Hegel's hope for the realization of reason and philosophy in history is proved to have been in vain—why the enlightened project of rationalizing society ended in Auschwitz. They inquire into what philosophy looks like, or *should* be, after Auschwitz, when the cognitive/material reality is different, when we know that Hegel's teleological philosophy and its doctrine of the unity of the subject and the object, the identity of reason and history, is epistemically false and sociopolitically disastrous.

Auschwitz, Adorno writes, "confirmed the philosopheme of pure identity as death" (1973, p. 362; see also Berman 2002, p. 119). In the face of the experience of disaster, Adorno states, "the assertion that what is has meaning and the affirmative character which has been attributed to metaphysics almost without exception, become a mockery; and in face of the victims it becomes downright immoral" (2001, p. 104). In other words, if, as the metaphysical system demands, there is a *telos* or an *arche,* if there is a meaning for the whole course of history, then meta-physics affirms Auschwitz as a determinate stage in this whole rational and meaningful development toward the good. Auschwitz appears as meaningful and good in its capacity. Hence, Adorno's rejection of meta-physics has a moral, a political, and an epistemic motif. From a political epistemological point of view, the sociopolitical context of the 1940s, the "situation," belies metaphysics: Metaphysics' meaning—or better, the lack thereof—is partially constituted by the situation. As Adorno states, "Situation affects not only metaphysical thought, but…the con-tent of metaphysics itself" (p. 105). It is within the sociopolitical "con-stellation" of the 1940s that metaphysics finds—or, better, loses—its meaning and truth content.

In *Dialectic of Enlightenment,* Horkheimer and Adorno offer a tran-scendental analysis and pinpoint the process that has, in part, made the disaster possible. They argue that *subjective,* or *instrumental, reason-ing* has been gradually concretizing in reality throughout the past 200 years. Subjective reasoning, in other words, is the cognitive constitu-ent of social rationalization, modernity's iron cage (Horkheimer 1974, p. 187). Throughout this process, instrumental reason that facilitates the mastery of nature has become universal, the whole reason, practi-cally as well as theoretically. It is this reification of subjective reasoning that has made the disaster possible. Arresting the dialectical unity of opposites—faith/value versus reason, matter versus consciousness, and so on—reified the Enlightenment reason that ahistorically dichoto-mizes opposites and ontologizes a self that knows the world only if it is rid of religion, values, myth, matter, interest, social engagement—in a word, the world (Horkheimer and Adorno 1988, p. 29). For Adorno and Horkheimer, such a mythical self, the Cartesian subject or the Kantian transcendent self that rises above its sociopolitical engagement and sit-uatedness, systematically misunderstands its object, since it overlooks its reciprocally constitutive relationship with the object.

Abstracted from the world, the subject has no choice but an irrational, practical faith in the reality of the world. Enlightenment reason, there-fore, depends on myths, though it rejects them: "Enlightenment still recognizes itself even in myths" (Horkheimer and Adorno 1988, p. 6). In other words, Enlightenment reason that, forgetting dialectic, reifies itself as the opposite of myth comes back to myth. This is the dialec-tic of Enlightenment: A dialectical return to—or *of*—myth takes place when Enlightenment reason disregards its responsibility—that is, crit-icism through and through—and reifies itself as subjective rationality. In *Dialectic of Enlightenment,* Horkheimer and Adorno make an effort to recover the vivid nature of Enlightenment reasoning, remove its reified and sclerotic instrumentality, and remind it that Enlightenment also demands a critique of the myth of instrumental reason. In other words, they seek a continuation of the genuine Enlightenment: the courage to know and critique everything, including rationality itself. This is the way Adorno and Horkheimer think about what philosophizing *should be* after Auschwitz. For them, rationality, and philosophy in particular, must resume its courageous critical function. After Auschwitz, philosophy should assume a "total" critique of subjective reasoning.

The dialectical materialist view, as we have seen, demands critique to be a critique of the object and the subject simultaneously. Orthodox materialism is nondialectical, since it abstractly dichotomizes genesis and epistemic validity. Accordingly, the *critique of ideology* aspires to illustrate that a theory or an idea is ideological, since it has not sufficiently transcended its context of genesis. Sharing this nondialectical position with materialism and abstractly separating "context of discovery" from "context of justification," positivist epistemologies offer the same explanation for falsity: a "fusion of power and validity," hidden behind the theory, makes it untrue. Habermas believes that the critique of ideology made Enlightenment reflexive, "for the first time," on its own theories. Through self-referential application of the critique of ideology to specific critiques of ideology, however, Enlightenment reaches a second level of reflexivity.

In Habermas's view, Adorno and Horkheimer radicalize and totalize the critique of ideology to "enlighten the Enlightenment about itself" (1982, p. 22). Now critique turns back on reason and investigates the material foundation, the sociopolitical context and constituent, of its reasonings. "The suspicion of ideology becomes total"; that is, the fusion of power and truth, genesis and validity, is located behind—or, better, is constitutive of—all reasonings and truth claims. Materialism is now substituted for by dialectical materialism. For Adorno and Horkheimer, the reified instrumental reason dismisses this fusion of power and truth. Assimilating itself to power, instrumental reason reduces truthfulness to pragmatic success—or, indeed, powerfulness. As a result, it drops the notion of epistemic validity and consequently ceases to be critical, since, as we have seen, criticism implies a truth claim. This evaluation of instrumental reason "is the final unmasking of a critique of ideology applied to itself" (p. 22). This is no relativism. Adorno and Horkheimer wish to retain the "performative contradiction" in which genesis and validity remain opposites in unity. They do not reduce one of them to the other. The performative contradiction, as Habermas argues, paradoxically uses Enlightenment rationality to show the limits of this rationality to itself. It, therefore, underlines the sociopolitical situatedness of any universal claim of validity.[15]

For the reified Enlightenment subject, the pure thinking, nature becomes an alien other that must be tamed and dominated. Looking into the epistemic content of this domination makes clear how abstraction, the universal concept's domination over the particular/singular, and the subject–object identity signify the cognitive constituent of modernity's iron cage. Let us first explore *why*, according to Adorno and Horkheimer, subjective reason purports domination. We also need to know *how*, epistemically speaking, the domination proceeds.

Domination and the Enlightenment

According to Horkheimer and Adorno, God's departure from the enlightened worldview left the European man alone in a meaningless world. Occult qualities and causes, sacred entities, and the animistic cosmos, surrendered their place to a chaotic universe emptied of any immanent pattern and design, motive, and telos (1988, p. 5). The European man was no longer a guest in God's world, but the "legitimate" owner and heir of it (p. 5). Now, in this originally meaningless world, everything enjoys its "being" (i.e., its existing *as* a certain thing) and tentative meaning only so far as man blesses it with both. The death of God meant the death of an entity that used to guarantee the truth of Descartes' perceptions and knowledge. Thus, the maturity of enlightened man (Foucault 1997, p. 306) was not only a "courageous" exit from someone else's authority; maturity also implied a daring to know the "truth" in the aftermath of God's death—the "dare to know" that he (the European man) is fully active in "making" the "truth" while giving order and discipline to the chaotic world.

In the absence of any other authority, the Enlightenment subject, the new master, has the right and feels the responsibility to change and dominate the amorphous world. The world is void of static essences that, according to the pre-Enlightenment worldview, were considered the ultimate limits of change and humans' (or even God's) manipulations. Hence, there is in principle no insurmountable barrier to implementing change. There is no boundary to the realm of the subject/knower's domination. According to Adorno and Horkheimer, the instrument of this domination is subjective reasoning (1988, p. 30). Thinking becomes a commodity when its "use value" lies in its ability to facilitate domination. The knowledge and even the art that this thinking produces is justifiable if its production follows a specific logical reasoning.[16] This reasoning is based on the premise that the rationales of justification must demonstrate the "usefulness" of a knowledge claim (Horkheimer 1972d, p. 207). Enlightenment rationality thus identifies itself with the business of use. All modes of behavior and knowledge claims that are incompatible with the logic of this business appear invalid, irrational, mimetic, mythic, and metaphysical (Horkheimer and Adorno 1988, p. 26). Engaged in the business of use, Enlightenment rationality knows and recognizes "things" so long as it can manipulate them, and thus power becomes the principle of all relations between the Enlightened knower and the thing as the colonized known (p. 9). The "power to manipulate" becomes the precondition of knowledge, and the subject/ knower is alienated from the object it dominates (p. 28).

The logic of this conqueror knowledge implies the removal of the incommensurability of entities and their dissolution into actual conformity (p. 12); that is, the will to domination makes the dissimilar comparable by reducing its elements to abstract quantities. What Adorno and Horkheimer call the "myth of quantity" implies the negation of anything new and different in individuals. According to Adorno, the different-in-the-object is the object's "qualitative moment" (1973, p. 43). Indeed, both the object and the subject have qualitative moments, the different-from-the-quantifying-conceptual/subjective moments. The reifying concept, however, quantifies and "reduces the knower to a purely logical universal without qualities" (p. 44). The logic of "quantification" limits the domain of possible experience (p. 13), since "Truth"—as the product of regulative and "category thinking"—needs this repressive equality in order to declare its universality. Hence, the untruth of Enlightenment is that it confounds thought and mathematics and puts aside the classical requirement of thinking about thought.

When this machinery thought takes society as its subject, men become mere species—each exactly like the next—through isolation in the forcibly united collectivity (Adorno 1973, p. 37). This absorption of factuality into mathematical formalism makes the new appear as the predetermined, which is accordingly old (p. 27). The constructed collectivity illustrates domination as a universal necessity and depicts the present division of labor and its correlated social injustice as the epitome of immanent reason. It not only discourages any resistance from dissolved individuals but also gives them the feeling of freedom and liberty in a "rational" society. Enlightenment's culture industry has the same function in manufacturing mass consent (p. 122). This is why Adorno and Horkheimer call Enlightenment a wholesale deception of the masses.[17]

Adorno and the emancipation of the nonconceptual

We also need to know, however, *how* abstraction together with the universal concept's domination over the particular/singular and the subject–object identity composes the cognitive constituent of domination. For Adorno and Horkheimer, dialectic of Enlightenment connotes the present moment, when the dynamism of reason is arrested so much so that the cognitive/material reality stands still, when subjective reason has become the sole source of meaning and conquers the *concept*, the medium of cognition.[18] It is in this very realm of the concept, that Adorno locates the points of resistance to the hegemony of subjective reason. It is the concept that Adorno wants to set into motion again, altering the fixed object into a field of tension. The way in which he strives to "get rid of concept fetishism" is immensely relevant to the project of political epistemology.

It has been argued that the highly pessimistic tenor of *Dialectic of Enlightenment* makes suspect any political attempt to resist domination and break free from the hegemony of instrumental reason.[19] According to this critique, critical theory has no clear political program, since domination is total—since subjective rationality implies obedience and "voluntary servitude" (Marcuse 1969, p. 13). From a dialectic materialist point of view, nonetheless, and according to critical theory's understanding of the theory–practice relationship, Adorno's plan to extinguish "the autarky of the concept" (1973, p. 12) is an epistemic and political activity at once. As Adorno states, far from being a static always-the-same universal, "the subject is an object as well; it only forgets, in its formal hypostasis how and whereby it was constituted" (Adorno 2000c, p. 147). The subject is also an object, that is, the subject has the "element of individual humanity" (p. 138) and has materiality: The subject lives and dies[20] and is mediated through by the very togetherness of humans in the polis. In its meaning and truth content, it is constituted, not self-sufficient.

Adorno wants to rescue the sociopolitical, as well as cultural and individual life, from the spell of subjective reasoning, or the *concept*, as he calls it. The *nonconceptual*, in this view, "is" ever-changing human life, society, politics, culture, art "before" they have been sucked up by subjective reason. The nonconceptual is the vivid reality with the prosperity of potentiality that must, ethically speaking, be freed from modernity's total administration. For Adorno, the nonconceptual is too abundant and dynamic to be totally assimilated and fixed by the concept.

Dialectical materialism implies that the reifying concept is indeed a specific "subjective moment in the object" (Adorno 1973, p. 170). By negating this moment, Adorno's negative dialectics seeks another moment of the object—a qualitatively different (subjective *and/or* objective) moment that is less violent, less reifying, and, in political epistemological terms, less new contradictory. Adorno's negative dialectics wishes to let the object's potentiality of being otherwise than what the concept dictates proceed its movement. Accordingly, there are subjective/cognitive moments constitutive of each step of this becoming. These dynamic subjective (and/or objective) moments involve the truth content and the meaning of the becoming/reality at a specific stage of movement. This is why, according to Adorno's dialectical materialist view, the "subjective moment is framed…in the objective one. As a limitation imposed on the subject, it is objective itself" (p. 180). In other words, the subject "has a core of object,…the subjective qualities in the object are all the more an objective moment." For "it is only as something definite that the object becomes anything at all" (Adorno 2000c, 143).

This "somatic moment of cognition" (Adorno 1973, p. 193) reflects Adorno's political understanding of knowledge. For, reaching a less new incoherent moment that harbors more truthful knowledge presupposes the alteration of the objective *frame*, the reality, into a more open one. It requires a political change of society, inasmuch as society is "immanent" to cognition (Adorno 2000c, p. 143). This political change, as I shall clarify later in this chapter, takes place in a "constellation."

The hegemony of instrumental reasoning means in part that in a totally administered society any access to reality that is not mediated by instrumental reason's categories of understanding is condemned and repudiated as untrue and irrational (Horkheimer and Adorno 1988, pp. 7, 25). In rejecting the hegemony of instrumental reason and reaching out for the nonconceptual, Adorno does not fancy gaining immediate access to the latter. What he rejects is instrumental reason's pretension of having monopoly over mediation. Adorno emphasizes the reciprocal mediation between the concept and the nonconcept: He stresses the social nature of mediation, the fact that the concept's meaning is mediated by the nonconcept, the reality, and the sociopolitical context that harbors potentiality and movement, inasmuch as it is always contradictory and nonidentical to itself.

To transgress the hegemony of instrumental rationality, Adorno points out that the concept is empty without the nonconceptual and that there is always a "remainder" in the object, the nonconceptual, that the concept cannot totally incorporate (1973, p. 5). Adorno's non-concept, however, is not the mystical ineffable (see Finlayson 2002, p. 16)—the beyond-language "unutterable" (Adorno 1973, p. 9) before which mystical silence is the only consistent reaction. (One cannot even utter that the unutterable exists.) Adorno is not to offer an ontology of the-beyond-language that would repeat the "dream of empiricism" in its "renunciation of the concept, of the a prioris and transcendental horizons of language." This dream "must vanish at the daybreak as soon as language awakens" (Derrida 1980, p. 148). Following Hegel, Adorno believes that all particulars are indeed universal/particulars. Adorno's nonidentity thinking seeks the otherwise-than-concept in the object, the inherent "potential that waits in the object" (1973, p. 19). This non-concept, however, is not the ineffable insofar as the latter is understood as the in-itself. According to Adorno's criticism, it is Heidegger's "empty" p. 157 and p. 379 subject, the being, which is "ineffable" (p. 79).

"Concepts alone," Adorno states, "can achieve what the concept prevents.... The determinable flaw in every concept makes it necessary to cite others; this is the font of the only constellations which inherited some of the hope of the name" (1973, p. 53). In other words, it is the alteration of the constellation—thus, the emergence of new concepts as well as new realities—which signifies Adorno's way of attending to the nonconceptual.

The nonconcept remainder is not an in-itself. Rather, it indicates the very potentiality within the reality/object to be different from what the concept aspires to fixate. In political epistemological language, the non-concept about which Adorno can actually talk indicates the very transcendental condition of the concept, the objective reality, which makes the concept possible. This objective reality includes society, which "comes before individual consciousness and all its experience" (1973, p. 181). This objective reality, in other words, signifies the "social a priori" of the concept (p. 190). Reality, Adorno maintains, harbors potentiality, and the nonconcept is the other name for this potentiality.

Adorno reminds the fetishized concept that it is not self-sufficiently meaningful. "Insight into the constitutive character of the non-conceptual in the concept," he states, "would end the compulsive identification, which the concept brings unless halted by such reflection. Reflection upon its own meaning is the way out of the concept's seeming being-in-itself as a unit of meaning" (1973, p. 12).

This "disenchantment of the concept" (Adorno 1973, p. 13) makes subjective reason realize its situatedness and historicity. It loosens the rigid and absolute claims of universal truth and relativizes meaning and truth to nonconceptual contexts. Negative dialectics, therefore, reflects Adorno's ontology of truth, the idea that there is a moment of materiality, a societal mediation, in the concept that gets suppressed under subjective reason's claims of universality and logical coherence.[21] This material moment, the nonconcept, is different from—or, in Hegel's term, opposite to—the universal concept. Though, according to dialectical materialism, the concept and the nonconcept unite in opposition, they never become identical. Identification of the concept and the nonconcept, the subject and the object, is either a positivistic idea or a teleological Hegelian notion. Whereas according to the former identification implies a denial of mediation, for the latter identification indicates a total fulfillment of reciprocal mediation, a final unity without opposition, a telos. Therefore, identification in both ways connotes a fixation of cognitive/material becoming. For Adorno, thus, Hegel's idealist misidentification of the concept and the nonconceptual consists in Hegel's inability to recognize *Geist* as society.[22]

According to dialectical materialism, as becoming, reality is always already ahead of itself, nonidentical to itself, and heterogeneous. Conversely, the identity thesis comprises the principle of the excluded middle: It does not tolerate the heterogeneous, the different, and the remainder (Adorno 1973, p. 5). Hence, "that which is simply differentiated, will be ignored...[and] appear divergent, dissonant, [and] negative" (p. 5). This is an epistemic/political violence to the different, a violence that forecloses the possibility of being otherwise. As closure, then, the conservatism—or *defeatism*, in Adorno's term—of subjective reason is politically violent. It is indeed the *feeling* of "all pain and all negativity" of the suppressed other that is one of "the moving forces of dialectical thinking" (p. 202). For Adorno, the "unhappy consciousness" (p. 203) makes radical critique possible. The unhappy consciousness knows that "suffering ought not to be, that things should be different" (p. 203). Adorno believes that, as a point of resistance and criticism, almost any individual consciousness in the modern period is an unhappy consciousness.[23]

Therefore, for Adorno, it is not the uniformity of a cognitive/material system but its openness to the otherwise that precedes truth: a "need to lend a voice to [the] suffering [object] is a condition of all truth" (1973, pp. 17–18). Adorno's concern is with the irrepressibility of being human and the capacity of being-otherwise. In a sense, negative dialectics attends to the negative aspect of what the human being, and the object, is *not*. Negative dialectics is to preserve the space of a certain negativity that refuses all positivity, all identification. In other words, "there is always a residue, an irreducibility, a fragment that cannot be incorporated."[24] Hence, doing justice to the nonconceptual is the precondition of truth, for "the matters of true philosophical interest at this point in history are those in which Hegel, agreeing with tradition, expressed his disinterest." "They are," Adorno explains, "nonconceptuality, individuality, and particularity—things which ever since Plato used to be dismissed as transitory and insignificant, and which Hegel labeled 'lazy existenz'." (p. 8).

Adorno's dialectical realism

For Adorno, the object/reality and the individual are always already effable: "The individual *Existenz* does not coincide with its cover concept of *Existenz* at large, but neither is it uninterpretable, another "last" thing against which cognition knocks its head in vain" (1973, p. 161). Adorno's "individual," the "more," and the "remainder" in the object are not other names for an in-itself that the autarkic subject cannot catch. After all, for Adorno, the subject is but a moment of the object and not an abstract thing. The "more," Adorno believes, is "immanent" to reality, to what exists (p. 161), while the ineffable does not exist:

> Whatever part of nonidentity defies definition in its concept goes beyond its individual existence; it is only in polarity with the concept, in staring at the concept that it will contract into that existence. The inside of nonidentity is its relation to that which it is not, and which its managed, frozen self-identity withholds from it. (1973, p. 163)

Hence, Adorno's nonidentity thesis is not concerned with—or better, is not targeting—the mystical, beyond-the-language "immediate reality," the supposedly ineffable-by-the-autarkic subject. Rather, it indicates the potentiality that inheres in the concrete thing/object/reality, a "possibility that sticks to the concrete" (p. 57). Therefore, we should understand Adorno's position by putting behind "the myth" (p. 186) of the autarkic subject and the ineffable in-itself.

For Adorno, reality is not a "dead thing" (p. 91). Identity thinking detaches the subject from the object, ontologizes each one as an inert substrate and turns objects into "immutable ones, into objects that remain the same," whereas "experience shows that they do not remain the same" (p. 154). What Adorno calls "unsuccessful realism," he writes, "seeks to breach the walls which thought has built around itself, to pierce the interjected layer of subjective positions that have become a second nature" (p. 78). In other words, "naive realism" (Adorno 2000c, p. 142) does not rectify the mistake of identity thinking in ontologizing the subject and giving it a second nature as a substrate.

Naïve realism, therefore, is unsuccessful, since it does not see the falsehood of the objective abstraction and the untruth of the autarkic subject. Idealism, the opposite of naïve realism, is also futile, since it too plays into the hands of the false objective reality. What I wish to think of as Adorno's *dialectical realism* must be simply différent.[25] As a non-teleological dialectical view, it should not be "positive" in its negation of idealism. In other words, the negation of the negation of naïve realism does not result in a synthesis of both that harbors their affirmative component, the autarky of the subject.

I believe Adorno's conception of freedom helps us form a better estimation. He states:

> The judgment that a man is free refers to the concept of freedom, but this concept in turn is more than it predicated of the man, and by other definitions the man is more than the concept of his freedom. The concept says not only that it is applicable to all individuals defined as free; it feeds on the idea of a condition in which individuals would have qualities not to be ascribed to anyone here and now. (1973, 150)

In other words, the concept of freedom "lags behind itself as soon as we apply it empirically" (p. 151). The concept of freedom reflects the object, the man, but simultaneously negates itself as covering what man really is. Through this negation, it testifies to the nonconcept in the object/ man as a potentiality of being otherwise than what the here-and-now definition of man/object determines. Man, the object, "is not what it says, then" (p. 151).

Perhaps Adorno's dialectical realism has to do with this understanding of the concept of freedom. The self-negating kernel of the concept of freedom is constitutive of any subjective moment of Adorno's object. And since the subject/concept is constitutive of the object, self-negation in the concept is the other name for the object's freedom to be different. Accordingly, when Adorno talks about potentiality, that is, the dynamism immanent to the object or to the nonconcept and the different-within-the-object, he does not allude to something positive and immediate within the object. Rather, he indicates negatively— that the object is a free becoming. His dialectical realism, therefore, is negative, not positive. Adorno's negative dialectics is to free dialectics from the urge to assimilate, or arrest, the nonconcept, and his dialectical realism is to underscore freedom/nonconcept/potentiality in the kernel of the object. Perhaps, I shall argue, this is how Adorno keeps open the possibility of genuine political activity against the dominance of instrumental rationality and its identity thinking.

Dialectical materialism cannot be a metaphysical account of the "final" structure of reality. According to Adorno, such an account—through the introduction of concepts and principles—eradicates genuine movement, the principal feature of reality. Through abstraction, metaphysical concepts give "unity" to different entities and make the otherwise identical. Movement, on the other hand, implies mutation, différence, and becoming (Adorno 1973, p. 96). In other words, metaphysics and its ontological concepts make the change/movement a "condition of being," a mere repetition of the eternal *arche*, and in so doing, they make the dynamic itself an invariant static (p. 87).

This point is of utmost importance. After all, politics has everything to do with concrete change in society, and if metaphysics, using the magic of the unifying concept, petrifies the object and arrests its genuine dynamism, any metaphysical articulation of realism will also nullify the possibility of genuine political practice and stay "conservative" (see pp. 89–92). From a political epistemological perspective, the untruth of metaphysics is also manifest in its political malfunction.

Let us see how the real and the possible/dynamic may entwine in a dialectical notion of realism. Adorno highlights the point that for Aristotle, *reality* is the form to be filled by the substratum, that is, the poor matter, the pure *possibility*. What Aristotle calls reality, however, corresponds to what we in our everyday language call possibility, that is, a form, a picture, or a plan that has not yet found content, "whereas, when we speak of *reality*, we mean *essentially* that which is filled by sensible material" (p. 37).

As discussed earlier in the chapter, Adorno underscores the fact that Aristotle, though a "mediating thinker," has his "Platonic moments" too: Aristotle is not a dialectical thinker. On the other hand, as Gramsci states, our contemporary commonsense and its associating language are "positivistic," not dialectical. If we radicalize Aristotle's mediation into a full-blown dialectical mediation and simultaneously distance ourselves from our commonsensical everyday language, then we may affirm that, like Aristotle's, our matter/reality is possibility, and we may simultaneously highlight the point that when we refer to matter/object/reality, we mean neither the "concept of matter" (i.e., the Aristotelian universal and unchanging form) nor some ineffable beyond-the-concept/ language secret. From this dialectical perspective, "there is no categorical form to which there is not a corresponding moment in matter which *calls* for it" (Adorno 2001, p. 66). It is in this sense of dialectical realism that Adorno talks about "the object's own dynamics" (Adorno 1973, p. 91) and of contradictions that "have filtered into the object" (p. 161) so that the real object is becoming; that which harbors the potentiality of being nonidentical to itself, to what the instantaneous form/ concept dictates and to *be calling* another form/concept. In short, for dialectical realism, matter is a "dynamic principle" (Adorno 2001, p. 63). Adorno believes that in his "Platonic moment," Aristotle kills reality's dynamism by *conceptualizing* dynamism as the movement of matter/ potentiality toward form/actuality. In so doing, Aristotle's metaphysics suppresses genuine political activity, that is, "miracle," the new beginning that breaks beyond the "automatic process" (Arendt 2006a, p. 78).

According to the Platonic Aristotle, the form is the immutable, the good, the truthful, and the beautiful. Therefore, the movement is predestined, and the change is but an affirmation of the everlasting structure.

From this dialectical perspective, the freedom or potentiality to change is inscribed in the concrete reality of the everyday life, in the constellation. As Horkheimer writes, critical theory "confronts history with that possibility which is always concretely visible within it" (1982, p. 106). For Adorno, therefore, political activity is accounted for by the very cognitive/material reality that harbors potentiality/the nonconcept—the "future-future," in Derrida's words—which cannot be captured by our concepts at the present. Such political activity is corollary to openness and to freedom (see Kohn 2000). It embodies *the promise* that the realm of reality, that is, the realm of the possible, exceeds the conceptual. Adorno, in other words, does not need to first contrive an ontology of political activity in order to show how politics is possible in the first place. Such an ontology forecloses on political activity as genuine change.

Openness to the nonconceptual as a precondition of truth

Openness is not a matter of immediate access to the object-in-itself (the object is always in-itself-for-us). Rather, openness demands more human modes of mediation between the concept and the nonconcept. Mediation is a social interaction, and, as we will see in the final chapter, the ethical character of mediation is a transcendental condition of truth.

Openness, in other words, refers to a mode of sociopolitical interaction that is ethical and of epistemic value.[26] Accordingly, new contradictions signify "the untruth of identity" (Adorno 1973, p. 5), a "wrong" state of affairs foreclosed on the nonidentical, the possibility of being otherwise. For Adorno, the iron cage of late capitalism embodies such a closure and untruth. Dialectic is "the ontology of the wrong state of things. The right state of things would be free of it: neither a system nor a contradiction" (p. 11).

Adorno thus seeks new coherence and rejects systems because of their closure. It is indeed the very closure of a system that promotes contradiction. Following dialectical materialism, Adorno believes that an object is this or that specific object only within a "constellation" of relationships. The object is indeed a "sedimented history" of relationships: "cognition of the object in its constellation is cognition of the process stored in the object" (163). Within constellations of cognitive/material interactions, connections between concepts are not reducible to logical consistency or inconsistency. The material moments of concepts, the sociopolitical constituents, also relate and connect concepts in constellations. These relations signify diverse reciprocal movements of mediation between concepts and material contexts that never end in identity. Reciprocal movements, therefore, remain as dialectical counterparts of real social antagonism and contradictions.[27] New coherence and new incoherence are two modes and moments of these reciprocal movements. Whereas the former indicates a more open-to-the-other reality, with relations of larger mutual support among its different conceptual and nonconceptual elements, the latter implies never-ending cognitive/material contradictions.

Adorno does not teleologically think of a final abolition of new incoherence. "To proceed dialectically," he states, "means to think in contradictions, for the sake of the contradiction once experienced in the thing, and against that contradiction. A contradiction in reality, it is a contradiction against reality" (1973, p. 145). The emancipatory and truthful is not a logically coherent system or a closed consensus. It is rather a never-resting political/epistemic struggle toward upper levels of new coherence. Since what is getting fixed as the object is indeed a "process restored in the object," doing justice to the object has to do with what the object may come to be. The concept cannot do justice to the object unless it, the concept, brings a promise of other relationships with the object: a promise that negates the present conceptualization/fixation of the object, a promise of transcending the status quo. This promise, Adorno asserts, is "the only form in which truth appears"

(1974, p. 98). The never-resting epistemic/political struggle toward upper levels of new coherence embodies this promise.

As J. M. Bernstein asserts, Adorno needs to develop a concept of "material inference" (2004, p. 45) to replace the simple logical inference among concepts. Political epistemology's notions of new coherence and new incoherence are attempts to address this need. New coherence and new incoherence are also modes of relation between the concept and the "totality."[28] This observation signifies the affinity between Adorno's dialectical materialist idea of society as a cognitive/material reality and hermeneutics. Cognition is always an "act" of cognition, and as such it belongs to the objective social context that must be apprehended. In other words, the totality embraces the very experience of the totality. This relationship between the totality and its moment, the cognitive act, is understandable not in a deductive but in a dialectical way. Indeed, Adorno's totality is a "constellation" of interactions whose constituent elements, including cognitive elements, cannot be understood without reference to the whole (see Jay 1977, p. 130). Adorno inspects the hermeneutical relationship between the general and the particular "in its historical concretion" (1976c, 77). Since historical developments are mediated by interacting and situated consciousnesses, and to the extent to which the objective meaning and the cognitive elements of a historical life context constitute that context, Adorno's materialist dialectical theory of society proceeds hermeneutically (Habermas 1976a, p. 139).

For dialectical materialism, the societal relations of historically acting "individuals"[29] are not reducible to law-like relations between things. Similarly, for hermeneutics, societal relations cannot be examined solely in terms of what social actors regard themselves to be. What Adorno formulates as "identity thinking" signifies a fetishized situation in which these two demands fail: a situation in which the conceptual system appears as a self-sufficient world of things "governed by its own laws," as "the objective world" (Sherratt 2001, p. 121). Identity thinking reigns in such an "objective" world where the particular, the singular, is "dictated by the principle of perverted universality" (Adorno 1973, p. 344). What Adorno connotes as the *particular* is very similar to what Derrida means by the *singular*: the "thing" that is covered up even by the very label of "the thing," or "the particular." As Adorno states, "the concept of the particular is always its negation at the same time; it cuts short what the particular is and what nonetheless cannot be directly named, and it replaces this with identity" (p. 173). It is this singular that gets epistemically as well as politically suppressed. And according to Derrida, it is the *impossible* emancipation of this singular that precedes truth. Adorno's "suffering consciousness" and Derrida's Marx are both "haunted" by the specter of this oppressed singular. Adorno's negative dialectic is in a sense an aspiration to transcend the concept in order to reach the nonconceptual, the nonidentical, the present damaged life, the "radically Other" (Cook 2005, p. 32), the immediate singular: a utopian agenda that is as impossible as it is necessary to follow. I shall develop this point in the last chapter.

Enlightenment reason and the birth of the abstract subject

Through abstraction, perverted universality systematically detaches the concept from its sociopolitical context of situatedness, removes its materiality, and in so doing destroys the subject/knower's potential of actually knowing and changing the "objective" world (Adorno 1973, p. 346). The forms of knowing that result from abstraction reify a world-in-itself in which the object is determined to be nothing more than a case of universal concepts. This "objective" world seems unchangeable, while its universals facilitate the subject's mastery over the object. What Adorno and Horkheimer signify as "dialectic of Enlightenment" embodies this reifying process that has historically ended in the birth of a transcendent subject and an objective world. The positivist epistemology that accompanies this ontology holds that in order to discover the truth of the objective world, the knower should not intervene in the world. By separating the subject from the world, identity thinking separates truth from politics. For negative dialectics, the crucial step is to break the "hardened" objective world by emphasizing its contingency. As Adorno asserts, "The means employed in negative dialectics for the penetration of its hardened object is possibility—the possibility of which their reality has cheated the objects and which is nonetheless visible in each one" (1973, p. 52). Here, politics as the art of the possible finds its epistemic value in breaking the spell of reification.

As we have seen, in Adorno's view, the exchange system is the sociopolitical counterpart of identity thinking that makes nonidentical singulars "commensurable and identical" (1973, p. 146). The conceptual reduction of use value to exchange value—that is, to an abstract concept—is the transcendental antecedent or, in Adorno's term, the "a priori" to the social act of exchange, and, through it, to all essential social events. That is, "the condition of exchange, which is objectively decisive, itself implies an abstraction, and in terms of its own objectivity, a subjective act" (Adorno 1976a, p. 15). As a result, abstraction discloses itself as a cognitive/material entity such that the abstract concept becomes immanent to the reified reality. Abstraction is identically preserved in the object, the social relations of exchange, and in the subject—the individual laborer. So the abstract and quantified object, alienated from the subject, appears as an invariant given.

This situation produces "individuals"—perceived as externally related subjects—who are linked together only by principles of exchange, that is, by the administrative rationality of the exchange society, the "category thinking" of positivist rationality. The transcendent subject originates when the reified consciousness, judging through these categories, fails to see the contradiction of the subject–object separation. Subjectivity, hence, emerges as domination through categorization over the world of objects. It implies ignoring the constructedness of categories, the self, and the world/object that appears as a given-in-itself.

According to category thinking and in a system, everything is already assimilated and familiarized in universals. System, following the logic of identity, performs its systematic function and opens no room for the unique and the different. In Adorno's language, identity thinking implies "the primacy of the subject." The primacy of the subject presupposes the subject–object and fact–value dichotomies. It amounts to the transcendence of the subject and the givenness of the object. The primacy of the subject demands that conceptual representation, loaded by the prescientific interest of control, assume the merit of epistemological validity. Even Georg Lukacs's proletarian consciousness, which could professedly grasp the whole truth of social totality, indicates the primacy of the "constitutive subjectivity" that creates the world by externalizing and objectifying its essence (Always 1995, p. 63). Mastery over the object is thus the precondition of the conceptual representation of the object that, in its turn, appears as "the subject's abstract other" (Adorno 2000c, p. 148). The logic of representation apprehends being "under the aspect of manufacture and administration" (Horkheimer and Adorno 1988, p. 84).

The primacy of the subject, the identity between the object and the concept, hence appears as the precondition of representational truth. The capitalist and socialist views alike, for example, objectify and re-present nature *as* matter, men *as* producers, and their interactions *as* products. The nondialectical version of the coherence theory of truth, like the positivist epistemological idea of correspondence, is knitted to the primacy of the subject. For Adorno, however, the primacy of the subject misses the point that the subject and the object are necessarily codeterminates. Neither mind nor matter could dominate the other as a philosophical first principle (Buck-Morss 1979, p. 81). Accordingly, truth does not rest ready at hand and immediate in either one. Rather, it resides in the cognitive/ material reality, the reciprocally mediating subject/object.

The transcendent subject, divested of any relation to the object of knowledge, needs method and methodology to ensure the validity of representing its wholly other, the object. At the same time, Adorno writes, "method must constantly do violence to unfamiliar things, though it exists only so that they may be known. It must model the other after itself" (2000b, p. 121). This is the crucial contradiction in the construction of an epistemology that is constantly polarized into the subjective and the objective moments and seeks the truth, as freedom from contradiction,[30] only in the reified sphere of subjectivity and among propositions.[31] The fault of the traditional version of coherence theory of truth becomes evident: So far as truth is conserved in the coherent web of propositions, the object is cognitively covered up and politically suppressed.

The nonidentity thesis and the reciprocal mediation between the subject and the object form Adorno's critique of historical epistemology. His critical method is in fact a "dialectics without identity."[32] Nonetheless, criticizing epistemology also means maintaining it. There is no justification for falling into skepticism. Indeed, Adorno would say that because, ontologically speaking, the subject and the object are codeterminates and are dialectically mediated through the totality of societal relationships, the subject's knowing the object is possible and indeed the case.

At the present stage, the main question before our interpretation of Adorno's political epistemology is about epistemological normativity. Which criteria, if any, would his political epistemology offer to distinguish between the true statement and the correct totality on the one hand and the false ones on the other? As mentioned before, Adorno himself does not provide a straightforward answer to this question. His negative dialectics, however, provides valuable insights and evidence that allows us to consider Adorno a participant in the project of political epistemology. Let me end this chapter with a reading of Adorno that acts to summarize my argument about the contributions of critical theory to the project of political epistemology.

Adorno as a participant in the project of political epistemology

In his search for truth, Adorno goes to the object to see the real contradictions within reality and between the concept and the object (which are mediating each other and, at the same time, constituting reality). Contradiction is cognitive/material; it is new incoherence. It is not reducible to the logical inconsistency among statements, though it is no stranger to the latter. Contradiction is in the "world" that has been wrongly "disenchanted" and become an in-itself by Kant's "transcendentalizing of appearances" (Bernstein 2001, p. 348), by Descartes' subject–object dichotomy, by identity thinking, and above all by the historical expansion of the capitalist mode of social relationships as the counterpart of these cognitive developments. It is true that the modern world has become disenchanted, but the disenchanted world, as a whole, is untrue, for, according to Adorno, it is antagonistic and strives to conceal its contradictions.

As we have seen, Adorno maintains that disclosing the cognitive/material contradictions, bringing rationality to the social reality, seeking upper levels of new coherence, and "siding with the object" are political emancipatory acts in the name of doing justice to the suppressed nonconceptual. They are simultaneously cognitive/epistemological attempts in the name of truth.[33] Social totality that is "immanent" in experience (Adorno 2000c, p. 163) is not a "rationally continuous object" (Adorno 1972, p. 145).[34] Totality as Adorno portrays it is a field of tension between the actual and the possible. The possibility, the reality, and the potentiality of the subject and the object—and history itself—exist only within a field of tension. This fragmentary characteristic makes philosophy drop its old desire to find the whole meaningful and rational (Adorno 2000a, p. 31). Due to the dialectical interchanges between the actual and the possible, moreover, society is always the ahead-of-itself. The possible, in its turn, is not merely the "not-actual." It is not the future that is already determined materially and formally.[35] The possible is also the negation of the actual. Adorno identifies the task of thought as projecting new possibilities, as looking differently and seeing the otherwise, which is covered up and subjugated. The possible that is to be built on rests in the "more" when Adorno says that society is both subject and object and more (see Adorno 1976a, pp. 32–4). It is the very fragmentary society of the modern era—no matter how totally administrated it might pretend to be—that provides points of resistance and possibilities of radical change. As Adorno's dialectical realism implies, "It is in the facts themselves[36] a tendency that reaches out beyond them" (p. 86).

Therefore, for Adorno there is—or, better, there ought to be—an exit from modernity's iron cage. The emancipatory praxis transcends the dichotomy of *is* and *ought to*. This praxis "is part of an effective striving for a future condition of things in which…the [natural] necessity of the object becomes the necessity of the rationally mastered event" (Horkheimer 1972d, p. 230). It is not the case, then, that Adorno and Horkheimer were paralyzed and petrified before all-embracing subjective reason.[37] Granted, they did not provide a straightforward political program of change to answer the question: "Where to?" As Marx states, however, "this very defect turns to the advantage of the new movement, for it means that we do not anticipate the world with our dogmas but instead attempt to discover the new world through the critique of the old," through "the ruthless criticism of the existing order—ruthless in that it will shrink neither from its own discoveries, nor from conflict with the powers that be" (1986, p. 398).[38] Philosophy after Auschwitz thus must criticize the material moment of the concept, the sociopolitical context of the present truth claims of Enlightenment reason. This criticism proceeds in the name of doing justice to the suppressed other, in the name of the truth of the otherwise.

As discussed above, contrary to naïve realism, Adorno does not wish to "place the object on the orphaned royal throne" once occupied by idealism's subject (1973, p. 181). His thesis of the primacy of the object passes dialectics to "the object's preponderance" and, in so doing, renders the subject–object dialectic materialistic (p. 192). In other words, Adorno's primacy of the object opens a site of possibility by initiating a *new moment* in the subject–object dialectical interdependence. Speaking from within this materialistic moment, Adorno writes that the subject and the object enter their dialectical mediation differently: While the object is conceivable only through the subject, it remains otherwise than the subject.

The primacy of the object, therefore, is not another first philosophy: It does not offer another "first" (this time, the object) as opposed to the concept which is the "first" of identity thinking (see Adorno 1973, pp. 136, 205). The primacy of the object thesis, therefore, is not a supposedly context-free metaphysics. As the materialistic moment of the subject–object dialectic, it is meaningful only from within a constellation. Accordingly, it is meaningless in another constellation, which, as Adorno argues, is the constellation of late capitalism, the sociopolitical reality of the exchange system. It is within this latter constellation that identity thinking, the primacy of the subject, finds its meaning. Or, better, it is this latter constellation, the exchange system of late capitalism, which is in part constituted by, and gives meaning to, the primacy of the subject.

From a political epistemological perspective, Adorno's constellation is akin to the "social a priori" (1973, p. 190) of meaning. The constellation signifies the very pattern of relationships that makes up society. The constellation is the other name for the cognitive/material reality. Adorno believes that presently, within the constellation or the cognitive/material reality of late capitalism, the subject–object dialectic experiences a bad (epistemically false and politically dangerous) moment: the moment of objective abstraction, the exchange system. Consequently, Adorno's initiation of the *new moment*, that is, the primacy of the object, underscores his political activity in opening a new site in which the possibility of change resides. Through the initiation of this materialistic moment within the course of mediation, Adorno is to change the present constellation. And this is a genuinely political activity because the subject and the object, and consciousness and matter, mediate through one another, and the trajectory of society is the course of this mediation: Implementing a change in the mode of mediation is at the same time implementing a change in social reality.

The primacy of the object is Adorno's different moment that is "articulated in dialectics" (1973, p. 184). The moment of the subject's primacy suppresses Adorno's different moment. This new moment, Adorno hopes, will bring to the level of our consciousness the forgotten fact that only because the subject "is not the radical otherness required to legitimize the object, is it capable of grasping objectivity at all" (p. 185). It is within this materialistic moment that we, the situated and framed-by-the-objective-reality subjects, recognize our mutually constitutive relationship with society and understand reality as a practico-inert. It is within this instant of realizing that reality is not natural and that another world is possible that the possibility of a political act comes to the fore. Accordingly, Adorno's "philosophy after Auschwitz" is a political activity that criticizes a specific material moment of the concept, the sociopolitical context of the present truth claims of Enlightenment reason.

At this point, the semantic bond between Adorno's conceptualizations of the constellation and the primacy of the object thesis comes into view. A constellation is the specific side of the object that the primacy of the subject thesis tends to ignore. Constellations, Adorno writes, "represent from without what the concept has cut away within: the 'more' which the concept is equally desirous and incapable of being" (1973, p. 162). Hence, the constellation is akin to the nonconcept.

Following dialectical materialism, Adorno believes that an object is this or that specific object only within a constellation of relationships.

He uses the example of language as a constellation and—in a way that has interesting resemblances to Jacques Derrida's reading of Saussure—states that language "is not a system of signs for cognitive functions." Rather, as a constellation, language puts concepts in plays of relationship, and it is the play of relationship "centered about a thing" that "lends objectivity to" concepts (1973, p. 162).

Adorno's dialectical materialism, on the other hand, amounts to the point that reality is linguistically mediated. Reality is linguistic, since consciousness and matter are mutually constitutive, since consciousness is linguistic through and through, and since lexis and praxis are "together" (see Alcoff 1996, p. 71; Coles 1995, p. 30).[39] The constellation, therefore, is where the subject and the object mediate, and a specific constellation is a specific mode and moment of their endless dialectical mediation. "The constellation changes," Adorno states, "in the dynamics of history" (1973, p. 306). Alteration of the constellation and historical change, therefore, are mutually implicative. Adorno's politics after Auschwitz, I believe, has to do with this mutual implication.

This observation explains why an object is this or that specific object only within a specific moment of a constellation of relationships in the linguistic, cognitive/material reality, the lexis/praxis ensemble. The specific object is indeed a "sedimented history" of relationships/ mediations, and "cognition of the object in its constellation is cognition of the process stored in the object" (Adorno 1973, p. 163). The dynamic constellation, the play of ever-changing relationships and mediations, is the transcendental precondition for the emergence of a phenomenal object and of meaning and truth content that partially, as the subjective side of mediation, constitute the object/reality. The constellation indicates the "more" in the object that the concept cannot swallow up, and the constellation's dynamism signifies the potentiality that Adorno's dialectical realism assigns to reality.

Adorno's constellation, therefore, is the site in which dialectics among opposites/differents (the subject and the object) takes place. Indeed, it is the very myriad of dialectical mediations that in their wealth and multidimensionality reflect the reality's potential to be different. The constellation is the lexis/praxis ensemble, the social, political, economic, and cultural play of relations.[40] It is an indissoluble nonconcept that accounts for Adorno's nonidentity thesis: *inside* this nonidentical constellation resides relation to that which it is not, that is, the concept. As reality, the constellation is nonidentical to itself because it is the unfixable myriad of mediations. Like society, it is always already *new contradictory.*

As mentioned above, the constellation is a site for the emergence of the object as this individual object. It is the opening in which the object appears. The fluidity of the constellation indicates that the object is indeed the sedimented history of previous moments *plus* the moves in the ongoing myriad of mediations. "This history," Adorno writes, "is the individual thing and outside it; it is something encompassing in which the individual has its place" (1973, p. 163). The object, therefore, is the "process stored in the object" within the ever-changing constellation. The new moments of this ever-changing constellation facilitate and become concretized as new moments in the process/object. The object is a "process" with "immanent dynamism" because it is the constellation that is always already *new contradictory*. It is society and its *new contradictoriness* that accounts for the potentiality *within* the object.

Adorno's dialectical realism, therefore, accords with the primacy of the object thesis and also with the fact that the constellation—that is, the linguistic/material play of relationships, the society—is always new incoherent. Unsuccessful/naïve realism seeks the object-without-constellation. Naïve realism forgets that the very meaning of its doomed project depends on a specific constellation: To talk about an ineffable object-beyond-constellation, naïve realism needs a constellation. It is the false constellation of the exchange system that makes identity thinking and naïve realism possible. This constellation tends to stand still, suppress the freedom of the object, and arrest its process, by introducing the exchange system as natural. This suppression is simultaneously linguistic, cognitive, and material. It is a social suppression, a "suffering under society," inasmuch as Adorno understands society as cognitive/material (1973, p. 67).

Adorno's political activity should be seen in his attempt to bring back movement to the current constellation of the exchange system. This attempt aims to free a site of possibility for the emergence of new objects and realities. Political activity is a move, a new enactment of the constellation by making new mediations. It implies new patterns of relationship between linguistic realities, the things. Therefore, it implies *new things*. The "potentiality within the thing/object" to become a new object is indeed the other name of the possibility of this political enactment: Each round of the enactment of the constellation can potentially make a new reality. Accordingly, a conservative enactment can reproduce and solidify the present constellation.

As one possible way of transgression, or strategic intervention, in the constellation, the introduction of new concepts, new interpretations, theories, and so forth affect the myriad of multidimensional mediations between the subjects and objects. This observation, I believe, highlights the political function of Adorno's primacy of the object thesis. Accordingly, and from a political epistemological perspective, the meaning and truth content of this thesis are partially constituted by this political function. Adorno's political action, therefore, targets the alteration of the superstructure, which, due to the dialectical interdependence of superstructure and structure, will result in the alteration of reality as cognitive/material.[41]

It is the dynamism of the rigid constellation of the exchange system that must be freed again. Situated within a specific moment of the constellation, Adorno had his own prescription for such an emancipatory political action. Caring about the different and placing value on distinction, as manifested in the principle of nonidentity—or the primacy of the object—orient Adorno's politics toward the "smallest things" (Always 1995, p. 69). According to this politics, the emancipation of the different is the precondition of truth. In this way, Adorno distinguishes his philosophy from an orthodox Marxian emancipatory vision with grand programs of radical change. He rejects both the universal truth claim and the radical political action based on the same reason: Forgetting the truth of the singular, radical political action fails to be justified. It commits terror.[42] Care for the "smallest things," however, must not distract us from considering their relation of reciprocal mediation with the social totality, the constellation. For this reason, Adorno would say, the emancipation of the object/nonconcept from the reifying spell of concept is the first step toward emancipating the social structure as a whole. Indeed, the dialectical materialist theory of society demands emancipation from antagonisms produced by this totality and its historical movement.

Adorno's contribution to the project of political epistemology becomes evident: Adorno holds that emancipating the nonconceptual and the damaged life cannot be abstractly isolated from emancipating its mediating totality, that is, changing the constellation into a less new incoherent one. Likewise, he implies that theoretical endeavors not only fail to remove antagonisms but also fall in the trap of abstraction and enhance the level of new incoherence.

3
Political Epistemology versus Sociology of Knowledge

Georg Lukacs traces the mutually constitutive relationship between positivist epistemology as a part of the reified consciousness and the capitalist mode of social life: The reified epistemological consciousness "corresponds" with the *fetishized* social reality. In other words, for Lukacs, positivism is the very process of "thingification" occurring in the social environment, which is carried to its logical extreme within a theoretical system. In the first section of this chapter, I explore the above point and argue that Lukacs's idea of the epistemic vantage point of the proletariat reflects one possible articulation of the constitutive relationship between sociopolitical context and knowledge.

The second section compares Karl Mannheim's to Lukacs's view. While Marx's and Lukacs's idea of the universality of the proletariat (and its embracing the truth of totality) is not a priori, Mannheim's intelligentsia is, by definition, epistemologically privileged: Mannheim's intelligentsia is the "universal class" for all seasons and has access to "universal" and "objective" truth. Here, I argue that Mannheim's account of the objectivity of free-floating intellectuals' truth claim about the totality of the social, political, and cultural bloc is not empirical but speculative.

Exploring the idea of the sociology of knowledge in Mannheim's writings, the following section discusses the problem of relativism in Mannheim's idea of relationism. Mannheim believes that relationism amounts to nonevaluative, sociological, and reflexive examinations of ideologies. In his view, the sociology of knowledge can investigate the productive relationships between the sociopolitical context and the idea without necessarily engaging in an epistemological/normative evaluation of the idea. This thesis of the epistemic neutrality of the sociology of knowledge, I will argue throughout the chapter, signifies the crucial point of theoretical weakness in the program of the sociology of knowledge.

The main question of the chapter is whether the project of political epistemology and the sociology of knowledge—and even the strong program in the sociology of knowledge—are basically the same. If yes, why bother to (re)articulate the project of political epistemology? And if not, then what are the differences among them? Does the project of political epistemology suffer from the same sort of relativism that plagues the sociology of knowledge? Does political epistemology, in order to be normative, offer a response to the allegation of relativism? In order to address these concerns, I divide the rest of the chapter into three parts. First, I investigate Marcuse's, Horkheimer's, and Adorno's critiques of Mannheim's thought. This section sheds light on the points of disagreement between participants in the project of political epistemology and the sociologists of knowledge. Here, I contend that contrary to Lukacs's, Mannheim's idea of the knowledge–society relationship is relativistic and nondialectical.

A modified version of Mannheim's sociology of knowledge is discussed in the next section. The strong program in the sociology of knowledge suggests that a true belief and its rationality are just as subject to causal explanations of the sociology of knowledge as error and nonrationality are. In other words, science, logic, and their truths must be included in the total conception of ideology. What is "strong" about this position is that even if there are some purely rational rules and rationales that are ultimately independent of sociopolitical causation, no such rules can be applied as independent variables in an explanation of knowledge. Indeed, the strong program rescues from Mannheim's thought the thesis of epistemic neutrality, the nonevaluative sentiment. It is interesting to see, however, that both the strong program and its sworn positivist critics share the same nonevaluative sentiment. The project of political epistemology challenges this very disposition.

The chapter to this point will argue that the sociologist has to understand the reasons that are embedded in social facts. The question is, however, whether he or she can approach validity claims in a purely descriptive, nonnormative way. The answer is negative. In order to substantiate this answer, I look into the nature of understanding in the next section, which studies Hans-Georg Gadamer's ontology of understanding and investigates the way in which Gadamer's hermeneutic philosophy contributes to the project of political epistemology. This investigation provides us with sufficient reasons to prove the falsity of the epistemic neutrality thesis.

The next section looks into the relativist nature of the strong thesis and examines the way in which the project of political epistemology rejects the nonevaluative fiat, thus differentiating itself from the strong thesis. The section makes the case that ideas like the sociologist's epistemic neutrality toward the object of study, the abstract separation between the reason and the cause, and the belief that both are external to meaning are just wrong. These ideas are corollaries to the strong program's epistemic relativism. Rejecting them, therefore, is a rejection of the program's epistemic relativism. I end this section by showing how the project of political epistemology's own account of knowledge is not relativist but normative.

Lukacs on epistemology and sociopolitical context

Human history is simultaneously an intellectual, moral, and material development. In Antonio Gramsci's words, history is politics and philosophy in the making (1971, pp. 352–7); that is, consciousness does not reside outside the real process of history. Hegel's inadequacy, according to Marx, was that he commissioned the absolute spirit as the only maker of history. Hegel's dualism of "spirit" and "mass," in its turn, put consciousness in a position of otherworldliness vis-à-vis the concrete realities of history.

Marx brought Feuerbach to Hegel. Feuerbach's materialism, however, was nondialectical in seeing matter as inert and the spirit as the effect of things. In Marx's view, Feuerbach's mistake is that he "wants sensuous objects, really distinct from the thought objects, but he does not conceive human activity itself as objective activity" (1972e, p. 107). Marx locates this mentality in the process of bourgeois society and opposes to it the notion of consciousness as "practical-critical activity" that, even when apparently interpreting the world, attempts "to change it." Marx demands that Feuerbach realize that the material realm is practico-inert, cognitive/material. Matter, in other words, is imbued by consciousness.

Working within the Marx's framework, Georg Lukacs focuses on the dialectical interdependence of consciousness and sociopolitical reality and views the commodification of labor in a capitalist economic system as reproducing itself not only in the consciousness of the worker but in society as a whole. Commodification of labor, indeed, is the point at which the cognitive/material nature of the capitalist mode of reality best manifests itself. It is the very point at which the *fetishized* sociopolitical relationship meets its indistinguishable twin, the *reified* consciousness.

According to Lukacs, capitalism organizes production through definite sociopolitical relationships between humans. These relationships take the character of things and acquire a "phantom objectivity, an autonomy that seems so strictly rational and all-embracing as to conceal every trace of its fundamental nature; the relation between people" (Lukacs 1971, 83). The reified or false consciousness associates a pattern of social relationships with elements—like bureaucracy, alienation, and inequality—that are seen as immutable, pure facts. False consciousness remains incapable of seeing its own contribution to the determinate sociohistorical essence of these "things" and loses the possibility of conscious human control over them. As a result, historically specific forms of human activity become reified and falsely viewed as "natural" facts of life, as "second nature." Accordingly, Lukacs would say, the object is experienced as immediate in-itself over and against a subject, which is now reduced from the active historical subject into a passive, abstract spectator.

This is the sociopolitical process that has historically ontologized the subject as the passive Cartesian knower. Ironically, the modern subject that actively seeks technical control over the natural and social worlds is sentenced to perceive itself as a passive spectator and define the objectivity of its knowledge—that is, the very means of active dominance over the world—according to this passivity. Such a notion of epistemological objectivity as a criterion of truth, therefore, has to do with the reified mode of social life in the capitalist period. Current epistemological analyses question the accessibility of objectivity, and indeed one might doubt if objectivity is a worthy political or epistemological goal at all.[1]

Lukacs's analysis thus traces the mutually constitutive relationship between positivist epistemology as a part of the reified consciousness and the capitalist mode of social life: the reified epistemological consciousness "corresponds" with the fetishized social reality. Positivism is the very process of "thingification" occurring in the social environment, which is carried to its logical extreme within a theoretical system. Lukacs's account of this dialectical interdependence displays how and in which sense the positivist consciousness is true: The reified epistemology/consciousness/ideology is true insofar as it coheres with fetishized social relationships.

Does Lukacs imply a kind of new coherence as the criterion of truth? If so, why does he call the positivist ideology *false* consciousness? He writes:

> If such methods [including positivist methodology] seem plausible at first this is because capitalism tends to produce a social structure

> which encourages such views....The fetishistic character of eco-
> nomic forms, the reification of all human relations, the constant
> expansion and extension of the division of labor which subjects the
> process of production to an abstract, rational analysis without regard
> to the human potentials and abilities of the immediate producers, all
> these things transform the phenomena of society and with them the
> way in which they are perceived. In this way arise the 'isolated' facts,
> 'isolated' complexes of facts, separate, specialist disciplines (econom-
> ics, law etc.) whose very appearance seems to have done much to
> pave the way for such scientific methods. It thus appears extraordi-
> narily "scientific" to think out the tendencies implicit in the facts
> themselves and to promote this activity to the status of science.
> (1971, pp. 5–6)

Lukacs, like Hegel, finds the falsity of a contingent consciousness in
its aspiration for universality and absoluteness. Ideology, Marx would
also agree, is partially true. It is a constituent of reality. It becomes
false when it forgets its historicity[2] and hypothesizes itself as a universal absolute that mirrors immediate reality. The bourgeois class consciousness, Lukacs argues, is prone to making this mistake: "We find
bourgeoisie and proletariat placed in an immediately similar situation.
But here too, it appears that while the bourgeoisie remains enmeshed
in its immediacy by virtue of its class role, the proletariat is driven by
the specific dialectics of its class situation to abandon it" (Lukacs 1971,
pp. 170–1).

While for the capitalist labor time is merely the objective form
of commodity—that is, a quantitative matter in the exchange of
equivalents—for the worker labor power is the determining form of his
or her existence as subject or as human being that gets commodified.
For the capitalist, this process of quantitative character moves toward
increased "rationalization, mechanization and quantification" in the
world of facts, commodities, and exchange values that immediately
exist. The worker, on the other hand, is forced to objectify his labor
power despite what his personality demands and sell it as a commodity.
"Because of the split between subjectivity and objectivity induced in
man by the compulsion to objectify himself as a commodity," "the situation becomes one that can become conscious" (Lukacs 1971, p. 168).
Lukacs points at "the factors that create a dialectic between the social
existence of the worker and the forms of his consciousness" (p. 168).
He shows that what renders the class consciousness of the bourgeoisie
"false" is objective: "It is the class situation itself" (p. 54).

According to the dialectical view of humanity and history, human beings are historical objects, formed and affected by historical process as much as the active subject of history. Like Hegel's, Lukacs's subject "knows its object only because it creates it, a subject that is no longer the individual 'I' but rather the 'we,' a subject that does not yet exist but would emerge at the end of a creative process" (Antoni 1972, p. 98). Lukacs articulates a dialectical course according to which the subject, which is simultaneously the producer and the product of history, can overcome the immediacy of reified reality and in so doing obtain true consciousness. For Lukacs, class performs this process because "it is able to discover within itself on the basis of its life experience the identical subject-object, the subject of action, the 'we' of the genesis, namely the proletariat" (1971, p. 149). The proletariat, on condition that it becomes the "class," the "we" subject of history, transforms the world through praxis. Because the proletariat's existential situation is one of alienation (the proletariat is itself an object of production), its self-consciousness becomes (unlike that of the bourgeoisie) consciousness of the nature of capitalist society itself. Hence, Lukacs contends, the proletariat's Archimedean point on reality (Sewart 1978, p. 344) is grounded in its own existence as the active producer of things. The proletariat sees social reality as a product of its own subjectivity, not as an aggregate of unconnected natural things. The proletariat does know the reality by living and doing it, though Lukacs and Gramsci would insist in their distinct ways that this knowing-how needs to be articulated, theoretically and strategically, by the party or by organic intellectuals.[3]

Praxis, therefore, is a conscious activity to change the present reality by resolving its contradictions. Its consciousness arises from a privileged epistemic point, from the truth that the proletariat upholds. It proceeds into theoretical, metaphysical, scientific, and other such articulations that are in part strategically and politically developed in order to alter the present. The truth of these articulations proves itself when they constitute and mediate, through praxis, the emerging reality in an upper level of new coherence. Now, participants in the project of political epistemology would argue that the new coherent reality and the praxis that mediates it are to be considered true.[4]

Lukacs socialized the "vantage point" from which true moral, cultural, and practical knowledge was possible. It is also in this sense that Karl Mannheim's sociology of knowledge has been traced back to Lukacs's arguments (see Kettler 1967, pp. 416–20). The project of political epistemology, too, shows great sympathy with Lukacs's analysis of the constitutive relationship between knowledge and the sociopolitical context. This leads to the question whether political epistemology can be considered basically the same project as the sociology of knowledge, or as the strong program in the sociology of knowledge. If so, is there any value in articulating the project of political epistemology? And if not, then how are they different, and does political epistemology suffer from some of the same weaknesses that have been identified in the sociology of knowledge? In the section that follows, I shall argue that, contrary to Lukacs's, Mannheim's idea of the knowledge–society relationship is relativistic and nondialectical, whereas the project of political epistemology promotes a nonrelativist and dialectical account of truth.

The position of the intelligentsia in Karl Mannheim's thought

In Lukacs's view, overcoming reification implies that one must understand the objects of the empirical world as mediated, as "aspects of a totality, i.e. as the aspects of a total social situation caught up in the process of historical change" (1971, p. 162). Lukacs's totality thus is a historical transient *reality*, not an ahistorical *knowledge*. Lukacs does not consider the truth of totality as universal and ahistorically objective. It is rather a truth that is to change the totality, and being the bearer of this truth has to do with the *ability* to establish a new reality. Accordingly, Lukacs's proletariat aims at actualizing this truth. It is, in other words, the proletariat that is universal, not the truth of totality.

The universality of the proletariat also has nothing to do with fulfilling Hegelian transhistorical norms. It simply refers to a class that attempts to be the subject of society's general consciousness. As Shlomo Avineri explains, "historical developments actually allow this class for a time to represent the *res publica*, society at large, but after a while, with changes in the distribution of social forces and in general conditions, this claim for universality no longer accords with the interest of society as a whole. The class, which had hitherto represented society, must vacate its place to a new class" (1968, p. 58).This interpretation of Lukacs's ideas mitigates the accusation of totalitarianism against him and his concept of the party.

Karl Mannheim refuses to accept what he perceives as Lukacs's view that the proletariat is the possessor of the totalistic moral-cultural-practical orientation. What is specifically important here is that Mannheim's idea of totality does not designate the transient and mediated historic bloc. As we shall see, by "totality," he means the absolute/universal knowledge that corresponds with reality as an in-itself. In fact, Mannheim disjoins Lukacs and dialectical materialism at this critical juncture. Furthermore, while Marx's and Lukacs's universality of the proletariat (and its embracing the truth of totality) is not a priori, Mannheim's intelligentsia is, by definition, epistemologically privileged; Mannheim's intelligentsia is the "universal class" for all seasons.

For Mannheim, totality is found in the harmonious integration of all the viewpoints that are represented by the collectivity of "free-floating intellectuals." Mannheim's intellectuals are not bound to any particular social band or a strictly caste-like organization. Rather, they occupy unstable social and economic locations in modern societies. It is their "participation in a common educational heritage [that] progressively tends to suppress differences of birth, status, profession and wealth" among intellectuals (1968, p. 155). "The socially unattached intelligentsia," Mannheim states, establishes an "unanchored, relatively classless stratum" (p. 155).

Mannheim entrusts the classless intellectuals with a view of the totality of sociopolitical structure. The mobility of intellectuals, he argues (Mannheim 1956b, p. 105), protects this view from the one-sidedness of the classes' views: "Since intellectuals are rooted *nowhere*, they are not single-mindedly engaged in one line of thought. But at the same time they feel in their fingertips the collective strivings of the epoch and they form them into a system."[5] Free floating in this way gains an epistemic value. Mannheim also "locates" himself—in terms of the sociology of knowledge and given the social and political situation in the Weimar Republic—in the "nowhere" of a free-floating intellectual who enjoys the epistemological privilege to talk about free-floating intellectuals and, more important, "scientific" politics. He writes: "It is only today, when we have become aware of all the currents and are able to understand the whole process by which political interests and *Weltanschauung* come into being in the light of a sociologically intelligible process, that we see the possibility of politics as science" (Mannheim 1968, 162).

A view from nowhere, however, is hardly a view at all. Mannheim himself rejects the isolated cogito and believes that "what is intelligible in history can be formulated only with reference to problems and conceptual constructions which themselves arise in the flux of historical experience" (Mannheim 1968, p. 71). Hence, how should we understand the "nowhere" of free-floating intellectuals consistently?

According to standpoint epistemology, all knowledge attempts, including the knower and the known, are socially situated, and "the observer and the observed are in the same causal scientific plane"

(Harding 1991, p. 1). Moreover, "some of these objective social locations are better than others as starting points for knowledge projects" (Harding 1993, p. 56). In terms of standpoint epistemology, Mannheim's classless intellectuals are capable, more than the members of any social class, of experiencing diverse social standpoints and thus maximizing the objectivity of their knowledge of the totality of a historical period, the *Weltanschauung*. The objectivity of intellectuals' knowledge, therefore, has to do with the abundance, not the abandonment, of standpoints. When it comes to understanding the totality of cultural and social phenomena, free-floating intellectuals who can take up and experience the totality of standpoints—who have all standpoints at their disposal—own the standpoint that is epistemologically best. The intelligentsia, according to Mannheim, is peculiarly well placed to consider matters from several perspectives: "Certain intellectuals have a maximum opportunity to test and employ the socially available vistas and to experience their inconsistencies" (Mannheim 1956b, p. 106).

According to Sandra Harding, standpoint epistemology "requires a critical evaluation to determine which social situations tend to generate the most objective knowledge claim" (1991, p. 142). This proviso implies scientific and empirical investigations of the causal relationships between historically located belief and maximally objective belief. For example, a less distorted science, Harding implies, depends on starting from a particular social perspective or standpoint—that of marginalized groups whose members have an interest in emancipation or in social equality. This standpoint is epistemologically privileged, for from it one can better identify culture-wide biases in the content of science. Standpoint epistemologists believe that the above proviso guarantees *strong objectivity* and defies judgmental relativism. It might seem that Mannheim would in principle agree with this logic, given his belief that the intelligentsia's social situation tends to generate the most objective knowledge claim about the totality. Nonetheless, he does not provide "a scientific and empirical account" for it.

Harding's account of strong objectivity, she argues, recognizes historical, cultural, and sociological relativism and simultaneously rejects judgmental or epistemological relativism. The means for evaluating objectivity, however—that is, the scientific and empirical account of the causal relationships between the historically situated belief and the maximally objective belief—needs to be objective as well. This fact suggests a kind of circularity in Harding's version of strong objectivity. In her view, this circularity is not a vicious one. The question, however, is whether her portrayal of strong objectivity leaves, beyond this circle, any recognizable room for independent reality's intervention in our scientific and empirical evaluations of objectivity. For a hermeneutical approach in natural and social sciences, such an all-embracing circularity represents no problem because "independent" reality is mediated linguistically. Harding, however, would hardly drop the idea of an independent reality as the subject and final arbiter of science.[6] She nonetheless cannot locate this arbiter out of the circle. In other words, Harding's inadequacy resides not in the viciousness of the circle but in the circularity itself.

Mannheim's concept of *objectivity* is different from Harding's. The former's objectivity does not primarily designate knowledge claims about specific realities: It indicates, rather, that the intelligentsia's knowledge claim about the totality is objectively true. This kind of objectivity cannot, in principle, be judged empirically, simply because each empirical assessment as a specific social practice falls within the category of social totality: The totality of social reality, as a totality, cannot be subject to empirical studies. Therefore, the objectivity of the free-floating intellectuals' truth claim about the totality of the social, political, and cultural bloc must be speculatively, not empirically, accounted for. Consequently, despite a few similarities, Mannheim's epistemological position on objectivity does not completely match the one of standpoint epistemologists.

For Mannheim, intellectuals' knowledge of the totality involves "the assimilation and transcendence of the limitations of particular points of view": Conflicting intellectual positions actually "come to supplement one another" in order to allow "the broadest possible extension of our horizon of vision" (Mannheim 1968, p. 85; see also Wolding 1986, p. 230). Transcending the limits of particular knowledges and thus knowing the totality is, indeed, the meditative excursion of Mannheim's intellectuals to the realm of the spirit. It is only after meeting with the spirit and catching the totality of the historic bloc that the truth of each specific social phenomenon discloses itself to the intellectuals (Mannheim 1952b, p. 146). Having already grasped the totality, Mannheim's intellectuals apply the sociology of knowledge to see the limits, the "functional meaning,"[7] and the conditional truth of the particular ideas, the ideologies.[8]

"The study of intellectual history can and must be pursued in a manner which will see in the sequence and coexistence of phenomena more than mere accidental relationships," Mannheim writes, "and will seek to discover in the totality of the historical complex the role, significance, and meaning of each component element." He adds, "It is with this type of sociological approach to history that we identify ourselves" (1968, p. 93). Hence, so far as the knowledge of totality is concerned, Mannheim tacitly brings Hegel back to secure its truth and objectivity.[9] His intellectuals witness the progressive revelation of reason in history (Bottomore 1956, p. 55). Their sympathy with and adaptation to the general trend of history therefore guarantees their objectivity.

Based upon this line of argument, Mannheim declares that the sociology of knowledge "does not signify that there are no criteria of rightness or wrongness in a discussion" (1968, p. 283). The intelligentsia's "broadest view of totality" provides these criteria. Indeed, Mannheim indicates that his "type of sociological approach"—that is, the sociology of knowledge—has an epistemological/normative dimension to it. In the middle of a relativist vortex, Mannheim evidently loads his free-floating intellectuals with heavy epistemological burdens!

The relativism of Mannheim's concept of relationism

Mannheim's involvement in the discussion of relativism follows his "new" theory of ideology. He distances himself from Marx's definition of ideology and, based on his new characterization of ideology, calls the philosophy of praxis an ideology: "With the emergence of the general formulation of the total conception of ideology, the simple theory of ideology develops into the sociology of knowledge. What was once the armament of a party is transformed into a method of research in social and intellectual history generally" (Mannheim 1968, p. 78). Mannheim also criticizes Lukacs because, according to Mannheim, Lukacs failed to go beyond Marx and "distinguish between the problem of unmasking ideologies on the one hand and the sociology of knowledge on the other" (p. 310). Here, "the total conception of ideology"—that is, the ideology of an age or of a concrete class—implies that "the thought of all parties in all epochs is of an ideological character" (p. 56). Therefore, all parties can analyze their opponent's position in ideological terms: Labels like "ideology" and "false consciousness" are no longer monopolized as "the intellectual weapons of the proletariat."

The main elements of the total conception of ideology are the following: First, the total conception of ideology does not exclusively rely on "what is actually said by the opponent in order to reach an understanding of his real meaning and intention ... the ideas expressed by the subject are thus regarded as functions of his existence." Second, "the total conception calls into question the opponent's total *Weltanschauung.*" Third, "the total conception refers to the theoretical or noological level." Finally, "the total conception uses a more formal functional analysis.... [it] presupposes simply that there is a correspondence between a given social situation and a given perspective," so the subject's knowledge is determined by its social existence (Mannheim 1968, pp. 56–8, 256–86).

This "modern" (Mannheim 1968, pp. 78–9) historical/sociological "insight" demands all historical thinking be bound up with the concrete position in life of the thinker. This is what Mannheim calls *relationism*. In his view, relativism emerges when the old epistemology, unaware of the interplay between conditions of existence and modes of thought— the epistemology that seeks criteria of absolute truth—encounters this new insight and ceases to accommodate it. For that reason, relativism must be considered as a historically transient epistemology (Mannheim 1968, p. 290) that needs to contemplate its own situatedness in order to surpass its relativist imperfection. Mannheim believes that relationism amounts to nonevaluative, sociological, and reflexive examinations of ideologies (pp. 86–7). In this view, the sociology of knowledge can investigate the productive relationship between the social context and the idea without necessarily engaging in an epistemological/normative evaluation of the idea.

Dynamic relationism emerges when Mannheim, aspiring to transcend the old epistemology and its associating relativism, extends the notion of relationism to the agent of epistemic evaluation and, therefore, introduces his version of "historicism" to epistemology. As a result, the arbiters who are sensitive to the existential determinacy of their own normative judgments, aware of relationism and of their own relatedness, apply the sociologically self-reflexive method and, in so doing, present social dynamism to epistemological evaluations.

These arbiters are indeed Mannheim's free-floating intellectuals. What provides them with epistemic norms of judgment is their access to the totality; what secures the historicity of the norms and evaluations is the sociological self-reflexivity of intellectuals. In line with the normative verdict of dynamic relationism, a theory is invalid if someone in a particular situation uses concepts and categories that belong properly in another historical phase and, on that account, inhibit that person from adjusting himself at that historical stage (Mannheim 1968, p. 95). Therefore, to Mannheim, social adjustment represents a normative concept. Accordingly, a knowledge claim is false if it does not give an accurate account of a new reality. Intellectuals, who grasp the "absolute in the process of becoming" and therefore know the reality in its totality, are the ones who assess the correspondence between the knowledge claim and the new reality, "the object itself" (p. 4). Though the totality is ever changing, in each phase of its change—that is, in each historic phase—the free-floating intellectuals recognize it. Therefore, Mannheim suggests that within the framework of a historic phase, the intellectuals' judgments about the correspondence between ideas and reality are non-relativist. I think this is what Mannheim means by the concept of *dynamic truth*.

It seems that Mannheim has delicately completed his theoretical jigsaw puzzle. Now, his sociology of knowledge, operated by free-floating intellectuals, happily lodges historicity, relationism, and epistemic normativeness together. Consequently, Mannheim's dynamic relationism, as a new epistemology, seems to reject relativism. Yet critics prove this judgment wrong. Investigating these criticisms points to the crucial differences between the project of political epistemology and the sociology of knowledge.

Critiques of relationism

Almost immediately after *Ideology and Utopia* was published, Herbert Marcuse underlined a problematic element of Mannheim's theory: "Mannheim accepts each particular historical stage as an ultimate, sociologically irreducible fact" (Marcuse 1990, p. 133). According to Marcuse, to call consciousness "true" when it corresponds to the given social reality indicates that Mannheim's understanding of society is nondialectical. In other words, Mannheim ignores the "intentional" characteristic of social beings and forgets the constitutive role of consciousness in the creation and alteration of reality: In Lukacs's terms, Mannheim reifies society as a given, as an in-itself, and thus falls back on pre-Marxian materialism in believing that a rigid reality nonreciprocally determines thought.

Mannheim's criticism of socialism as ideology is also misled, for, Marcuse points out, socialism is self-conscious about its own relatedness and does not claim unattached universal validity. Marcuse insists that socialism is definitely a historical corollary of the proletariat's situation, but the crucial matter is that the proletariat struggles to "actualize" the truth of socialism, and "its deed aims to be true deed" (Marcuse 1990, p. 132). Mannheim's theory of correspondence, however, cannot encompass the notion of "actualizing truth." It cannot epistemologically account for the utopian thought and practice that aspire only to change current reality but not correspond with it.

According to Marcuse, the sociological method

> must not accept the historical stage of existence simply as a given base and as an ultimate authority on questions of truth…a historical situation…is historical only in so far as it can be perpetually and concretely actualized; i.e. the consciousness, which according to Mannheim, aims to "correspond" or be appropriate to it, *causes* this situation in the first place and precisely in the sphere of its concretion, in what distinguishes it as a particular historical stage. (1990, pp. 133–4)

This is to say that dialectical historicism indicates that the present is not final, and "in its very historicity, it points beyond itself."

In fact, Mannheim's total concept of ideology implies that the structure of the worldview, like the Kantian categories of understanding, depends on the subject. Moreover, the subject is not to be perceived unconditionally and generally, but determined by historical and social conditions. Accordingly, Mannheim's historicism amounts to the social determinedness of categories of reason (see Mannheim 1952a, p. 91). There is no real dialectical connection between theory and practice, and between categories and social reality, in Mannheim's concept of historicism.

Max Horkheimer further developed this vein of criticism in the following years. In Horkheimer's view, Mannheim's sociology of knowledge represents a return to metaphysics, since the general claim of it is that "there exists a foundation of history outside history" (Horkheimer 1993b, p. 137; see Mannheim 1968, p. 92). Thus, disclosing truth requires that we seek the traces of the extrahistorical in mundane history, "mute and meaningless" per se. Horkheimer concludes that the central idea of Mannheim's sociology is "the dubious belief" (1993b, p. 137) that all "standpoints and contents…are part of a meaningful overall process" (Mannheim 1968, p. 93).[10]

This analysis demonstrates well how and in what sense Mannheim's theory is traditional: It prefers to explain the overall movement of history rather than changing a specific sociopolitical reality. Drafting metaphysics, however, is hardly consistent with Mannheim's own total conception of ideology: Metaphysics is a luxury the situated thinker cannot afford.[11]

Marx called Hegelian metaphysics an idealist illusion and launched his criticism against its sociopolitical functions: "Because the fates of human beings are extremely unequal, 'to think of a totality as the unified context of meaning' mitigates the real sufferings of economically underprivileged classes" (Horkheimer 1993b, p. 139). Therefore, what Mannheim calls a total context of "unity and meaning" (1968, p. 92) of "the whole" (p. 106) is theoretically illusive and politically dangerous: It disguises the fragmentary nature of social reality and conceals its contradictions.

In Adorno's terms, Mannheim's total and unified context of every particular meaning amounts to a totalitarian system in which "planning directed at maintaining the system leads to the barbarous suppression below the surface of the contradictions it inevitably produces" (1967, p. 48). In other words, Mannheim's intellectuals, despite their free-floating movements, do not recognize and embrace the plurality of contexts of meaning: "Although it is precisely they which comprise the life-process of 'society,'" contradictions disappear in the unified theoretical system (p. 38). Social contradictions are cognitive/material. They are new contradictions. In Adorno's view, the problem of Mannheim's undialectical sociological theory is that it "translates dialectical concepts [like social new contradictions] into classificatory ones." And, "since in each case what is socially contradictory is absorbed into individual logical classes, social classes as such disappear and the picture of the whole becomes harmonious" (p. 41). Therefore, the free-floating intellectuals reach their coherent total knowledge by abstracting from the very social reality that they aspire to know. This abstraction is violent theoretically and politically.

Furthermore, Mannheim's dynamic relationism examines the epistemic value of a particular idea based on its adaptation to and correspondence with the totality. It consequently subjugates any expression of the unsatisfactory condition of reality as an untrue claim. Hence, Mannheim's concept of ideology implies that a particular idea cannot express political criticism and expect to be called true simultaneously. To Marx, Mannheim's very definition of ideology, his static ontology, and its accompanying epistemology are all *ideological*.[12] Ironically, Mannheim appeals to a dogmatic metaphysics to support his "revolutionary" sociology. The failure of this dogmatic metaphysics proves Mannheim's distinction between relativism and dynamic relationism to be superficial.

As we have seen, in order to distinguish relationism from relativism, Mannheim ponders an impossible demand. He strives to situate all partial ideologies within a total vision that gives those relative meanings. In so doing, Mannheim wishes to move from the nonevaluative conception of the pure observer to an evaluative one. As Paul Ricoeur asserts, "Once again we are led back to the impossible request for total knowledge....Relationism and relativism are thus divided by a disgraced Hegelianism" (1981, p. 241). It seems that to escape relativism, Mannheim becomes an idealist.

In addition, Mannheim contends that free-floating intellectuals synthesize particular ideologies and have access to social reality in its entirety at the end of processes of "assimilation and transcendence of the limitations of particular points of view." He also believes that a partial ideology finds its own relative meaning only after being contextualized in the total vision. This circularity, which finds no exploration in Mannheim's work, further problematizes his epistemological criterion of truth. While the total vision and the particulars are hermeneutically interdependent, Mannheim cannot consider the intelligentsia's vision of totality as the final arbiter of the particular's truthfulness.

The above discussions on Lukacs and Mannheim should have made it clear that though they both emphasize the role of the sociopolitical context in the makeup of consciousness, their articulations of this role are dramatically different. While Lukacs believes in the mutual mediatedness of thought and sociopolitical reality, Mannheim does not show any interest in this dialectical view. For Lukacs, the human being is both the subject and the object of history, whereas for Mannheim, the human being is the object of a history that itself moves according to an extrahistorical entity. Mannheim's epistemological theory of dynamic relationism, moreover, follows his static ontology and takes the present as the ultimate epistemic authority. It thus cannot reconcile with an idea of truth that promotes changing the present. Hence, Mannheim's sociology of knowledge is a traditional theory. As earlier chapters have shown, the project of political epistemology has close affinities with critical theory. These observations underline the differences between the sociology of knowledge and the project of political epistemology. Let us study an updated version of Mannheim's epistemology and see how it is different from Mannheim's theory and, at the same time, relativist.

The strong program in the sociology of knowledge

David Bloor and Barry Barnes interpret Mannheim's distinction between what he calls *conjunctive* and *communicative* knowledges as a sign of weakness in Mannheim's sociology of knowledge. By *conjunctive*, Mannheim means moral-cultural-practical knowledge, the *Geisteswissenschaften*. Its antithesis, *communicative knowledge*, indicates the mathematical and physical sciences, with their goal of mastering nature. The second type of knowledge, Mannheim contends, develops according to "immanent laws" derived from "the nature of things" and from "pure logical possibilities." In other words, he believes that mathematical and physical sciences are free from the "existential determination of thought." Mannheim writes:

> The existential determination of thought may be regarded as a demonstrated fact in those realms of thought in which we can show...that the process of knowing does not actually develop historically in accordance with immanent laws, that it does not follow only from the "nature" of things or from "pure logical possibilities," and that it is not driven by an "inner dialectic." On the contrary, the emergence and the crystallization of actual thought is influenced in many decisive points by extra-theoretical factors of the most diverse sorts. (1968, pp. 239–40)

The notion of an immanent law or logic that supposedly directs the evolution of mathematical and physical sciences gives Bloor evidence to consider Mannheim's sociology of science to be teleological (1973, p. 178). According to the teleological approach, man has a natural propensity toward discerning and knowing the truth. Hence, it is only false belief that requires explanation: The truth of a true belief is all that is needed for its explanation. Whereas erroneous belief lacks rational justification and, as such, requires causal explanation, the rational justification of a true belief is the same as its causal explanation. Therefore, truth is the reason *and* the cause of a true belief, whereas a variety of "extratheoretical factors" cause deviations into ignorance or error.

Mannheim parallels sociopolitical causes with extratheoretical factors. To him, the truth and the content of mathematical and natural sciences are independent of the sociopolitical contexts in which theories emerge. Following a Platonic/Realist view, Mannheim indicates that even if there were no human beings or society, the mathematical and physical sciences, though undiscovered by man, would remain exactly the same. Contrary to the project of political epistemology, according to which the social context partially constitutes meaning, Mannheim's position implies that the social context has nothing to do with the semantic content, meaning, and truth of genuinely scientific theories.

Mannheim himself never equated the existential determinedness of an idea with its irrationality or falsehood (1968, p. 71). Subsequent articulations of his original distinction, however, exposed this positivist tendency in his work. Positivists believe that the rationality of natural sciences, embodied in their methodological logic, adequately explains not only the content but also the historical development of real sciences. Imre Lakatos, for example, underscored his own favorite philosophy and methodology of science as the innate rationality that directs scientific procedures. In his view, the historiography of cases that conform to this normative logic—that is, the timeless, universal, and ahistorical methodology of research programs—establishes the "internal history" or the "rational reconstruction" of science. Lakatos maintained that the truly scientific aspects of science, its truth content and growth, can be fully accounted for by means of internal explanations, though "all of theses normative reconstructions may have to be supplemented by empirical external theories to explain the residual non-rational factors" (1970, p. 105). Therefore, untruth and mistakes, together with other nonrational elements like "the speed, locality, selectiveness etc. of historic events *as interpreted* in terms of internal history" (p. 105), must be externally explained by social, political, and psychological causes.[13] Thus, the real subject of Mannheim's sociology of knowledge is not the genuine, but the pseudo knowledge, the error. It is indeed the "sociology of error" that his "weak" sociology of knowledge harbors (Bloor 1973, p. 180).

Unveiling the positivist tendency of the "weak" sociology of knowledge also makes conspicuous an inconsistency in Mannheim's thought. Mannheim's positivistic belief in the nonsocially induced truth of mathematics and physical sciences is itself a nonmathematical theory. As such, and according to his total conception of ideology— which implies that *all* beliefs about man and society are existentially determined—it must undergo self-reflexivity and consequently be socially contextualized. In other words, since Mannheim's sociology of knowledge is committed to the total conception of ideology and self-reflexivity, it cannot embrace the positivist epistemology. Thus, Bloor's critique finds more support when we add that Mannheim's teleological/weak sociology, or the sociology of error, is not just incomplete but inconsistent.

The *strong thesis* of the sociology of knowledge suggests that a true belief and its rationality are just as subject to the causal explanations of the sociology of knowledge as error and nonrationality are. In other words, science, logic, and their truths must be included in the total conception of ideology. What is "strong" about this position is that even if there are some purely rational rules and rationales that are ultimately independent of sociopolitical causation, no such rules can be applied as independent variables in an explanation of knowledge. Rational beliefs are not self-explanatory.

This is a crucial observation. Bloor and Barnes would definitely agree that the total conception of ideology results in denying the existence of society-independent rationales. Using the argument from "underdetermination," however, they insist that *even if* there were pure reasons and theories, even if there were positivist distinctions between reason and cause, between rational and social, and so forth, science—the "hallmark of rationality" in Popper's terms—could not proceed without employing "causal/irrational" factors.

According to the *underdetermination thesis*, scientific theories are never logically determined by data: There are always sets of theories that meet with the data more or less adequately. Data are *overdetermined* by theories. In other words, a given body of data is incapable, in principle, of singling out a unique theory. Therefore, mere exposure to data is not enough to explain why the community of scientists finds a theory justified. Extratheoretical factors are required to complete the explanation. The theory, as Bloor states, "is not given along with the experience it explains, nor is it uniquely supported by it." He continues: "Another agency apart from the physical world is required to guide and support this component of knowledge. The theoretical component of knowledge is a social component, and it is a necessary part of truth, not a sign of mere error" (Bloor 1991, p. 16; see also Barnes, Bloor, and Henry 1996, p. 27). Barnes also upholds that "any number of theories may explain a given set of data" (1974, p. 11); hence, "the theory may be partially determined by social factors" (p. 13).[14] For Bloor and Barnes, underdetermination implicitly means that the scientist's cognitive commitments are not purely rational. They are, rather, socially caused, and thus in need of sociological explanations.[15]

In "Two Dogmas of Empiricism," Willard Quine argues that the extraempirical criteria for what counts as a good theory can always be manipulated to save any theory from falsification by contradictory data (1964, p. 43). Furthermore, no theory reaches the "facts of the matter"—if it even makes sense to speak at all of the "facts of matter." We can only describe the facts using theoretical conceptual frameworks. Quine also repudiates a priori/analytic truth. According to him, extraempirical criteria are neither empirical nor analytic. As Mary Hesse states, "It is only a short step from this philosophy of science to the suggestion that adoption of such criteria, which can be seen to be different for different groups and at different periods, should be explicable by social rather than logical factors" (1980, p. 33).

Following this line of thought, a proponent of the strong thesis could argue that social causes are involved in the very processes that finally determine the rationality and validity—or, rather, credibility—of theories. So social causes precede the epistemic judgment of theories: Prior to this causal involvement, the truth or falsity of beliefs and the rationality of theories remain undecided. Furthermore, because the epistemic evaluation is yet to come, the social causes that precede it are themselves neither true nor false, neither rational nor irrational. As I understand it, this is more or less what Bloor and Barnes mean by the *nonevaluative* nature of the strong thesis (as manifested in the impartiality and symmetry principles): The sociological study of a belief goes on under the veil of epistemic ignorance.[16]

The nonevaluative nature of the strong program

For the positivist tradition, including logical empiricism and critical rationalism, the distinction between contexts of discovery and justification provides the very basis upon which philosophical reflection on knowledge becomes possible. Karl Popper introduces the distinction using two types of historical processes that usually take place one after the other: The process of discovering a theory and the process of its epistemic evaluation (1959, ch. 1, section 2). Though the second process takes place in a period of time, it indeed has no history. For according to the positivist/realist view, the context of justification is the realm of time-independent formal logical assessments of theories. What counts as a justification or critical test at some point in time counts so forever. In this realm, norms and methods of justification inspect the truth and the rational plausibility of theories to see whether they correspond with an independent, static reality.

The context distinction is indeed a distinction between the factual and the normative. The history of science reveals that the processes are intimately intertwined.[17] Nevertheless, on a positivist account, in order to avoid cognitive relativism, it suffices to believe that the contexts are at least analytically distinct.

The context distinction is also regarded as a separation between epistemology on the one hand and the external historiography, psychology, and sociology of knowledge on the other. According to the realist/ positivist account, the latter empirical set has to learn from the former philosophical context the result of the evaluation of a belief in order to know what is in need of causal explanation. Epistemology, however, needs to learn nothing from the latter disciplines, for justification is exclusively a matter of logic and reasoning. In other words, from a positivist perspective, the cause–reason dualism accords by definition with the discovery–justification partition, and ultimately, the context distinction is also a distinction between the sociology of error and epistemology, between the external and the internal histories of knowledge, between "mob psychology" and rational reconstruction, and so on.[18]

The strong program's factual–normative distinction accompanies a specific discrimination Bloor makes between the cause and the reason. He distinguishes "rational" from "irrational" causes and regards them as two different species of causes (1981, p. 206). Bloor also separates the descriptive "natural rationality" from the evaluative "normative rationality." In his account, "natural rationality refers to typical human reasoning propensities; normative rationality refers to patterns of inference that are esteemed or sanctioned. The one has reference to matters of psychological facts; the other to shared standards or norms" (p. 207). For Bloor, the natural world is "neutral" (1991, p. 10), so values, normative beliefs, and reasons are ontologically separate from nature and, as such, they cannot causally explain the existence, the credibility, of a belief. This is why the symmetry principle implies that rational beliefs are not self-explanatory.

As Warren Schmaus points out, Bloor suggests that reasons and causes be considered as different metaphysical realms: "Reasons, he seems to believe, are but causes of this latter sort [i.e., metaphysical causes] and best not thought of as causes at all" (1985, p. 191).[19] Indeed, Bloor and Barnes contend that reason functions differently from other sorts of causes in the explanation of beliefs. What is essential, nonetheless, is that according to the strong program's argument from underdetermination, whatever the metaphysical nature of causes might be, they could not be prevented from penetrating into the context of justification. Even if reasons are not causes ipso facto, justifying a belief requires cooperation among causes and reasons (even if they arrive from different metaphysical realms). The strong thesis thus departs from the current context distinction, allowing causes to infiltrate the context of justification and, therefore, localizing methodological investigations to bring historicity and contextually to epistemological criteria of justification. This departure indicates that the rules of argument and criteria of truth are internal to the social system. Therefore, the strong program embraces the context distinction to the extent that the latter connotes the factual–normative and the (new version of) cause–reason dichotomies. If the distinction amounts to any discrimination between epistemology and the sociology of error, or between internal and external history, Bloor and Barnes would certainly dismiss it.

From the positivist/realist view, the context distinction is a precondition of any normative epistemology that avoids relativism. The core of the context distinction, nonetheless, is the factual–normative dichotomy. All other distinctions rest on this basic dichotomy. The accurate description of what is the factual case (e.g., a historical event or process, a theory or belief, or even a norm) is supposed to contrast with the normative perspective on the subject matter. The normative perspective evaluates the extent to which cognitive claims are justified, as well as the method of their justification. (Though even factual descriptions of something must proceed under certain norms of accurate description, following rules is assumed to be different from evaluating them.)

The concept *normative* often indicates "a distinction, not between the good and the bad (or between the right and the wrong, the correct and the incorrect) but rather between the good-or-bad (or right-or-wrong), on the one hand, and the [merely] actual, possible or usual, on the other" (Railton 2000, p. 1). Therefore, the normative–factual distinction implies that the context of discovery is a realm in which nonevaluative descriptions of a belief take place. According to the context distinction, then, a belief is a belief prior to its epistemic evaluation, and it stays so afterward: The belief's meaning, the belief's being this belief, does not change before or after an epistemic evaluation of it. Consequently, as a "thing," the belief might be investigated under two distinct perspectives (i.e., the normative versus the descriptive views), while the subject matter, the thing/belief, remains the same.

Bloor and Barnes affirm the nonevaluative nature of factual descriptions, and to this extent they welcome the core concept of context distinction: the normative–factual dichotomy. The symmetry principle of the strong thesis underlines this position:

> What matters is that we recognize the sociological equivalence of different knowledge claims. We will doubtless continue to evaluate beliefs differentially ourselves, but such evaluations must be recognized as having no relevance to the task of sociological explanation; as a methodological principle we must not allow our evaluation of beliefs to determine what form of sociological account we put forward to explain them. (Barnes 1977, p. 25)

Hence, for the strong thesis, a belief is something factual and in-itself, independent of our epistemic evaluation of it. This is why Bloor and Barnes "effectively entail the 'de-epistemologizing' of cognitive sociology" (Laudan 1981, p. 186). Their "equivalence postulate" demands that all sociological investigations "can and should be answered without regard to the status of the belief as it is judged and evaluated by the sociologist's own standards" (Barnes and Bloor 1982, p. 23). The epistemic neutrality of the strong thesis implies that questions of truth and falsity, and rationality and irrationality, "are epiphenomenal matters on which believers make a judgement by the standards of their local context, without that judgement reflecting or initiating any relevant causal connection" (Pettit 1988, p. 84). Thus, the strong thesis and the proponents of context distinction equally share a nonevaluative conviction, which implies that a belief is what it is prior to any epistemic judgment of its content.[20] The project of political epistemology, however, proves this sentiment false. Before exploring this point, it is worth considering how the nonevaluative conviction reappears even in a "modest" version of the strong program.

According to the modest version, the strong program shows a tendency to drop the notion of epistemic validity and concentrate instead on the idea of credibility. Knowledge for Bloor and Barnes is a "system of beliefs that a community collectively accepts as knowledge" (Bloor 1991, p. 3). They use this concept of knowledge to ultimately secure a nonrelativist character for the strong program.[21] In their view, all forms of relativism hold to a "symmetry thesis" or an "equivalence postulate," each of which assigns some property to all beliefs. For example, a certain equivalence postulate holds that all beliefs are equally true—or equally false—and another maintains that all beliefs are exempt from any kind of rational justification. Hence, Barnes and Bloor offer their own symmetry thesis, which, applying the concept of credibility, aspires to circumvent relativism. According to their own version of symmetry, "all beliefs are on a par with one another with respect to the cause of their credibility." They explain:

> It is not that all beliefs are equally true or equally false, but that regardless of truth or falsity the fact of their credibility is to be seen as equally problematic. The position we shall defend is that the incidence of all beliefs must be accounted for by finding the specific, local causes of this credibility. This means that regardless of whether the sociologist evaluates a belief as true or rational, or as false or irrational, he must search for the causes of its credibility. In all cases he will ask, for instance, if a belief is part of the routine technical competencies handed down from generation to generation. Is it enjoined by the authorities of the society? Is it transmitted by the established institutions of socialization or supported by accepted agencies of social control? (1982, 23)

Bloor and Barnes contend that their concept of knowledge is epistemologically impartial (see Bloor 1991, 40). Therefore, "there is no reason…why philosophers should adopt this conception of knowledge for their epistemological purposes" (quoted in Haddock 2004, p. 23). Consequently, and significantly, the strong program's idea of credibility is supposedly nonevaluative. According to this "modest" version of the strong thesis—which aspires to put all epistemological aspirations aside—the sociologist of knowledge asks "Why does a person or a community hold a particular belief true?" not "Why does a person or a community hold true?" To the strong thesis, the latter question involves the sociologist's epistemic judgment about the content, that is, the validity, of a belief. The former question, however, asks about the credibility of a belief in a nonevaluative way.

Sympathetic readings usually underscore the nonevaluative concept of credibility in order to exempt the strong thesis from making an epistemological choice between realism and relativism.[22] Nonetheless, the nonevaluative conviction does not suggest that the modest version retreats to the sociology of error.

To summarize the above discussion, the relativist and modest versions of the strong thesis indicate that the same sociopolitical (or probably, biopsychological) causes that are in effect in the context of discovery also affect the mechanisms of reasoning and theory choices in the context of justification. The modest version, though marking a metaphysical distinction between the reason and the cause, does not equate the cause–reason dichotomy with the discovery–justification distinction. With respect to epistemic relativism, the modest version apparently refrains from position taking and remains "justificationally atheist" (Rehg 2000, p. 34). The immodest version embraces epistemological relativism. At the core of both versions, however, resides the nonevaluative sentiment. Indeed, it is more accurate to consider the nonevaluative sentiment together with its corollary, the normative–factual distinction, as the crux of context distinction. The strong thesis accepts the context distinction to the extent that the latter distinguishes between the factual and the normative, as well as between the nonevaluative and the normative epistemological evaluation.

It is interesting that both Bloor and Barnes and their sworn positivist critics share the same nonevaluative sentiment.[23] The project of political epistemology challenges this very disposition. Let us first look into the relativist nature of the strong thesis and then examine the way in which political epistemology rejects the nonevaluative fiat and thus differentiates itself from the strong thesis. I shall finally demonstrate how the project of political epistemology remains normative and nonrelativist.

The relativist nature of the strong program

Bloor and Barnes maintain that relativism is "essential" to sociology and that the scientific understanding of knowledge and cognition necessitates belief in relativism. In their view, "the simple starting-point of relativist doctrines is 1) the observation that beliefs on a certain topics vary, and 2) the conviction that which of these beliefs is found in a given context depends on, or is relative to, the circumstances of the users" (1982, p. 22). Relativists and nonrelativists alike grant the fact that beliefs vary, so it is in fact the second clause that motivates relativism. Causation and dependence are relational, and it is easy to conclude that what a person believes is relative to his or her circumstances: Beliefs fluctuate as social causes change. To this extent, the second conviction, the metasociological clause, imparts Mannheim's relationism and is compatible with the sociology of error. Hence, the second clause does not entail any substantive relativism of truth. The modest version of the strong thesis, too, agrees with this mild relativism. As discussed above, the modest version concentrates on credibility and approves of contextualizing credibility and bringing historicity to it. Its relativism is supposedly the relativism of credibility, not of validity.

The relativity of credibility requires, however, that even the modest version of the strong thesis discard the question of whether the epistemological criteria of truth or the methodological rules that cause one to believe in something are valid. The rules thus can be modus ponens, induction, or any similar fallacy.[24] Bloor and Barnes hold:

> For the relativist there is no sense attached to the idea that some standards or beliefs are really rational as distinct from merely locally accepted as such. Because he thinks that there is no context-free or super-cultural norm of rationality he does not see rationally and irrationally held beliefs as making up two distinct and qualitatively different classes of things. (1982, p. 27)

This skeptical idea about the rational justification of rules of reasoning promotes contextual (as opposed to context-independent) validity.[25] A methodological relativist claims that rules and methods are variable with respect to social, political, cultural, psychological, and economic contexts. Accordingly, there are but local judgments of beliefs that take place within specific contexts wherein beliefs can be ranked based on their credibility. In other words, methodological relativism denies any universal, a priori,[26] and context-independent truth claim or way of reasoning.[27]

Methodological relativism conforms to ontological realism, and Bloor and Barnes identify themselves with both: "The general conclusion is that reality is, after all, a common factor in all the vastly different cognitive responses that men produce to it" (1982, p. 34). The basic version of ontological realism upholds that something exists in a mind-independent way. This version is compatible with the strong program's constructivist (or conventionalist) explication of the specific "real" objects that are supposed to exist relatively. According to Barnes and Edge, "no body of knowledge, nor any part of one, can capture, or at least can be known to capture, *the* basic pattern or structure inherent in some aspect of the natural world." They explain, "Nature can be patterned in different ways….Specific orderings are constructed not revealed, invented rather than discovered, in sequences of activity which however attentive to experience and to formal consistency could nonetheless have been otherwise and could have had different results" (1982, pp. 4–5). Therefore, the strong thesis is an epistemologically relativist view that implies that the contents of our beliefs and theories are constructed (or determined) relative to the sociopolitical context. This is a full-blooded truth relativism that contextualizes both the content and the truth criteria of knowledge.

The strong thesis is also self-reflexive in its claim of truth relativism. That is, its belief in the contextuality of belief evaluations is itself declared relative to the truth criteria of a specific culture. Now if this specific culture grants the strong thesis, the latter is true relative to this specific culture. The strong thesis would have become self-refuting had it maintained that its claims are absolute. Critics have frequently portrayed Mannheim's sociology of knowledge and the strong thesis as universal truth claims and criticized them for being self-refuting (see, for example, Grunwald 1990). Considering the locality of the strong thesis, however, we might conclude that its relativism is not an absolute epistemological relativism: The strong program is relativist for rejecting an absolute epistemological realism. It is, however, a local voice (not an absolute voice) that rejects a presently dominant absolute. According to the project of political epistemology, the partial truth of the strong thesis, including its (indexical) epistemological relativism, resides here.

As indicated, the strong program's nonevaluative sentiment is indeed the very positivist factual–normative distinction that is applied to beliefs and theories. The nonevaluative sentiment envisions the belief as a factual "thing," an in-itself, which exists independent of our normative accounts of it. This thingification of belief is central to the strong thesis, which eschews any concern with the epistemological condition of what is to be studied sociologically: Bloor and Barnes assign an above-the-battle neutrality to the sociologist, who avoids any involvement in the thing/belief he or she studies.

A critique of neutrality

The strong program's relativism is a logical corollary of its reified concept of belief: A belief is believed to remain the "thing" it already is despite the different normative and epistemic values that people assign to it in different sociopolitical contexts. Hence, according to the strong thesis, the same belief can be judged as true in one context and as false in another.[28] The strong thesis indicates that a sociologist can distinguish between a belief and its semantic content on the one hand and its epistemic value or reason on the other. Epistemic value and reason are allegedly external to the meaning of a belief. In a sense, the reification involved in the strong program's concept of meaning also suggests that even the causes of a belief/thing (let us accept for the sake of argument that the cause and the reason are genuinely separate) are external to the belief and its meaning.

The project of political epistemology finds the above characterization of belief unacceptable. In what follows, I shall argue that ideas like the sociologist's epistemic neutrality toward the object of study (i.e., the belief), the abstract separation between reason and cause, and the idea that they are both external to meaning are just wrong. These ideas are corollaries to the strong program's epistemic relativism. Rejecting them thus leads to a rejection of the program's epistemic relativism.

The strong thesis works only if understanding a belief could allow a strict separation between questions of meaning and questions of validity—if neutral, nonevaluative epistemic atheism were possible. Yet epistemic judgment does not come to sociology from the outside but breaks out from within. According to the dialectical view of the project of political epistemology, understanding is ontologically constitutive of social reality. Sociological descriptions, moreover, are themselves parts of the society. As Anthony Giddens points out,

> The generation of descriptions of acts of everyday actors is not incidental to social life as ongoing *Praxis* but is absolutely integral to its

production and inseparable from it, since the characterization of what others do, and more narrowly their intentions and reasons for what they do, is what makes possible the intersubjectivity through which the transfer of communicative intent is realized. (1976, p. 151)

He continues, "It is in these terms that *verstehen* must be regarded, not as a special method of entry to the social world peculiar to the social sciences, but as the ontological condition of human society as it is produced and reproduced by its members" (p. 151). Whatever social reality Bloor and Barnes would put their fingers on as the causal explanatory variable is in part constituted by *verstehen*. The social reality is cognitively structured, and this is another way of saying that social reality is cognitive/material or practico-inert. The very subject matter of sociology, the social reality, embraces the processes of reaching understanding among social individuals who, as agents, form the social reality by their purposive acts, speech acts, and cooperation. Social individuals' interpretations of each other's behaviors and intentions, and of texts, materials, goods, techniques, events, and so forth, affect the varying ways in which they respond to their condition, communicate and exchange reasons, and so generate (indirectly) configurations that are self-stabilizing. These interpretations, moreover, promote institutions, social systems, and personality structures (see Berger and Luckmann 1967, ch. 2).

Hence, in order to know the cognitively structured social reality, one must grasp the meanings and the reasons that partially compose it. Even if the strong thesis were right and social reality really was the "determining cause" of beliefs, the sociologist would still be compelled to look into the reasons and meanings that constitute this "cause." In other words, dialectical ontology and the idea of society as cognitively structured reality imply that reasons and causes are interdependent and only abstractly separate.

And if the sociologist has to understand the reasons that are embedded in social facts, the question is whether he or she can approach validity claims in a purely descriptive, nonnormative way. The project of political epistemology's answer is negative. In order to substantiate this answer, however, we need to look into the nature of understanding. The following section addresses this need: It considers Hans-Georg Gadamer's ontology of understanding and investigates the way in which Gadamer's hermeneutic philosophy contributes to the project of political epistemology. This investigation uncovers the falsity of the epistemic neutrality thesis.

Gadamer's ontology of understanding

In *Truth and Method*, Gadamer investigates the ontological commitment that is, according to him, involved in all understanding. The nature of this commitment reveals what happens to us when we attempt to interpret and understand. Like Kant, Gadamer inquires about the conditions of our knowledge, its extent, and its epistemic validity: He asks how understanding is possible at all. Unlike Kant, however, Gadamer focuses not only on that which precedes the subject's understanding (e.g., methodological activity, objectivity-seeking endeavors, and so forth) but also on that which precedes the birth of subjectivity itself.

For Gadamer, hermeneutics is not a methodological tool that a disengaged subject would use to leap over the gap between itself and the "external/independent" world or to understand the "intrinsic" meaning that dwells in the text or resides in the author's mind. Rather, Gadamer observes the conditions necessary for understanding to be possible. "The question I have asked," he writes, "seeks to discover and bring into consciousness something which methodological dispute serves only to conceal and neglect, something that does not so much confine or limit modern science as precede it and make it possible" (Gadamer 2002, p. xxix). Hermeneutics is "not to develop a procedure of understanding, but to clarify the conditions in which understanding takes place" (p. 295).

Gadamer's hermeneutics thus offers a transcendental analysis of understanding. The certainty-seeking methodology of Descartes does not appeal to Gadamer, who, following Heidegger, rejects the ontological background of Cartesian epistemology. The separation of knowing and the known, the subject–object dichotomy, the idea of the thing-in-itself that is the object of inquiry, and the exaltation of method as a means to grasp reality are all part of this ontological background. In Gadamer's view, preoccupation with a route of access is contingent upon a prior ontological portrayal of knowing that categorically separates the disengaged subject from the real object and, in so doing, attempts to measure and bridge the epistemic gap between them.

Gadamer rejects the Cartesian presupposition that we can separate ourselves from our assumptions, prejudgments, and situatedness. Our situatedness is within a tradition that, according to Gadamer, enables us to know and, at the same time, limits our horizon of understanding. The historicity of understanding, the locatedness of all understandings in historical contexts, is what the Cartesian metaphysics misses.

In other words, the historicity of understanding implies that the content of understanding simply depends on the historical context. This means, moreover, that the very "event of truth" is constituted, in part, by social, political, and historical elements.

The historicity of understanding invalidates what Gadamer calls "historicism," the idea that understanding a text consists of reacquiring *the* meaning that resided at a past historical moment. "Historicism tempts us...to regard understanding as a kind of reconstruction which in effect repeats the process whereby the text came into being," Gadamer writes (2002, p. 373). When regarded in this way, the past historical moment, or the author's meaning and mentality, appear as a thing-in-itself distinct from the knower, who applies methodology to retrieve them. Gadamer's conception of the historicity of understanding suggests that for metaphysical reasons (the knower's being-in-the-world-with-others), both ahistorical and historicist accounts of understanding are wrong. It holds, moreover, that the ahistorical and historicist accounts unjustifiably assign universal authority to the social and political (contextual) elements of present and past. As such, these metaphysical errors, historicist and ahistorical accounts, are also politically dangerous. Reifying one specific understanding—the author's one—as the uniquely true, historicism indeed aspires to prioritize one set of contextual sociopolitical elements over all possible others that actually contribute to alternative understandings.

As we shall see, Gadamer's idea of understanding as an interactive fusion of horizons reminds us that the set of unjustifiably prioritized sociopolitical elements is not completely that of the author: It also includes specific contextual elements of the present that are involved in whatever interpretation that allegedly "corresponds" to the author's meaning. Therefore, historicism and ahistoricity alike prioritize some sociopolitical elements of the present context while denying, in their own separate ways, that they do so. While the former yearns to leave its own historical moment and leap into the author's historical context, the latter longs for absolute detachment from any historical situatedness. Gadamer believes, however, that every understanding of a past or present text (and of its context) involves a new dialectical interaction with its contextual elements. In other words, understanding begins with negating the absolute and universal authority of both past and present contexts. Understanding thus has a radical feature, and Gadamer aspires to enact the emancipatory potential of a post-Enlightenment rationality that accompanies his ontology of understanding (Caputo 1987, p. 111).

These considerations suggest that truth or falsity cannot remain innocent of the sociopolitical context of understanding. Gadamer's ontology of understanding, therefore, paves the way for a political epistemological reading of hermeneutics. Let us now consider how, in Gadamer's ontology of understanding, the "consciousness" that interprets and knows is always "historically effected" by, and engaged in, sociopolitical reality.

There are four major themes that together form Gadamer's ontology of understanding: prejudgments, the fusion of horizons, the centrality (or virtuality) of language, and the historically effected consciousness. Gadamer locates the essence of the Enlightenment in its "prejudice against prejudice itself, which denies tradition its power" (2002, p. 270). For him, prejudice does not necessarily lead to false judgment, however. It can have either a positive or negative epistemic value. The Enlightenment's prejudice, informed by the Cartesian quest for certainty, upholds that the prejudgment has no foundation in the thing-in-itself: It is unfounded. Accordingly, while all authority is assigned to a supposedly prejudice-free reason, the truth of tradition seems contingent upon the credibility that reason accords. Removing the prejudice of the Enlightenment, Gadamer says, "opens the way to an appropriate understanding of finitude which dominates not only our humanity but also our historical consciousness" (p. 276). Finitude, for Gadamer, is our belonging to history, our "historical life," our understanding ourselves "in a self-evident way in the family, society, and state in which we live" (p. 276). The Cartesian detached subjectivity is a "distorting mirror," Gadamer explains, and "that is why the prejudices of the individual, far more than his judgments, constitute the historical reality of his being" (p. 276).

Prejudices, handed down to us by tradition, constitute us. In part, we *are* our prejudgments, our tradition. Our identity as a finite and historical entity does not emerge *ex nihilo* (see Wachterhauser 2002). Contrary to the Enlightenment prejudice, neither any other reality nor we are identifiable as pure in-itself. Following Hegel, Gadamer maintains that the very act of identification mediates the in-itself and makes it in-itself-for-us. This is why even the most ultimate unit of what is "given" in consciousness is named "Erlebnis not sensation" (2002, p. 65): This naming indicates that units of experience, realities that *are*, are at the same time units of meaning; that is, the known objects are not separate from the knower and the process of knowing. Prejudgments, therefore, are units of meaning that partially make up the world and us.

Gadamer's idea of prejudgments is no stranger to the notion of herme- neutic fore structures that together form what Heidegger calls the "her- meneutic situation" (1962, p. 275). Fore structures are our prethematic interpretations of the world of everydayness: Forehaving, foresight, and foregrasping conjure up the understanding that we, as beings-in-the- world, "always already" possess. "Inheriting" these forestructures, or being "thrown" in a hermeneutic situation, resembles what Gadamer calls having a tradition: "We are always situated within traditions, and this is no objectifying process—i.e. we do not conceive of what tradi- tion says as something other, something alien. It is always part of us" (2002, p. 282). Tradition also refers to the broadly historical legacy and the entire set of practices of which we, as individuals, are only a part, and in relation to which we can articulate our prethematic interpreta- tions of the world and ourselves.

Gadamer's concept of tradition also shows similarities with Kuhn's idea of paradigm. According to both, using reason in acts of under- standing and evaluation is possible only within a common body of guiding assumptions, frameworks, methods, practices, and, broadly speaking, only within shared forms of life. In Gadamer's view, "the meaning of belonging—i.e. the element of tradition in our historical/ hermeneutic activity—is fulfilled in the commonality of fundamental enabling prejudices." He writes, "Hermeneutics starts from the position that a person seeking to understand something has a bond to the sub- ject matter that comes into language through the traditionary text and has, or acquires, a connection with the tradition from which the text speaks" (2002, 295).

According to Gadamer, tradition is not a homogeneous and consis- tent entity.[29] Our situated consciousness "is always filled with a variety of voices in which the echo of the past is heard," and "only in the mul- tifariousness of such voices does it exist: this constitutes the nature of the tradition in which we want to share and have a part" (2002, p. 284). Mutual understanding, however, like interpreting a text, requires some shared elements of tradition. Under the condition of absolute incom- mensurability, we can not even understand and articulate the differ- ences (see MacIntyre 1977, pp. 45–74).

When we share elements of tradition with a text or a partner in dia- logue, we find ourselves open to them. Openness thus has an epistemic dimension, though it is not limited to it. Openness is indeed not totally involuntary. Morality constitutes the second dimension of it. Gadamer writes: "All that is asked is that we remain open to the meaning of the other person or text. But this openness always includes our situating the other meaning in relation to the whole of our meanings or ourselves in a relation to it" (2002, p. 268). Openness thus involves a creative (see O'Murchadha 1992, p. 127) and active appropriation—a morally loaded engagement in an I–Thou relationship—and a courageous willingness to change one's prejudices. According to Gadamer, there are three ways of knowing or "experiencing" the other: The first is treating him or her as a predictable object of natural sciences. This behavioristically oriented experience of the other contradicts the "moral definition of man," however (Gadamer 2002, p. 358). The second is claiming to understand the others better than they understand themselves and thus trying to absorb them into ourselves. In other words, what the other says or does has no autonomy or legitimacy of its own, but can be acknowledged only in its identity with us (Warnke 2002, p. 92). "In this way the Thou loses the immediacy with which it makes its claim," Gadamer explains. "It is understood, but this means it is co-opted and pre-empted reflectively from the stand point of the other person" (2002, p. 359). The third is "to experience the Thou truly as a Thou—i.e. not overlook his claim but to let him really say something to us" (p. 361).

Only this latter kind of openness to tradition—which "is the characteristic of historically effective consciousness"—is moral. Here, one neither instrumentalizes the other nor claims to speak for him or her, and so one remains sensitive to the other's "alterity." This kind of sensitivity "involves neither neutrality with respect to content nor the extinction of one's self, but the fore-grounding and appropriation of one's own fore-meanings and prejudices." "The important thing," Gadamer emphasizes, "is to be aware of one's own bias, so that the text can present itself in all its otherness and thus assert its own truth against one's own meaning" (p. 269). An open engagement with a Thou implies that I myself "must accept some things that are against me, even though no one else forces me to do so" (p. 361).

Here, Gadamer's openness shows its two dimensions together: The morally enforced acceptance of "some things that are against me" accompanies the epistemic need for coherence. Moreover, an I–Thou relation is a historical event. As a relationship between situated human beings or between them and a situated text, it takes place within a sociopolitical context. It is this context that in part makes openness (im)possible.[30] Consequently, the demand for practical realization of such a relationship compels us to ask what it is that blocks, distorts, or facilitates openness at a historical moment. Gadamer writes, "What man needs is not just the persistent posing of ultimate questions, but the sense of what is feasible, what is possible, what is correct, here and now" (Gadamer 2002, p. xxxviii). The question of the feasibility of openness indicates its third, political dimension. Hence, for Gadamer, openness as a constitutive element of the event of understanding and truth is an epistemic/moral/political entity. As a result, an appropriate epistemological analysis of understanding needs to take into consideration the political dimension of openness.[31]

Human finitude is best mirrored in the historical dimension of humans' capacities. Finitude thus means man's being in a historical horizon—or, better, his or her being a historical horizon. According to Gadamer, *horizon* indicates the range of vision that includes everything that can be seen from a particular vantage point. It limits what we can see and allows us to see anything at all. Horizon, therefore, has a dialectical relationship with the phenomenon of understanding. This is why understanding is always a cohappening of disclosure and concealment.

For Gadamer, tradition must be primarily considered not as the past but as a restless movement from the past through the present and future. (This movement is not a linear transition from the past to the present and future. It is rather circular: Our past helps us constitute the present and future, and our idea of what our present or future is, or should be, modifies what we realize as our past.) The connectedness of tradition to the present lies in the fact that tradition is basically a dialectical fusion of historical horizons that receives its driving force from us whenever we are engaged in the event of understanding. And when indeed are we not?[32] Tradition is the fusion of vantage points of past and present. Here resides the crux of Gadamer's ontological idea of understanding (and truth): Understanding is an event, a dialectical happening of fusion; it is interactive, practical, and, as we shall see, dialogical and linguistic. An epistemological glance identifies the sociopolitical dimension, which this ontology assigns to the event of truth.

When understanding a text, our current interpretations and the historical horizon of the text intertwine as part of a common tradition. This is why understanding "happens" not at the point of the text itself but at a point of interaction between the text's—or the other partner of dialogue's—horizon and ours. As Gadamer says, "The true locus of hermeneutic is this in-between" (2002, p. 295). The idea that human beings are always already engaged in the practice of understanding testifies to the point that what is called tradition in Gadamer's ontology of understanding is essentially the same entity that the concept of fused horizons refers to. In other words, tradition as an entity is but the endless movement of the dialectical fusion of horizons that epitomizes the very event of understanding in which human being is "primordially thrown."

It is thus due to an analytic abstraction that we talk about the horizon of text—or of the other partner of dialogue—versus our horizon as though they are two distinct things-in-themselves. This specific understanding, the idea that there are, or should be, two horizons that will later fuse into each other, is itself an understanding that takes place *before* we reach "the two in-itself horizons": We are always late for understanding, for the fusion of horizons and for the language. Wherever we go to see what there is prior to the fusion, we find out that understanding and fusion have already arrived before us. This is why "thing(1)s" become "thing(2)s" within the process of understanding and through the dialogical happening of truth in language. This also shows why Plato's idea of dialogical dialectics, rather than Hegel's monological dialectics, conforms more properly to the Gadamerian notion of fusion.[33]

Out there, before fusion, there "are" no separate horizons that are warming up to intertwine dialectically. The same goes for the separation of subject from object: "Our line of thought prevents us from dividing the hermeneutic problem in terms of the subjectivity of the interpreter and the objectivity of the meaning to be understood. This would be starting from a false antithesis that cannot be resolved even by recognizing the dialectic of subjective and objective. To distinguish between a normative function and a cognitive one is to separate what clearly belong together" (Gadamer 2002, p. 311). In Gadamer's view, the Hegelian dialectical mediation between the subject and the object is still guilty of a sort of Cartesian metaphysics, under the spell of which Hegel expects certainty—the "whole of truth"—when the dialectics reaches the telos (Ambrosio 1987a, pp. 28–9). For Gadamer, the interaction of understanding is an endless dialogical process through which truth and untruth (disclosure and concealment) go hand in hand. No one is ever the owner of whole truth: "To be historically means that the knowledge of one can never be complete" (Gadamer 2002, p. 302). In other words, it is the interactive nature of understanding that implies its open-endedness.

A tradition persists due to the interactive fusion of horizons, the recurring event of understanding. In result, tradition is not a rigid and unchangeable "thing." In Gadamer's words, "Understanding is not merely a reproductive activity but always a productive activity as well" (2002, p. 296). Finitude, openness, and impermanence always accompany horizons and traditions that in turn owe their existence to understanding. Accordingly, there cannot be a final correct meaning for a text: There is only the unfolding history of interpretations generated by different horizons of understanding. Like a musical fragment that, literally speaking, "comes" into being, afresh and unique, each time an interpretation/performance happens, meaning and truth come into existence, anew and specific, each time an interaction of understanding takes place. A musical fragment *is* a historical chain of each-time-anew interpretive performances. Likewise, the being of a text *as* a text and its textual meaning come alive through different readings over time: Understanding is not so much reproductive as it is productive; it cocreates the meaning and being of what it understands (Guignon 2002). Of course, we seek nothing less than to perform the *same* musical fragment, nothing less than to understand the *same* text, the *same* person, or the *same* thing. But the meaning of what we seek to understand is not "self-contained." It does not exist *an sich* (Bernstein 1982, p. 827). It is only realized through the happenings of understanding. This is why Gadamer tells us that to understand is always to understand *differently* (2002, p. 297).

As we have seen, such understanding is only possible because of the prejudices and prejudgments that are constitutive of what we *are*—our own historicity. In other words, such understanding is possible only because of our active participation in the practice of fusion. Our participation "incarnates" (see Figal 2002, p. 114) the meaning and truth and lets the very *same* thing that we seek to know reveal *itself*. Hence, according to Gadamer, our participation is not an independent variant or a precondition that could be located within the "context of discovery" of the truth. It is rather a constitutive element of meaning and truth—the element that in part contributes to the meaning of the thing and, therefore, makes up what the thing truly is. Meaning and truth thus are path dependent, and this path is of sociopolitical nature. Again, it is a very short passage from this ontological position to a political epistemological reading of Gadamer that accordingly takes the politics of our participation into its normative account of truth.

In Gadamer's view, understanding, interpretation, and appropriation are three moments that together and simultaneously (Gadamer 2002, p. 308) facilitate the fusion of horizons. Understanding is an active interpretation and appropriation of the text to the reader's own horizon. According to Gadamer, the appropriation of the text to a given situation (e.g., the context of the reader), and thus making the "play" of to-and-fro movements between two horizons happen, is an act akin to what Aristotle calls *phronesis*. Phronesis is a form of knowledge that enacts the mediation between the universal and the particular. This mediation is not a matter of applying technical rules, or what Descartes would imagine as method. It is rather a form of "ethical know-how" in which both what is particular and what is universal determine each other. To the process of understanding, phronesis contributes a deliberate choice about what must be affirmed as true (Ambrosio 1988, p. 176).

Phronesis is not an "objective" knowledge detached from one's own being and becoming. As opposed to technical knowledge, the application of ethical knowledge is never straightforward because the ideal to which one looks in acting is never independent of the action itself. Means and ends here are not separable as they are in technical skills (where one can distinguish a skill from its ideal result). Accordingly, a person becomes a certain sort of person in the course of his or her ethical action. This is why, as an ethical move, Aristotle's phronesis shapes the being of the *phronimos*. Similarly, Gadamer's appropriation that leads the process of understanding forms the knower. Far from the Cartesian reifying dualism, the practice of knowing constitutes the knower and the known. The interactive relationship thus is prior to the determination of relata: Herein resides the main difference between phronesis and techne (see Warnke 2002, pp. 83–5).

Furthermore, the moral dimension of phronesis results in openness and thus becomes constitutive of understanding:

> It appears in the fact of concern, not about myself, but about the other person. Thus it is a mode of moral judgment....The question here, then, is not about knowledge in general but its concretion at a particular moment. This knowledge also is not in any sense a technical knowledge or the application of such....Once again we discover that the person who is understanding does not know and judge as one who stands apart and unaffected but rather he thinks along with the other from the perspective of a specific bond of belonging, as if he too were affected. (Gadamer 2002, p. 323)

In Gadamer's account, mediation implies the knower's engagement in a process through which both the particular and the universal become codetermined and integral to the very being of the phronimos. For Gadamer, this process is characteristic of *all* real knowing. As discussed above, the practice of understanding is part of a process through which meaning and truth come into being. Like phronesis, and as moral-practical knowledge, understanding becomes constitutive of what we are in the process of becoming. Accordingly, the authentic hermeneutical understanding, the open play of free interaction in which ethics implies respect toward the alterity of the other, truly humanizes us and becomes integrated in our very being, just as phronesis forms the being of the phronimos (Bernstein 1982, p. 832). Therefore, the truth of our interpretation is not reducible to a simple coherence among propositions. Meaning and truth have ethical constituents and constitute the human beings who interact understandingly. Much more than representing reality, meaning and truth intervene in it and affect it. Truth and meaning thus are parts of reality—they are *real*.

Here, the emancipatory nature of Gadamer's hermeneutics comes to the fore. An authentic hermeneutical understanding is political insofar as it shapes the praxis of social individuals and social reality. The social nature of phronesis as a moral-practical discipline is of key importance here. Gadamer complains that in modern society the hegemony of a deformed techne has changed the contemporary understanding of praxis, and as a result, the application of science to the technical control of society has subjugated phronesis, "practical philosophy," and practical wisdom. He writes:

> In a scientific culture such as ours the fields of techne and art are much more expanded. Thus the fields of mastering means to pre-given ends have been rendered even more monological and controllable. The crucial change is that practical wisdom can no longer be promoted by personal contact and the mutual exchange of the views among the citizens. Not only has craftsmanship been replaced by industrial work; many forms of our daily life are technologically organized so that they no longer require personal decision. In modern technological society public opinion itself has in a new and really decisive way to become the object of very complicated techniques—and this, I think, is the main problem facing our civilization. (Gadamer 1975, p. 313)

Gadamer's ontology of meaning helps us realize the depth of the problem: It is not just a matter of external imposition of power and "technical" control over society. It is, indeed, the ways in which modern human beings conceive themselves and understand the meaning and truth of their sociopolitical relationships that dialectically makes modern society an iron cage. As Gadamer's ontology of meaning demonstrates, the very way we "know" the meaning and truth of ourselves—that is, the scientific understanding and its correlated instrumental rationality—forms our life and society the way they are.

Modern knowledge, meaning, and truth partially constitute the power over us. They *are* the power over us. It is, using Foucault's term, the problematic of power/knowledge.

Gadamer's hermeneutic philosophy aspires to defend practical and political reason against the domination of a science-based technology. Hermeneutics is in this sense "the heir of the older tradition of practical philosophy" (Gadamer 1975, p. 316). Hence, Gadamer's hermeneutic philosophy is an emancipatory political attempt to formulate and practically realize a post-Enlightenment rationality. It emphasizes freedom and solidarity that include all human beings:

> The principle that all are free never again can be shaken. But does this mean that on account of this, history has come to an end? Are all human beings actually free? Has not history since then been a matter of just this, that the historical conduct of man has to translate the principle of freedom into reality? Obviously this points to the unending march of world history into the openness of its future tasks and gives no becalming assurance that everything is already in order. (Gadamer 1982, p. 37)

Our political epistemological reading of Gadamer suggests that his version of truth is new coherentist. Understanding, agreement, and consent are the concepts that inform Gadamer's idea of *Verstehen* (Weinsheimer and Marshall 2002, p. 14). For him, as we will see, understanding is coming to an agreement with someone dialogically. "Agreement" connotes consistency and coherence between the different opinions of the partners who participate in the event of understanding. For Gadamer, understanding, meaning, and truth are practical events. They do not merely refer to a set of propositions that "represent" reality: They also affect and intervene in reality. Accordingly, agreement as a moment in the event of understanding entertains a sociopolitical makeup. Gadamer's criterion of true understanding (i.e., coherence), therefore, extends itself beyond the web of propositions and takes into account the question of mutual support among sociopolitical elements in a hermeneutic interaction: Gadamer as a participant in the project of political epistemology believes in the new coherence theory of truth.

The sociopolitical nature of phronesis, and thus the political attributes of meaning and truth, become clearer when Gadamer highlights the virtuality of language. Gadamer formulates the idea of hermeneutical experience in terms of the ontology of language. To him, prejudgments, horizons, and their fusion; tradition and its continuity; phronesis; openness; play; meaning; truth; and even the "being" of entities are to be conceived from the central point of language (Gadames 2002, p. 389). It is language that makes them all possible. Gadamer believes in the ontological priority of language in every event of truth and experience of understanding, whether philosophical, aesthetic, historical, or even "scientific" (Ambrosio 1986b, 132). The centrality of language also alludes to the decentralization of method as the primary path to truth.

For Martin Heidegger, similarly, language opens a space for things to come into their being. It does not name a substance that has already shown itself, but is itself the opening up of a clear space and the lightening of the entity that appears in it. The identity of a thing *as this specific thing* becomes disclosed in language, where the specificity of the thing and its very being emerge together. In other words, the specificity, the identity, or the this-thingness of the thing, has no ontologically prior standing apart from its being and existence. For Gadamer, language constitutes a "point of mediation" out of which man and world emerge together: Language "centers" the event in which this togetherness takes place. Language has no independent life apart from the world that comes into view within it. "That language is originally human means at the same time that man's being-in-the-world is primordially linguistic," he writes (Gadamer 2002, p. 443). Thus, acccording to Gadamer,

> In language world itself presents itself. Verbal experience of the world is 'absolute.' It transcends all the relative ways being is posited because it embraces all being-in-itself, in whatever relationships (relativities) it appears. Our verbal experience of the world is prior to everything that is recognized and addressed as existing. *That language and the world are related in a fundamental way does not mean, then, that the world becomes the object of language.* Rather the object of knowledge and statements is always already enclosed within the world horizon of language. That human experience of the world is verbal does not imply that a world-in-itself is being objectified. (2002, p. 450)[34]

Gadamer's response to the accusation of relativism follows this ontological description: the *real this thing* comes into being within the practice of language *together* with the meaning and truth. Hence, truth is not a matter of correspondence between a truth claim and the *real this thing.* Gadamer does not suggest that outside of language there is no thing, nothing, no in-itself. He is not antirealist in this sense. He rather says that outside of language we cannot *say* anything about a presumably thing-in-itself. Indeed, the thing in-itself also has a linguistic makeup due to previous linguistic practices that have brought it into light—due to our very talking about it right now at this moment. This is why ontology is always late for language. We cannot transcend language and see what *is* behind: We have *said* yes to language before saying yes to anything else.

For young Heidegger, and for his student, Gadamer, the meaning—that is, an existential of Dasein—is found only so far as Dasein projects a horizon that gets filled by entities. Meaning and truth are found so long as there is Dasein. Outside of Dasein, there is not the absurdity of substances without forms, natures, and identities, but nonmeaning, silence. Dasein is linguistic through and through, just as it is social through and through.[35] Therefore, in Gadamer's view, just as in Foucault's discourse, it is language that opens up a field of objects.[36]

Gadamer takes the dialogical movement of conversation to be the original form of language. This dialogue is only possible because both parties to it share a common language that is the language of the tradition to which the interpreter listens. The belonging-together (or togetherness) of the entities with their meaning in language is also contingent upon the belonging of the interpreter to the tradition. Accordingly,

> truth for Gadamer is the emergence into language of the human relationship to the world as a virtual whole of meaning....The structure of truth happening in language is "virtual" in the sense that all beings which appear within the world are already "embraced" and "enclosed" within the world-horizon of language as their absolute condition. (Ambrosio 1986a, p. 31)

Now the idea of fusion of horizons finds its proper articulation in the dialogical interplay of questions and answers. The idea of fusion as a dialogical movement between questions and responses rectifies the aforementioned error of abstracting the existence of two horizons as in-themselves before their fusion.

Openness also turns out to be linguistic in nature: The more authentic the conversation is, the less "its conduct lies within the will of either partner." "A genuine conversation," Gadamer writes, "is never the one that we wanted to conduct" (2002, p. 383). Openness, listening to one another, and addressing one another, are an essential constituent of a conversation that render it both unpredictable and fruitful. In a successful conversation, Gadamer asserts, the matter at hand takes the lead (p. 383) and comes to language if the partners act such that the conversation is not hindered. Questioning provides the possibility "of avoiding the pressure of opinion." It indicates and presupposes (p. 366) the freedom of conversation. As such, it also implies that truth is not a private relationship in possession of few. In addition, the freedom to question demands that we ask about the sociopolitical context that blocks or fosters it.[37]

The art of questioning, Gadamer believes, "makes object and all its possibilities fluid" (2002, p. 367). This is why the truth of the question is always more than the one of answers: The question opens up the possibility of new disclosures. Each answer in its dialogical relationship to the question fulfills a possible disclosure among many and simultaneously covers up the ways in which different answers could have participated in different disclosures of the *same* subject matter. Within the event of meaning in a conversation, the thing that comes to words at the same time "withdraws"[38] and thus gives the happening of truth, *aletheia*, its historical dimension. Following Heidegger, Gadamer believes that the question holds this "hermeneutical priority" (2002, p. 362) in thought because it takes ontological priority in human existence. It is finally those questions "as our very mode of being as persons, which give rise to every pre-reflective ontological commitment and consequently to the very reflective formulation of the questions and of any answer" (Ambrosio 1986b, p. 142, note 13).

Within a conversation, *moral-practical phronesis* refers to the ability of partners to pass from indeterminacy and universal openness (question) to determinacy and concreteness (answer). Phronesis includes a deliberation in which universal norms are applied to individual situations. It is the power to find the universal in concrete circumstances and to know what is demanded by the particular situation. Phronesis is not just a matter of moral decision, which concerns the alterity of the other partner and, in so doing, guarantees the openness of the conversation. It is also a decision, which appropriates and contributes a specific answer out of the set of possible responses.[39] It is in this second dimension that phronesis better reveals its communal nature.[40]

Social reality is constructed out of the meanings, fused horizons, and traditions of social individuals. It "is not *expressed* linguistically, but simply it *is* linguisticality" (Alcoff 1996, p. 36). In other words, being-in-the-world-understandingly means being-in-the-world-with-others-linguistically. Therefore, the social relations within which we are situated are in part contingent upon the meanings through which we understand our social engagements. And meaning, as Gadamer demonstrates, is linguistic—that is, meaning is an event with practical dimensions in society itself. This circularity—or, better, the reciprocal constitutiveness of meaning and social relations—affirms the familiar fact that truth is contextual.[41] On the other hand, it also testifies to the less familiar, but equally sound, conclusion that social relations and political reality are truthful.

That he claims truthfulness for the political reality might mistakenly make Gadamer seem to be a conservative. We must remember the specific meaning that Gadamer gives to meaning and truth as linguistic/social events, however. For Gadamer, a linguistic event is the very social practice that finds its meaning in—and simultaneously gives movement to—a linguistic interaction. In other words, linguistic interactions are not abstract events that transcend social reality. They *are* social reality. Moreover, as Gadamer implies, *every* social reality is linguistic, simultaneously. The interwovenness of linguisticality and social reality shows a "difference without distinction" (Weinsheimer 1985, p. 282) and, as Gadamer states, "everything that is language has a speculative unity: it contains a distinction between its being and its presentations of itself, but this is a distinction that is really not a distinction at all" (2002, p. 475).

For socialist thinkers, the interdependence of power relations and meaning has always been at the center of attention. Karl Marx's idea of ideology as a constitutive part of both the means and the relations of exploitative production, Louis Althusser's notion of the ideological state apparatus and his definition of *interpellation*, and Antonio Gramsci's idea of hegemony and his concept of the political power as Centaur are widely known. They all attest to the mutual constitutiveness of structure and superstructure. Gadamer, I think, would agree to be interpreted accordingly. Gadamer is a Hegelian conservative if he assigns totality, permanence, and purity to (the whole of) truth, if his idea of the authority of tradition implies a homogeneous and ahistorical tradition; if his dialogical dialectics is, like Hegel's, teleological; and finally, if he forgets Heidegger's doctrine that concealment is the hidden ground of disclosure, that truth is always already untruth. But as we know, Gadamer leaves these ifs unfulfilled. Rather, his idea of truth is in harmony with Adorno's statement that "history is in the truth, the truth is not in history" (quoted in Buck-Morss

1979, p. 46). Gadamer's truth, as a social interaction, is historical: Historicity is a part of his ontology of truth. Accordingly, Gadamer's historically effected consciousness—Gadamer's own consciousness, for example—has the privilege of knowing the historicity of whatever it regards as true.

The notion of the historicity of truth, its sociopractical nature and its fusion with untruth, helps us perceive Gadamer as a participant in the project of political epistemology, inasmuch as he studies the sociopolitical, and the linguistic, conditions of the possibility of meaning. Moreover, Gadamer can be seen as a participant in the project of political epistemology because, besides offering an ontological description of what understanding is, he suggests a criterion for evaluating it. Gadamer's normative position is coherentist since he locates the standard of truth in the agreement between the partners of conversation (Gadamer 2002, pp. 180, 291). And finally, Gadamer is a new coherentist since for him agreement is not a logical consistency among propositions, but a sociopolitical happening.

Gadamer's identification of true understanding as an agreement follows the logic of experimental transcendental analysis: It looks into the sociopolitical factors that constitute the truth and make it possible. As a result, the ontological fact that the events of disclosure and concealment go hand in hand gets translated epistemologically into a normative idea. This normative idea encourages truth-seeking practices to proceed endlessly from a lower level of new coherence toward an upper one. This process is endless because Gadamer's dialogical dialectics is not teleological. For each understanding is simply different, and a different understanding is not necessarily synthetically different. Here lies the difference between something that is dialectically teleologically different—that is, something that shares a teleological partial truth with its opposite—and what is just simply different without having a Hegelian negation–affirmation relationship with its other.

This normative epistemology might remind us of epistemological pragmatism. According to pragmatism, increasing coherence is an epistemic value because it maximizes our understanding of reality. Gadamer, I think, would not deny this interpretation provided that the concept of coherence is not understood just as a characterization of the process of understanding because, for him, coherence is also "an ontological component of understanding" (see Alcoff 1996, p. 51). Reminding us of Lukacs, Gadamer implies that proceeding toward upper levels of new coherence is a movement with both superstructural and structural dimensions. It presupposes, and enacts, the freedom of conversation that is closely knitted to the justness of society. Social freedom and justice together "warrant" the movement of authentic hermeneutical understanding toward upper levels of new coherence. They, therefore, have epistemic value. Gadamer's ontology of understanding shows that truth, social freedom, and justice cannot be separated. For him, truth dwells in the realm of lived reality and makes rationality, morality, and politics meet each other. Gadamer's "practical philosophy" laces together epistemic normativity and politics and in so doing contributes to the project of political epistemology. It knits "truth" to the "good" again.

Evaluation of the epistemic neutrality thesis

Now that the sociologist has to understand the reasons that are embedded in social facts, the question is whether he or she can approach validity claims in a purely descriptive, nonnormative way. The project of political epistemology's answer is negative. Following Gadamer, the project of political epistemology identifies understanding with agreement (2002, pp. xvi, 293). Agreement, in its turn, occurs in light of reciprocally raised validity claims in dialogical interactions. In Gadamer's view, moreover, the "anticipation of completeness"—or openness—is a precondition of understanding. Openness implies that the sociologist, as a reader of text, when studying a belief must take its truth claims seriously (2002, pp. 261–2). In other words, in order to understand the reasons that are already involved in the constitution of cognitively structured reality, the sociologist must engage in the process of evaluating validity claims. For understanding a reason and knowing why it is or is not sound are indeed one and the same process, and "the *description* of reasons demands *eo ipso* an *evaluation*" (Habermas 1981, pp. 116, 132). The attempt to identify the *what* of a belief inevitably includes comprehending the *how* and *why* of it.[42]

Bloor and Barnes recommend, on the other hand, that the sociological account refer to reasons descriptively and not normatively, that it must "mention" validity claims but not "use" them as reasons (see Gutting 1984, p. 98). This requirement amounts to the neutralization of validity claims and, as such, to not understanding the reasons at all. This is why the nonevaluative sentiment of the strong thesis, if taken seriously, makes sociologists misunderstand the very social reality that is supposed to help them explain a belief.[43]

Gadamer's ontology of understanding indicates that in the interaction of knowing, the knower participates from his or her hermeneutic situation in a social/linguistic event. The objectivity of understanding, therefore, "is endangered precisely to the degree that the interpreter is seduced by the illusion of objectivism into concealing from himself the methodologically indissoluble bound to the hermeneutic initial situation" (Habermas 1977, p. 344). Objectivism forgets the indexicality of the "historically effective consciousness" and overlooks the chain of past interpretations (including epistemic judgments) that—through the prior understanding of the knower—objectively mediate with their object of study at hand. The strong program's symmetry and neutrality tenets embody objectivism.

As we have seen, the process of understanding interweaves meaning and validity and connects them both with reasons. The concept of cognitively structured social reality, moreover, reflects the reason–cause interdependence. At this level of analysis, and while meaning, validity, and cause twist together, the context distinction and the factual–normative dichotomy become meaningless.[44]

To the extent that the cognitive structure of reality and cause–reason interdependence are ignored, the strong thesis hypostatizes social reality as something that exists in itself. It, therefore, fetishizes the object of investigation and ignores that the sociologist partially constitutes the context that he or she analyzes as an object.

The thingification of belief and the reification of social reality go hand in hand. They both result from the static ontology of the strong thesis. Consequently, and contrary to the strong program's articulation, the historicity of truth and the indexicality of normative evaluations connote the mutually constitutive relationships between semantic contents and sociopolitical contexts and denote the cognitive/material complex of society. In other words, the notion of the historicity of truth and epistemic assessments cannot be reduced to the one-directional, causal, and deterministic connection between the sociopolitical context as an in-itself and the belief as an effect. Rather, according to political epistemology, the sociopolitical context as the transcendental precondition of a *belief*'s semantic content is simultaneously (and linguistically) constituted in part by participation of *believers*.

Social reality, according to Gadamer and the project of political epistemology, and as discussed in the previous chapters, is itself linguistical, not just expressed linguistically. It is structured out of the fused horizons, shared meanings, and traditions of interactive social individuals. Traditions produce meanings and are in their turn produced by meanings. Meaning, inseparable from epistemic validity judgments, gets created, each time anew, when an event of understanding takes place. Furthermore, understanding is "essentially a historically effected event" (Gadamer 2002, p. 300), which implies not merely reproducing fixed meanings of the text, of the other person's behavior or assertion, and of sociopolitical phenomena, among other things. Rather, Gadamer believes that understanding is "always a productive activity as well" (p. 296). Thus, each understanding is an understanding "in a *different* way" (p. 297). Tradition, moreover, is not simply an immutable precondition of understanding. Rather, "we produce it ourselves in as much as we understand, participate in the evolution of tradition, and hence further determine it ourselves" (p. 293). Therefore, the semantic content of a belief is somehow and to some extent creative of, and also unique to, the specific interpretive event—that is, to the sociopolitical interaction in and through which understanding proceeds. Indeed, the ontological circle of understanding insinuates that each time a semantic content emerges, a new and different cognitively structured social reality comes forth—and vice versa. The unconcealment (truth) of each meaning formation is indexed to its specific cognitively structured social reality. It is in fact the complex of cognitive/material social reality that harbors the epistemic values of truth (unconcealment) or falsity (concealment).

This dialectical/hermeneutic idea contains the pluralism of actual and possible cognitively structured realities (including meanings, semantic contents, and epistemic values—not the relativism of free-floating epistemic evaluations. When "the genesis in thought and historical genesis coincide,"[45] the relativism of a "representative" notion of truth becomes meaningless. There is, however, another kind of relativism, which is also to be rejected. Political epistemology must offer normative criteria in order to compare different cognitively structured social realities so as to deny both the epistemic equality and the incommensurability of all cognitively structured social realities.

In light of the dialectical position, the project of political epistemology may reread Mannheim and understand him *differently* when he writes: "Theories do not refute each other simply immanently: they can cancel each other only in 'real dialectic' that is, existentially. In this view one existential situation overcomes another, and a theory overcomes another theory only as part of such an existential situation" (1990, p. 44). Mannheim was also quite right in saying, "Only a philosophy which is able to give a concrete answer to the question of 'what shall we do?' can put forward the claim to have overcome relativism" (1952a, p. 129).

The point thus is to integrate the utopian into epistemology in order to reject the defeatism and relativism of positivism. The project of political epistemology pursues this path of thought when—introducing the upper level of new coherence—it attempts to compromise and combine the epistemic evaluation with the ethical assessments of actual and possible cognitively structured social realities. In the following chapter (Chapter 4), I shall argue that there is a close relationship—akin to identity almost—between the epistemological/normative criterion of new coherence and the ethical/normative (messianic) idea of justice.

4
Différance, Deconstruction, and the Project of Political Epistemology

As we have seen, subject–object dialectical interdependence and the linguistic nature of cognitive/material reality are of canonical importance to political epistemology, a research project with a strategic function. The project of political epistemology learns from critical theory that the dialectical contingency of the present cognitive/material reality allows, and indeed promotes, political actions to change the present. The political measure, however, should not be understood as a merely coercive and physical act. Since the in-itself-for-us reality is at once cognitive *and* material, political attempts to change it should address both aspects of reality. In order to understand the politics of cognitive change in reality, I begin the present chapter with an inquiry into the nature of contingency. The notion of contingency of language, consciousness, and reality opens up a site for studying the relationships between political acts, ethics, and epistemic normativity. Within this site, I believe, Jacques Derrida's ideas of *différance* and deconstruction can contribute valuable insights to the project of political epistemology. They can help us envision a pattern of the relation of mutual implication between epistemic normativity as new coherence, radical ethical normativity as openness, and political activity in the name of doing justice to the other.

To investigate the very meaning of contingency, I begin with Richard Rorty's idea of contingency of language and discuss his rejection of metaphysics, first philosophy, as universal truth. I argue that though Rorty denies any essence for meaning, he is not a dialectical thinker and, as such, does not believe in the reciprocally constitutive relationships between meaning/truth and material reality. His "liberal ironist" thus ceases to be a dialectical epistemologist. The next section investigates Jean-Francois Lyotard's idea of the contingency of language and understands him to be a Hegelian dialectician without teleology. Lyotard's interpretation of contingency reveals the politics involved in language. He underscores, and scorns, the suppression of the *differend* at every act of linkage between phrases and in so doing shows how each and every act of linking up between two successive phrases is political in suppressive *and* emancipatory senses. I make the case that Lyotard's notion of the contingency of linkage teaches political epistemology to see the ethical decision making and political acts together as involved in the practices of meaning and truth formation.

In the section that follows, I trace social and political features of the contingency of language in Jacques Derrida's idea of *différance*. Here, I show that Derrida's play of differentiation, *différance* should not be understood as a mere semiological phenomenon abstract from other constituents of cognitive/material reality. Derrida can be seen as a *nominalist dialectician*[1] who rejects Hegel's teleological essentialism. Consequently, the section promotes a materialistic reading of Derrida's *différance*: It demonstrates that Derrida's *différance* has to do with the very sociopolitical context of meaning/truth or, better, the very cognitive/material reality. Derrida thus contributes to the project of political epistemology by providing it with yet another supporting argument: the idea of a play that holds the interdependence of meaning/truth and sociopolitical context. Indeed, here I propose that Derrida's would-be theory of knowledge is a sort of political epistemological theory.

The following section inquires into the intersubjectivity of the self through Emmanuel Levinas's and Jacques Derrida's idea of the self as mediated by, as hostage to, the other. Here, the contingency of self–other relationships, and also of the self-other others relationships, reveals the political makeup of the self. The argument is that Derrida's deconstruction is a political and strategic response to the radical ethical, *ethical*, responsibility toward the other. This radical ethical responsibility, openness to the other, is also a condition of possibility for the unconcealment of the truth of the other. Accordingly, my argument goes, deconstruction is a political activity with an ethical motivation that opens the horizon for the truth. Deconstruction thus is of epistemic value. I explore the way in which Derrida's notion of deconstruction offers a model of coexistence between the political strategic act, ethical responsibility, and epistemic normativity. A deconstruction is a reconstruction too. That is, a political act in the name of doing justice to the other is ethically motivated by, and epistemologically conducive to, truth embodied in an upper level of new coherence.

This much, however, is not enough. Though the idea of openness as a radical, ethical, *ethicical* norm is proved to be of epistemic value, I also need to demonstrate how new coherence, political epistemology's specific criterion of truth, and ethical openness mutually imply each other. This is why I articulate the meaning of contradiction as closure in the next section and demonstrate that openness and new coherence imply each other. Political epistemology endorses political actions in increasing the level of new coherence in the cognitive/material reality. Deconstruction, I believe, as a political action that happens whenever we feel "haunted" by the call of justice-to-come and truth-to-come, gathers the political, the ethical, and the epistemic aspects of such an act together. In the rest of the chapter, I give reasons for the idea that an ethics-without-universal-principles is the kind of moral normativity that accompanies the political act of movement toward upper levels of new coherence.

The final observation of the present chapter is that political activity in search of justice, the ethical mode of relating to the other, and the epistemic pursuit of truth cannot be abstracted from each other.

The contingency of language

The concept of the contingency of language indicates that we cannot stand outside the multiplicity of languages and reach a metalanguage that gives an ultimate account of all possible languages, vocabularies, ways of judging, and criteria of decision making: It implies the impossibility of metaphysics as the first philosophy. Furthermore, the linguistic nature of meaning, truth, and reality indicates that epistemic properties like truth and falsity refer to cognitive/material reality. Language is a constitutive part of cognitive/material reality, and the contingency of the former means that it is indeed the very cognitive/material reality itself that is contingent and, moreover, that truth and meaning are situated. It also testifies to the fact that there is no perspective outside the sociopolitical context or beyond language from which a final account of society/reality is possible. Accordingly, the untruth of metaphysics (or any other totalitarian theory) can be located in its claim of universality, in its denial of its own contingency.

The linguistic "nature" of reality, and the contingency of this nature, give us good reasons to believe that changing language and other social practices (e.g., changing the way people describe the world and make themselves at home in it) might produce new human beings. Such changes, therefore, are truly political moves ending in "changing the world." As we have seen, the project of political epistemology is attentive to the politics and ethics of these changes. The present chapter further analyzes the way in which changes of meaning and reality manifest their mutual inference and investigates how this phenomenon has concurrent political, epistemological, and ethical countenances that mutually implicate each other.

Language is neither a tool for representing independent external reality—the object—nor a medium for expressing the internal ideas, emotions, and other aspects of the subject. The subject–object dichotomy is itself constructed and meaningful only within a specific language. Indeed, the subject–object dichotomy is real. It is a real constituent of a historic reality—a passing one, we hope. It is thus truthful, insofar as it is a part of cognitive/material reality.

When language conceives of itself as a mirror that passively reflects two independent "things" (i.e., the objective reality of the world and the subjective realities immanent to the subject), it finds itself transparent and invisible and tends to overlook its effective engagement in both sides. According to this traditional understanding, a core self/subject is supposed to hold, decide among, and manipulate a web of beliefs and desires. This web, in its turn, must cohere internally and also correspond with exterior reality. Hence, there are two essential things presupposed in the traditional understanding of language: the core self/subject and the independent reality. There is also granted a mirror-like language in which the expression of the former and the representation of the latter take place, interact, and finally form the true web of beliefs. If language is not a means of expression and representation, or a third thing intervening between the self and reality, however, the subject and the object are not independent things but realities that are mediated by language—realities that are linguistic. The contingency of language, therefore, suggests that the self and reality are contingent.

The contingency of the self, I shall argue, is the precondition of ethics. By *ethics*, I do not mean the Kantian ethics of a universal principle that accompanies a divine-like, universalized self as the consciousness of morality. The contingency of the self, rather, is the transcendental precondition of the self's ethical relationships with the other. These ethical relationships, I argue, are the locus of the unconcealment of truths. They are at the same time social relationships. They are deeply political. It is in fact the contingency of the self and reality that makes politics, as an activity to change the world and the self, possible. The contingency of language, in other words, is the transcendental precondition of ethics, politics, and truth.[2]

The contingency of language is a crossroad at which ethics, politics, and meaning-making processes meet. In order to clarify this point, we need to investigate the different meanings and aspects of the contingency of language. Let us start with Richard Rorty's idea of the contingency of language.

Richard Rorty and the contingency of language

Richard Rorty states, "To have a meaning is to have a place in a language game" (1989, p. 18). Rorty's elaboration of this statement represents the difference between his epistemological position and the one of political epistemology. In Rorty's view, to dismiss the idea that language, as a third entity, mirrors the world within the web of beliefs, and to deny that the world in-itself, as the fixed and factual prelinguistic reality, can be reached by the knower amounts to the epistemological attitude of a liberal ironist. For a liberal ironist, the world is out there: "It is not our creation," our human mental state. The truth, however, according to the liberal ironist, is not out there, for "where there are no sentences there is no truth…sentences are elements of human languages, and…human languages are human creations" (p. 5). In Rorty's view, language *describes* the world, and "only the descriptions of the world [not the world itself, on its own] can be true or false."

Rorty's liberal ironists drop the "absolute criteria of rationality" that is associated with the mirror concept of language and that indicates the correspondence of linguistic true beliefs with the world in-itself. Because there is no activity as epistemological choice among rival language games, paradigms, and so forth performed from a neutral point of view outside a language game and "neutral between vocabularies" (p. 48), Rorty's liberal ironist cannot be accused of traditional relativism or irrationality. "There is no way to rise above the language, culture, institution and practices one has adopted and view all these as on a par with all the others," he writes (p. 50). A liberal ironist who sees his or her language, consciousness, morality, and supreme hopes as contingent metaphors combines commitment with a sense of the contingency of his or her commitments (p. 61).

Rorty's liberal ironist maintains that truth is not a constitutive part of reality. The liberal ironist is in fact a *subject/being-in-the-language*, not a *being-in-the-world*. For Rorty, the world, language, and the subject are not in dialectical relationships. They do not constitute each other. Hence, Rorty's epistemology "is,"and claims to be, apolitical: For Rorty, seeking (local) truth and liberal political action do not imply each other. It is thus in principle possible for a liberal ironist to perform political acts and change the sociopolitical world into a liberal one and, simultaneously, to remain playful toward the truth of diverse linguistic descriptions that emerge in such a society. Such a liberal society is indeed marked by this very playful attitude toward truth. A liberal ironist, who pretends to "know" that truth is Nietzsche's "woman,"[3] is committed to a society in which everyone behaves playfully toward the "woman"—truth. The liberal ironist does not claim truthfulness for this very commitment, moreover, and precisely here resides the irony of a liberal ironist. He or she knows that there can be no valid justification to prove that, compared to its rivals, the epistemological attitude of a liberal ironist is more truthful (Rorty 1989, p. 57). Hence, for a liberal ironist, truth is a private property,[4] whereas political activity belongs to the public sphere. Consequently, the liberal ironist's political actions do not proceed in the name of truth.

The project of political epistemology, on the other hand, sees the knower, the truth, and the world in a relationship of dialectical interdependence: Truth is not a mere product of language or a property of statements. It is rather a constitutive part of reality. It is the reality, and not the "descriptive proposition," which is true or false. It is the reality that is linguistic (not linguistically described). From a political epistemological perspective, the epistemic search for truth and the political act toward justice and ethics mutually implicate one another.

The project of political epistemology understands the statement that "to have a meaning is to have a place in a language game" as follows: To have a meaning is to be conditioned by endless connections of words and concepts, to be situated within the semiological plays of differences and idiosyncrasies, and to be positioned within the play of forces, within the web of sociopolitical relationships. The project of political epistemology ties the truthfulness of contingent moments of plays to their justness and *ethicity* (Derrida's term for an *ethics-without-ethics*: an ethics otherwise than following a set of principles) and accordingly offers its normative criteria of truth. The project of political epistemology strives for a truth that, contrary to Rorty's, is not our production—a truth that comes to us from the height, *from beyond* the language, from the nonconcept (in Adorno's term), and shatters our preformed horizons of language and expectation.

Jean-Francois Lyotard and the contingency of language

The contingency of language manifests itself best in the dark abyss of "nothingness" (Lyotard 1988, p. 138) that "separates" two phrases, two genres, or two language games, where and when the first phrase has taken place and the second is yet to arrive. The contingency of language means that the way we link up the second sentence to the former is always unsettled and indeterminate. It is not a rule-governed happening. As Jean-Francois Lyotard states, "The linking of one sentence onto another is problematic," and, more importantly, "this problem is the problem of politics" (p. 11). Language interactions include diverse multiplicities of linkages that do not follow "correct principles" of linking. When a phrase has taken place, something must happen: Something must advance from the void that detaches two sentences (p. xii). This happening can be a respectful silence, a rejecting reticence, a waiting, a disregarding, or it can be another phrase. We cannot choose not to link; this choice would still be a sort of linking (p. 66). In other words, to link is an "obligation" that is not implemented by a set of ethical principles, simply because ethical principles are but specific genres, and a contingent linkage happens exactly where the genre is absent, where two genres are to be linked up.[5] To link is an obligation-without-principles.

Something must arrive. "What" arrives, however, is contingent. Lyotard calls this "the necessity of contingency" (see Prado 1991, p. 92). Therefore, the arriving of a sentence as well as what the arrived sentence is are both contingent. Meaning and truth claims as the outcomes of diverse linkages throughout linguistic communications are contingent upon the ways in which linkages take place.

The linguistic nature of reality and the fact that meaning and sociopolitical reality are mutually constitutive indicate that the contingency of linkage has to do with the contingency of sociopolitical reality constituted by meaning. The necessity of contingency means that one must decide under the condition in which there is no rule or ethical, categorical principle, in order to link up two genres where there is a structural discontinuity between two games. From a political epistemological point of view, the sociopolitical factors that affect a decision, or contextualize a contingent act of linkage, also give meaning to it and partially constitute the meaning of the arriving sentence. They become, using Gadamer's terminology, constituents of the horizon of the text, of the chain of linked sentences—a horizon that is never a unity or a totality: an open horizon that harbors the multiplicity of contingent passages. More accurately, they, the sociopolitical contexts, the constituents of every linkage in the text, become part of the text itself.[6]

Therefore, it is only through an ignorant, retrospective look at a chain of successive phrases that one can envisage a genre, a totality, and a unique game with rules that are assumed to have been followed at each passage from one sentence to the other. This ignorance, as we shall see, is politically violent and epistemologically wrong. Lyotard asserts,

> Genres of discourse are modes of forgetting the nothingness or of forgetting the occurrence, they fill the void between phrases. This nothingness is, nevertheless, what opens up the possibility of finalities proper to the genre. If the manner of linking were necessary (filled in), there would not be several possible modes. (1988, p. 138)

In other words, the contingency of linking over the void is "necessary" to language, to the formation of genres. But the ignorant look tends to forget this fact. The genre of metaphysics is famous for its ignorant look. It dreams of touching the arche, the necessary unchangeable structure of reality, and reflecting it into a genre that is universal. The contingency of linkages makes metaphysics impossible.[7]

What Lyotard calls the *differend* dwells in the abyss of nothingness, where there is no language—in between two phrases. The abyss of the between-two-phrases is not a phrase. It is an enigmatic reality beyond language. The differend is a "name" for this beyond-language. Lyotard has a "taste" for (see Derrida and Ferraris 2001), a "sentiment" about it (1988, p. 56)—a "feeling" that amounts to a faith, and hope, that language is not "the house of Being." The project of political epistemology shares this faith and, simultaneously, keeps in mind that the reality is linguistic. The differend, Lyotard asserts,

> is the unstable state and instant of language wherein something which must be able to put into phrase cannot yet be....In the differend something "asks" to be put into phrases, and suffers from the wrong of not being able to be put into phrases right away. (1988, p. 13)

The differend makes us recognize that "what remains to be phrased exceeds what [we] can presently phrase, and that [we] must be allowed to institute idioms which do not yet exist" (p. 13).

Since each act/decision of linkage "actualizes" one possibility among innumerable "potential" passages, a contingent passage unconceals one among innumerable unique "beings" (singulars) obliterated or simply threatened in their power-to-phrase, one among those silent shadows who have been "wronged" and whose memory claims the impossible reparation. A passage thus conceals, silences, subjugates, and excludes innumerable beings that reside in the nothingness. It is the intersubjective sociopolitical engagements of the interlocutors that partially perform this violence. The contingency of the link obliges us to decide how to link. Consequently, the decision to link is an obligation toward the differend, an obligation that can be performed responsibly and ethically or irresponsibly and wrongly. A passage that denies its own contingency does "wrong" to the differend. The wrong is a harm accompanied by the loss of the means to prove it.[8] The contingency of linkage hence implies the contingency of language. Also, the obligation toward the differend demands the negation of the metaphysics of presence.

Nothingness, the sphere of the nonlinguistic, is not empty. It is not "nothing." It is only a quasisilence. The other, the threatened other (Adorno's damaged life) who "calls" us to lend an ear to it, to give it voice, to bring it into phrases, "is" there. The differend, the other, "is" there waiting to get disclosed and become unconcealed through passages in language. The other "is" there waiting to give us its truth via coming into language. Therefore, the obligation to link, as a linguistic/political act, if performed responsibly to the call of the differend, if performed ethically, is also of epistemological relevance.[9] Among the diversity of possible passages, the project of political epistemology loves the ones that are singled out by the ethicopolitical stakes of justice.[10] The project of political epistemology tries to say, to let it be said, what cannot be said at every passage, what gets concealed, what the universal totalitarian (meta)narrative, as a specific contingent chain of passages that forgets its contingency, denies existence to.

Jacques Derrida and the contingency of language

The contingency of language and the linguistic nature of reality imply that the covenant between the signifier and the signified is indeed instituted, and not natural. Rather than a set of exterior signs that mirror already formed interior thoughts, language comprises a group of repeatable marks or traces that are found from within, particular units of meaning as "effects." Accordingly, meaning is contingent upon differential and multiple connections or possibilities that the contrast of words with each other—what Jacques Derrida calls "the systematic play of differences" (1982, p. 11)—puts into effect. There is no unique meaning behind the words: The differential and multiple connections of words are unstable and so is the meaning. For a transcendental analysis of language, meaning, speech, and truth claims, Derrida examines the chain of "differential marks" that makes meaning possible. Translated into Derrida's terms, the idea of the linguistic nature of reality partially means that what we call experience is not the perception of phenomena that are present to self-consciousness. Experience is rather "produced" by the chain of differentially ordered signs or "marks" that produces and precedes meaning.

According to the classical semiology, signs stand for things and simultaneously represent ideas. A sign represents a thing that is itself absent and different from the sign. Therefore, the classical idea of the sign is founded on a notion of difference, a deferral, between the sign and the reality, the thing. As Derrida states, the traditional idea of the sign regards it as secondary, derived from a lost presence: "The sign represents the present in its absence. It takes the place of the present. When we cannot grasp or show the thing, state the present....we go through the detour of the sign....The sign in this sense, is deferred presence" (1982, p. 9). The classical view perceives the sign also as provisional, as a movement of mediation toward the lost presence.

In contrast to the traditional semiology, Derrida believes that Saussure's linguistics locate the foundation of general semiology in arbitrariness and differentiality, the two "correlative" characters of signs. According to Saussure, the sign is arbitrary only because it is differences in terms that constitute a system of signs. It is the network of opposition that establishes and relates the elements of signification. Derrida concludes that the principle of difference, the play of differentiation among signs, affects the totality of the sign and makes it both the signifier and the signified (1982, p. 10). Derrida quotes an excerpt from Saussure with approval:

> In language there are only differences...a difference generally implies positive terms between which the difference is set up; but in language there are only differences *without positive terms*. Whether we take the signified or the signifier, language has neither ideas nor sounds that existed before the linguistic system, but only conceptual and phonic differences that have issued from the system. The idea or phonic substance that a sign contains is of less importance than the other signs that surround it. (p. 11)

Hence, every concept is inscribed in a chain in which it refers to the other within and by means of the play of difference. This view surpasses the secondariness of the sign and substitutes for it the originality of *différance*, the play of differentiation, the transcendental precondition that makes the very conceptuality, meaning, and signification possible.

Meaning and reference thus become functions of the distance, the differential "spacing," between traces. By means of, and within, this play, the users of language make sense and communicate. Like a dictionary, and unlike it, *différance* is "the relation of the interval or the spacing to what is lodged in it to be received in it" (Derrida 1995b, p. 125). In a dictionary, the meaning of a term discloses differentially, in relation to the meaning of other terms. Each term has a location in a dictionary that is a function of graphic spelling and, concurrently, a location that is its semantic place within the play of connotations and denotations in relation to the semantic positions of other words. To obtain a meaning, no term in a dictionary detaches itself from this play and grasps the thing-itself, the allegedly "signified" beyond language. A dictionary, therefore, is a "spacing," a differentiated spacing.

Nevertheless, *différance*, the play of difference, is not a concept. It is "the opening of the space," the spacing, in which conceptual systems emerge. In other words, ontological systems, the metaphysics of presence, the Cartesian subject, Heidegger's ontic–ontological dichotomy (see Caputo 1988, p. 531; Dallmayr 1981, pp. 113–14), the self, the same, the consciousness, diverse social and scientific theories, ordinary language concepts, and so forth are, far from falling from the heavens, all contingent "effects" constructed by the playing movements of *différance*. *Différance*, if there is such a *thing*, is older than metaphysics,[11] the *arche*, and the universals. Universals, in other words, are tentative constructs of specific moves of the play. They are indeed situated universals (see Caputo 1987, ch. 5).

Each round of sense making and communication thus is a set of moves within the space that the play opens. These moves enact the play and extend it. They become possible due to the "openings" that the play provides and are simultaneously capable of changing the differential relationships within the fluidity of the play. In other words, the play is not a substance that "causes" the sense-making moves. The play *is* play*ing*—that is why each move is indeed the continuation, or, better, the play*ing*, of the play. The play is not a timeless essence or structure. It is a play insofar as it is getting enacted by the differents. An actor, on the other hand, is this specific actor insofar as he or she is in the play playing his or her specific role vis-à-vis other actors. Being positioned in the play is the same as actually playing it. The play thus is the very (sociopolitical, as we will see) interactions of the actors.

There is no play without playing, without actual actors. These interactions are rule bound—bound by the rules of grammar (Derrida 1976, pp. 27–73), the law, linguistic norms, and so forth—though the play is open-ended, and in principle it is always possible for it to be repeated differently. Thus, rules do not govern the play. They are contingent effects of the fluid play, inscribed in the an-arche of *différance*. This is one reason that *différance* is indeed the "quasitranscendental"[12] of meaning. The play makes, constructs, meanings, but all meanings can be unmade and deconstructed. There is no finality to the play of difference. Each move can bring about new differences, new nuances of meaning, and, as such, change the whole system of differential relationships between signs.

There is no final vocabulary, no final play. The play just plays. As such, Derrida's "philosophical and transcendental theory" about the play is indeed meaningful only through a set of specific sense-making moves of differentiation. This is why it is not a "metaphysical theory proper" that would dream of fixing, or "arresting," the play and, in so doing, offering the final "secret" of meaning-making phenomena. This quasitranscendental theory is in fact a "strategic" set of moves within the play. It is political in the sense that it affects the play and promotes new patterns of differentiation. It is a political movement within the play that, at the same time, produces new meanings, new truth claims. As Derrida asserts: "In the delineation of *différance* everything is strategic. Everything is strategic and adventurous" (1982, p. 7).[13]

This is the point that the project of political epistemology tends to read in Derrida's quasitranscendental theory of *différance*. The project of political epistemology pinpoints politics, truth, and ethics in a relation of mutual implication here, at the unfixable conjuncture of *différance*. As such, it ties contingency to truthfulness without dropping the normative criteria of truth. (Political praxis and ethics are also involved in this reconciliation.) Following this pattern of argument, the project of political epistemology sheds light on the epistemological relevance of Derrida's ideas of *différance* and deconstruction.

Therefore, the key question seems to be of connections between Derrida's condition of possibility of meaning, *différance*, and the project of political epistemology's condition of possibility of meaning and truth, the sociopolitical context. While *différance* is the condition of possibility of language, sociopolitical reality is linguistic. As a result, *différance* and sociopolitical reality cannot be total strangers: the sociopolitical-linguistic relationships of individuals to each other are possible because of the play of differentiation (see Derrida 1976, p. 60). The semantic differences that make up the meaning associate the phonic and graphic differences among signs. Political epistemology, however, sees the sociopolitical relations of power as another aspect of this association: The semantic differences that make language possible are in reciprocally constitutive relationships with the differential play of sociopolitical relations. The network of sociopolitical relations is indeed a site of play of differential forces. Social individuals are situated in this play. They enact it and, concurrently, get positioned in it (the idea of social reality as practico-inert). Their acting in this play is their praxis, their social, political, economic, and cultural interactions that are interwoven with, partially constituted by, and constitutive of their linguistic interactions (lexis). The differential play of sociopolitical forces is not just relations of power as brute coercion. Indeed, the Foucauldian idea of discursive regimes of meaning/power in which power moves in all directions "throughout the entire social body" (Derrida 1980, p. 119) is an apt portrayal of the sociopolitical network as a play of forces. What Foucault calls the "discursive formation" or the "economy of discourses" is also a site, a space, an opening, in which diverse discourses of P/K emerge.

In the same vein, Derrida states:

> For me it is always the question of differential force, of difference as difference of force, of force as *différance* (*différance* is a force *differee-differante*), of the relation between force and form, force and signification, performative force, illocutionary or prelocutionary force, of persuasive and rhetorical force, of affirmation by signature, but also and especially of all the paradoxical situations in which the greatest force and the greatest weakness strangely enough exchange places. And that is the whole history. (1990, p. 929)[14]

According to a demythologized Heidegger, the truth of Being is the way historically situated people "dwell." The clearing of Being, *aletheia*, refers to the constellation of arts, science, and socio-politico-economic institutions of a historic bloc. There is no secret to the Being and its cycles of disclosure and withdrawal. "Being" is but the very concrete sociopolitical, economic, cultural, or other form of life in an epoch. The truth of Being, therefore, indicates the manner in which situated people in a historic bloc settle into an understanding of the world, of God, and of themselves (see Caputo 1989a, pp. 56–7). Accordingly, *aletheia*, the "opening" that in Heidegger's view grants the epoch's truth, has to do with the sociopolitical mode of life, that is, the manner in which Being is *presencing*. Therefore, sociopolitical reality is the *presencing* of the Being, the playing of the play (in Derrida's—as well as Heidegger's—terms), the "opening" for the emergence of meaning and truth. The sociopolitical reality "is" *différance*.

Yes, a demythologized Heidegger is Derridean, and he shows a great sympathy with the project of political epistemology. Derrida writes: "In a certain aspect of itself, *différance* is certainly but the historical and epochal unfolding of Being or of the ontological difference. The *a* of *différance* marks the movement of this unfolding" (Derrida 1982, p. 22). Needless to say, "ontological difference" is the differential play of forces, the very sociopolitical network of relationships, that is, what the project of political epistemology calls the transcendental condition of possibility of meaning and truth.

Sociopolitical institutions, sexuality and gender relations, the body, and so forth, all carry the "marks" of differentiality and spacing (Derrida 2002, p. 35; 1982, p. 18). There are differential plays of "locations" in social institutions: the head quarter, the common room, the top floor, the pulpit, the throne, the first row, and so forth. There are also differential plays of family (the head, the godfather); of clothes (official, casual); of cars, bodies, colors; and so on. Occupying positions within these plays defines the role, the social status, the right and responsibility, the voice, the share of social production (John Rawls's justice is a differential play of distribution), and the identities of social individuals. A social individual concurrently lives in a multiplicity of plays. Or since a play is an opening and not a thing that can be demarcated and contrasted to other thing-like plays, it is more accurate to say that a social individual is always already inscribed and situated in an endless differentiality.

Derrida defines text qua context as the entire "real-history-of-the-world" (1988, p. 136). In Derrida's account, *text* refers to "history, to the world, to reality, to being." In other words, institutions of the sociopolitical context are integrally internal to the general text. Far from being external, they inhabit the innermost structures of the text. Derrida declares:

> What I call "text" implies all the structures called "real," "economic," "historical," "socio-institutional," in short: all possible referents. Another way of recalling, once again, that "there is nothing outside the text."…It does mean that every referent and all reality has the structure of a differential trace,[15] and that one cannot refer to this "real" except in an interpretive experience. (1988, p. 148)

A text is a differential play within which meaning emerges. However, the text, the socio-politico-historical reality, is not present as an in-itself. Rather, it is mediated through language and meaning. That is, any reference to this reality, to the text as the referent, is also an effect inscribed within the space that the differentiality of the text opens. A text, the socio-politico-historical reality, is differential, and it is its differentiality that allows us to meaningfully state that "the text is differential."

While investigating the connection between the sociopolitical text and *différance*, the previous sentence seems to be repeating the project of political epistemology's tenet, the dialectical interdependence of the sociopolitical text (context) and meaning. *Différance* thus seems to be withdrawing again from the scene of this dialectics.[16] It is true, in a way. We should bear in mind, however, that the very discussion of the relationship between *différance* and the sociopolitical context (text) is meaningful because of *différance*, and that *différance*, the play of dif-ference, is not a substance that would possibly like to follow the socio-political text, and the meaning, in entering the scene as a third entity. *Différance* "is" the sociopolitical text in a way that the latter is an alle-gory for the former. This is the "truth" of *différance*—though, as Derrida says, there are no truths, only texts. That is, talking about the "nature" of *différance* presupposes it. We cannot talk about *a difference*-without-*différance*—no "Truth" of *différance* beyond the differential text. There is only text. Derrida once said that *khora* is *différance*'s surname (1995a, p. 95). According to the project of political epistemology, *différance* is the sociopolitical context's middle name. A middle name withdraws or gets ignored most of the time.

To conclude this section, let me affirm that I tend to understand Derrida's idea of the play as the very sociopolitical transcendental condition of meaning and truthfulness. I believe that Derrida's *dif-férance* opens the possibility of this political epistemological interpre-tation. In order to further support my position, I need to show that Derrida's ideas of *différance* and deconstruction also secure an episte-mic normativity and offer new coherence as the criterion of truth. To those who see no difference between *différance*, deconstruction, and epistemic relativism, tracing an epistemic normativity in Derrida's works is but a futile attempt. I shall argue in the following sections, however, that Derrida's idea of deconstruction opens up a novel per-spective to look at the reciprocal implications between ethical norma-tivity, epistemic normativity, and emancipatory political activity.

Openness and the *ethicity* of *différance*

The contingency of language and the contingency of consciousness[17] are conditions that make responsibility and decision making possible for the self. In Derrida's view, this responsibility is "radical" (Michelfelder 1989, p. 49). It precedes the construction of the subject, the ego and its freedom, right, and so on as tentative effects of the play of difference. In other words, since the other mediates the self, the way in which the intersubjective relationship of the self and the other goes affects the very selfhood of the self at each single moment of the self–other dialectic. Therefore, an intersubjective relationship that harbors the radical responsibility to the other forms a specific self different from the one that emerges out of different kinds of intersubjective relationships. It is in this sense that radical responsibility, or *ethicity*, precedes the construction of the self. It is thus not a matter of temporal succession or causal relationship between the radical responsibility and the self: They are of the same existential order.

Since the project of political epistemology has established its kinship with Derrida's play, we may now expect this radical responsibility and decision making to be of epistemic value and to involve the disclosure of truth. In fact, the political epistemological view indicates that the "ethical" operation of the play, the "morality" of the sociopolitical context, the *ethicity* of *différance*, advances cognitive functions. (Now that the play of difference, *différance*, and the sociopolitical context are proved to be the same "thing," for the sake of brevity I will use the term *play* in the rest of this chapter and, unless specified otherwise, intend the project of political epistemology's reading of *différance* by it.) *My* Derrida would definitely agree with this point that there is a radically ethical moment in the act of understanding.

As discussed in previous chapters, understanding, the fusion of horizons, is an interactive "happening" with sociopolitical dimensions. According to the project of political epistemology, the disclosure of truth through the "happening" of understanding is indeed a phenomenon with political, ethical, and cognitive dimensions. The dimensions of a spatial body do not reduce or resolve into each other. They do imply each other, however, and, altogether, constitute the spatial body. Following this allegory, the project of political epistemology underlines the relation of mutual implication among these dimensions.

The dialectic of master and slave helps us clarify this point. For Hegel, in *each and every* social encounter, the self finds the other as the limit of its own freedom, because the other is free to have his or her own understanding and judgment of the self, which is not necessarily the same understanding the self has of itself.[18] The self and the other, Hegel believes, are the limits of each other's freedoms. Consequently, in the presence of the other, the self loses certainty about its self-consciousness or about what the self "knows" as "truths" or "values" attributed to the self. The desire for "objective truth" that would return the lost certainty to the self, Hegel says, emerges at this very moment: the self needs the other's *recognition* of the self's self-consciousness, truths, and values in order to alter the subjective certainty of existing "for itself" into the universal truth (1974a, p. 70). Hegel maintains that there is no objective truth without this mutual recognition (p. 73).

What the relationship between master and slave lacks is this very recognition. To see this, let us analyze the relation from the master's point of view. The master is not the only one who considers himself as master. The slave also considers the master as such. Hence, the master is recognized in his human reality, freedom, and dignity. But this recognition is one-sided, for the master does not in turn recognize the slave's human reality and freedom. The master is recognized by someone, the slave, whom the master does not recognize. This is what is insufficient and "tragic" in this situation, for the master can be satisfied only by recognition from one whom he recognizes as worthy of recognizing him. The nonfree slave's recognition does not confirm the picture of "the Lord" that the master has of himself; thus, the "mastery" of the master does not become an objective truth. The master can be recognized as such *only* by making the other his slave. But the slave is (for the master) but an animal or a thing. The master is, therefore, "recognized" by a thing. The master must free the slave and deny his own being as master in order to win the recognition he seeks: The master cannot be recognized as master unless by negating his being as such.

The dialectic of master and slave is a sample of countless relations of domination that social individuals experience in their being-in-the-world-with-one-another. It is a "death struggle" insofar as in it, the one denies the otherness of the other and desires to transform and manipulate the other, to neglect its being otherwise and exclude the other qua other, who enjoys the freedom of judging, accusing, and demanding justification from the one. Reciprocally, in a death struggle, the other desires to treat the one in the same violent way. A death struggle is thus "agonistic" and filled with "fear" (see Kojeve 1980, ch. 1). Since subjectivity and truth are intersubjective, the project of political epistemology also reads into Hegel's master–slave dialectic the point that radical responsibility, being radically responsive to the call of the other (a call to consider him or her as wholly other and different, to let him or her be), or radical ethical openness toward the other (*ethnicity*), is a condition of possibility of truth: The exclusion of the other by the *sovereign* self amounts to the closure of truth, for here the other is prevented from contributing to the intersubjective happening of understanding. As such, the disclosure of truth is prevented. Openness toward the other means that in a "death struggle," the self will be ready to see its own death rather than trying to survive at the cost of the other's death, at the cost of taking away the freedom of the other. This readiness for one's own death is the gist of what Gadamer calls "experience." Experience, therefore, means a readiness to risk one's own life with *hope* for a truth-to-come through one's ethical, *ethicical*, encounter with the other. Radical responsibility, hope, readiness for death, and the experience of truth are all different moments of the same intersubjective dialectic.

The master–slave dialectic reveals that against the setting of social relations of coercion, truth and politics alienate one another. Moreover, the project of political epistemology reads into the master–slave parable that the self's identity embraces a difference.[19] The self needs a different subject that is free and respected in his or her difference. In other words, the self—even for the sake of his or her own identity—needs a specific *différance*, a *différance*—a play of forces—which is not closed to the other. Consequently, even the self's fight for his or her own identity implies a fight, a "political praxis," for the freedom of the other. This political praxis is motivated by a desire for truth. It moves in the name of ethics and promotes the freedom of the others. Far from a sovereign/ egocentric idea of politics and its associated utilitarian ethics, the politics of responsibility is concerned about the other and commits to *ethicity* of social life. Political epistemology, therefore, adopts the aspect of openness to the other from Hegel's parable and simultaneously, and strategically, denies that the "death struggle" has only one outcome, that is, the enslavement of the other at the tragic cost of truth. For radical responsibility can actually affect the destiny of the struggle. The self's radical responsibility, its readiness to see its own death, opens the horizon for truth.

The other interrupts the egocentric monism of the self: by noticing that the other is "looking" at me, I "know" myself being obligated to justify myself.[20] The other limits my freedom (Levinas 1987). By his or her unchosen "height," the other makes me responsible and accountable for his or her life, "disrupts my being at home with myself so that my selfhood is my being-for-the-Other." Peperzak elaborates, "The whole of my concrete—corporeal, sensible, kinetic, emotional, contemplative, striving—existence is determined by my orientation towards the Other: I am demanded, disposed, obsessed and inspired" (1993, pp. 24–6).

The radical ethical moment in the act of understanding takes place when the subject/knower "welcomes" the other, becomes a "host" (Levinas 1969, p. 300), and even realizes that "the subject is hostage" (Levinas 1981, p. 112) to the other. Radical ethics is ethics *as* hospitality. It is a more practical than a thematic "welcoming." It is, as Derrida states, "the first gesture in the direction of the Other" (1999, p. 25), the right way of being. A radically ethical subject practices a *responsible* way of acting in the play. Levinas calls this mode of being-in-the-world-responsibly-toward-the-other "existent" and underlines the "philosophical priority of existent over Being" (1969, pp. 51, 79).[21] In the project of political epistemology's language, Levinas's assertion means that the radical ethical mode of engagement in sociopolitical practices, the play, is partially constitutive of meaning.

Ethicity is the hospitality and affirmation that makes it possible for the other to come and contribute his or her share in the interactive happening of understanding. After the coming of the other, after welcoming the other, comes understanding, meaning, knowledge, *theories* of ethics (as a discipline),[22] and diverse truth claims. The otherness of the other and the new unconcealment come to us through language. Hence, an open *différance* (i.e., a language without closure, an ethical/nontotalitarian sociopolitical play of differentiation)[23] is the medium of an endless emergence of new voices of the other. The face of the other "calls" for response before any unity of knowledge about the other gets constructed (see Derrida 1980, p. 138). The subject/knower is subject to this call. As Levinas says: "The I is not simply consciousness of this necessity to respond…rather the I is, by its very position, responsibility through and through" (1996, p. 17). *Ethicity* is to be able to hear this call, to be open to it before and without knowing who is calling. *Ethicity* is saying yes to the unknown, to the other's voice that has not yet been heard. *Ethicity,* as a transcendental condition of the happening of meaning, has epistemic value.

Language, the voice of the other, and the ontology of the singular

Language, *différance*, is the opening in which the voice of the other, the singular, should be welcome and hosted. Language also conceals the singular, however. Every word in a linguistic assertion, insofar as it is a repeatable signifier that can be restated in other linguistic contexts, is a universal. Hegel argues that the most particular words, like "here" and "now," are indeed universal: They can mean anywhere and anytime based on the context of their application. As Hegel states, "By saying 'this Here,' 'this Now,' 'an individual thing,' I say all Thises, Heres, Nows, or Individuals" (see Solomon 1983, pp. 329–37). Hence, disclosure, that is, coming into the phrase, requires that the singulars enter into the particular–universal dialectic and, accordingly, get concealed. In other words, the singular does not come to language as singular. The aporia thus is to respect the singularity of the singular while bringing it to language, to *différance*, and having it drop its singularity in order to get disclosed (and concealed). What makes the situation more complicated is that even the term *singularity* is a linguistic effect inscribed in *différance*. We cannot meaningfully talk about the existence of a singular-without-*différance*. The singular stays "inaccessible" and—like the other in his or her otherness that limits the self's freedom of manipulation—resists being absorbed by language without remainder. The aporia is not solvable by taking sides between realism and nihilism (relativism) as two ontological doctrines that *talk* about the status and existence of the singular beyond *différance* or language. These positions are inscribed in *différance*, and whatever they say is a trace, a particular/universal effect or concept. In contrast to these two ontological positions, our aporia "talks" about "something" *beyond* language and *différance*: the singular as referent-without-difference. And exactly here resides the impossibility and paradox of the aporia.

Traditional epistemology follows ontology and falls in the same trap of aporia. Participants in the project of political epistemology, however, bear in mind the similarity of the play of differentiation and the socio-political context, the fact that metaphysics is but a constructed trace. Therefore, they should not aspire to construct a new ontology, a new metaphysics. They should not wish to be realists in saying that there is, there does exist, a singular other beyond language, simply because whatever might be considered as the ontological status of this entity—for example, its "existence" or "nonexistence"—is but a trace of the play of differentiation.

As participants in the project of political epistemology, we should follow Wittgenstein's advice: "What we cannot speak about we must pass over in silence" (1974, p. 152). That is, we should stop producing ontology about the singular and its existence (or nonexistence) beyond language. Nonetheless, this does not mean that we should also stay inert, neutral, and indifferent toward the singular. The singular is always and already overlooked, structurally left out and excluded—either when it is denied a voice (the wrong imposed on the differend) or when it has been brought into language and been concealed by the particular–universal dialectic. In the name of doing justice to the other, in order to actually do the impossible aporia, political epistemology addresses the singular-beyond-language. It does so not by ontology but by *ethicity*, by an affirmative yes to a yet unheard voice, the "call." This "unconditional" affirmation "is not to be found in dialogue," Derrida writes. "It is not a verbal 'yes.'…[It is unconditional because it] is not accounted for in the structure of dialogue."[24] This affirmative yes is in fact the *ethicity* of the moment in the play of differential forces, the sociopolitical *différance*.

In this sense, the project of political epistemology is neither realist nor relativist, for these two are effects that come after language. The project is indeed hyperrealist[25] in its ethical affirmation of the singular differend and in its "respecting, loving even, the invisibility that keeps the Other inaccessible" (Derrida 1995b, p. 74). This love is simultaneously a love for truth and for justice, a love that motivates emancipatory political practices. It is so because the happening of meaning and truth also depends on the coming of the other from afar as an "event" that we cannot control, an event that interrupts the horizon of possibility that metaphysics—or any totalitarian act in the play of forces—wants to stabilize.

The structural injustice that happens to the singular other intensifies when the metaphysics of presence attempts to comprehend the singular, still the play, and pretend that what is coming is but a case of what is, and has always been, already present, the "presence." The "presence," however, is a combination of fetishized ethical-ontological hierarchies constructed by specific unjust and unethical (*unethicical*) moves of *différance*. In political epistemology's language, the metaphysics of presence is a set of unjust moves and acts in an unjust play of forces through which subordination and violence toward the other proceed.[26] Therefore, according to the *normative* political epistemological judgment, the metaphysics of presence is untrue due to its violent closure toward the other, due to its fetishism that makes it believe that it is a noncontingent mirror that reflects the referent-without-difference. The moment of the play of forces, the sociopolitical *différance* that produces the metaphysics of presence as a trace and simultaneously continues the play by this move, is closed toward the other. This closure is unjust and false and, at the same time, has political danger of exclusion.

Therefore, we may conclude that from a political epistemological view, ethical, epistemic, and political dimensions imply each other. This much is not enough. I still need to show that this relation of mutual implication is conducive to a specific epistemic normativity, new coherentism. I should also highlight the contribution that Derrida's idea of deconstruction makes to the project of political epistemology.

Before taking these next steps, I wish to include a brief clarification. Using Derrida's language, I will frequently apply the expression "the voice of the other"—or the less accurate expression "the truth of the other"—in the following sections. As formerly discussed, for participants in the project of political epistemology, meaning is a collective and intersubjective happening that takes place within the play of differentiation, and the truth content of this happening is constitutive of reality. The voice of the other, however, is heard only within a play. It is within a play that the voice of the other finds words and becomes *a voice* in the first place. The voice of the other is not a different-without-*différance*. Accordingly, to participants in the project of political epistemology, the expression "truth of the other" does not denote a truth prior to the intersubjective happening of meaning. Truth happens when the other, as one among many participants in the play, contributes in the making of a less (new)incoherent reality. Hence, from a political epistemological perspective, and for a combination of diverse reasons, I do not intend to grant an epistemic privilege to the oppressed other. (This point highlights a difference between standpoint epistemology and the project of political epistemology.) Truth emerges only through the intersubjective happening, and an other before participation in the play and in the happening does not hold a truth. Indeed, the other-before-participation is a fetishized in-itself: The self and the other mediate through each other, and the other is always already an "other-than-I." Moreover, an oppressed (mediated) other might well be totalitarian and oppressive toward other others. Adorno's famous statement on this topic, I believe, is put very carefully: "The need to lend a voice to suffering is a condition of all truth" (1973, pp. 17–18). The voice of the other does not automatically hold the truth. Rather, hearing this voice within the play is a *precondition* of truth: Without saying that the oppressed already has a prior-to-dialogue truth (whatever such an expression might mean), we need to be open and let the oppressed talk. This is a precondition in the sense that truth emerges only through the happening of the intersubjective practice of understanding when the new coherent reality takes place. And after the happening, it is not the truth-of-the-oppressed, but the *truth*, simply.

Radical ethical openness and new coherence

Closure toward and exclusion of the other produces contradiction. This consideration opens a new angle on political epistemology's criterion of truth. The idea of new coherence indicates, in part, a relation of mutual constitutiveness between sociopolitical contexts and meanings: New coherence is not just between propositions but among unities of cognitive/material entities. Accordingly, it is the practico-inert—social reality together with meanings that get concretized in it—which should be called true or false. New coherence theory has two tenets. First, meaning and reality are dialectically interdependent (*mutual constitutiveness*); second, the truth of a cognitive/material reality has to do with the relation of *mutual support* among the constituents of a cognitive/material unit. In other words, it is not enough to say that meaning and sociopolitical contexts affect each other. Rather, for epistemological, ethical, and political reasons, it is necessary to normatively distinguish true cognitive/material realities from false ones. The idea of mutual support fulfils this latter task.

Like consistency, contradiction is also inscribed in, and is a trace of, *différance*. Contradiction is indeed a specific enacting move of the play of differentiation—an unjust move through which a universal (concept, system of thought, system of law, and the like) tries to swallow the singular without remainder, surpassing the contingency of language and reaching the "presence" beyond language. The singular other, however, is the idiomatic that resists the equalizing power of the universal (Derrida 1984, p. 117). This resistance is best manifested when contradiction happens. A contradiction among theories and concepts signals that the singular is partially disclosed (and concealed) within the particular/universal concepts/moves of the play. The particular/universal concepts are inscribed in tentative moments (traces) of contradiction (though each concept/move—forgetting its situatedness and contingency upon the play—dreams of digesting the singular without remnant).

In other words, contradiction happens because each side (or at least one side) is totalitarian. The totalitarian pole of contradiction claims that it exhausts the whole truth, the truth-without-difference, of the singular, and hence there is nothing left to be further (partly or totally) exhausted by another concept or theory: Two universality claimers cannot tolerate each other.

Metaphysics assigns itself to a privileged position, a nowhere-beyond language, and forgets that this very self-appointment is a move inscribed in the play. The project of political epistemology stresses that there is another way to resolve contradiction: Drop the universality claim and remember that your truth claims, like others', are indexical to, and situated within, the play.

As discussed above, the play is indeed the play of differential forces: Reality is linguistic, and *différance* has to do with the sociopolitical play of differentiation. Therefore, a contradiction within the web of propositions should be simultaneously seen in relation with a *new contradiction* within the web of cognitive/material reality, in the play of forces. New contradiction, hence, is a cognitive/social reality that harbors cognitive as well as political totalitarianism.

Now, if new contradiction is a consequence of closure toward the other, *new coherence* demands *opening* to the singular as otherwise. Contradictions are traces in the cognitive/material play of forces. Theoretical paradoxes and dilemmas, political unrest and struggles, class contradictions, social violence, and the like are traces at which we feel[27] the "wrong" that happens to the differend, the singular. The relation of *mutual support* among the constituents singles out a new coherent cognitive/material reality. The proviso of mutual support prevents the closure toward, and the exclusion of, the other. Hence, the project of political epistemology's criterion of truth, that is, the proviso of mutual support, is indeed the same as opening to the other.

It is in fact the singular's resistance against the *cunning of the universal* that makes us make an *exception*. New contradiction signals the resistance of the politically as well as epistemically suppressed singular. Contrary to the disrespect that the totalitarian and universality-seeking move in an unjust moment of the play shows to the *exceptional*, participants in the project of political epistemology should love the *exceptional* as a "nonsite" for the coming of the other, for another happening of meaning. The exceptional is "the event" that interrupts the reified play and shatters the present horizon of intelligibility. What is coming is always to-come: It is not a future-present, a "case" of the ever-present "presence"—the arche.

The project of political epistemology makes clear that the present cognitive/material reality is contingent: It cannot claim finality unless through violence and contradiction. Therefore, the happening of new meaning and truth demands the coming of the otherwise than the present, the arrival of the unforeseeable within the present horizon: Truth is "the event" that surprises us. Preparation for hearing the voice of this wholly other is a permanent political, ethical, and epistemic praxis. It involves boundless measures in actually making the play of sociopolitical forces open-ended and revisable. It entails exposing the cognitive/material reality to the risk of future, to a "new beginning" that "breaks into the world wholly unexpected and unforeseen" (Arendt 2006a, p. 76). This endless politico-ethico-epistemic praxis the invention of other is what Derrida calls "deconstruction" (1989, pp. 53, 59–60).

How is deconstruction political?

For the project of political epistemology, the present new coherence is always unsatisfactory. It is not pure, and it contains contaminating contradictory elements that strive for totality and closure. Consequently, the new coherent cognitive/material reality, in order to be truthful—that is, in order to maintain relationships of mutual support among its constituents—must be open to the voice of the other. Hence, truth happens *differently*, within a different cognitive/material reality, within a different play that is always to be established by our politico-ethico-epistemic praxis/lexis.

Deconstruction, therefore, suspends the fetishized hegemony of a particular set of moves in the play and *makes* truth actually happen by bringing new moves and changing the play of differentiation accordingly. Deconstruction is an endless set of moves that enact the play of difference (repeat it differently) and proceed toward the happening of unforeseeable meaning and truth. As Derrida asserts,

> what is hastily called deconstruction *as such* is never a technical set of discursive procedures, still less a new hermeneutic method operating on archives or utterances in the shelter of a given and stable institution; it is also, and at the least, the taking of a position, in work itself, toward the politico-institutional structures that constitute and regulate our practice, our competences, and our performances. Precisely because deconstruction has never been concerned with the contents alone of meaning, it must not be separable from this politico-institutional problematic, and has to require a new questioning about responsibility, an inquiry that should no longer necessarily rely on codes inherited from politics or ethics. Which is why, though too political in the eyes of some, deconstruction can seem demobilizing in the eyes of those who recognize the political only with the help of prewar road signs. Deconstruction is limited neither to a methodological reform...nor, inversely, to a parade of irresponsible or irresponsibilizing destruction. (1992, pp. 22–3; Caputo 2003a, p. 3)

Deconstruction, in other words, is a "strategic" move, a political and institutional intervention with overt political and ethical reasons. "Deconstruction," Derrida says, "is not *neutral*. It *intervenes*" (1981, p. 93). For the project of political epistemology, this strategic intervention is also of epistemic value when it is an invention of the other and when the ethico-political reason behind it is justice. Indeed, we can understand the very philosophical "system" that Derrida developed throughout his whole life as deconstructive moves within the Western play of thought.[28] For example, Derrida's new articulation of the concept of *text* is indeed a deconstructive move. It changes the play of differentiation, and in the wake of this change, even our understanding of deconstruction changes.

Derrida shows how he has decided to invent a new meaning for the signifier *text*.[29] He writes:

> An hour's reading, beginning on any page of any texts I have published over the last twenty years should suffice for you to realize that *text,* as I use the word, is not the book. No more than writing or trace, it is not limited to the *paper,* which you cover with your graphism. It is precisely for strategic reasons (set forth at length elsewhere) that I found it necessary to recast the concept of text by generalizing it almost without limit that *is*. That is why there is nothing "*beyond* the text." That is why South Africa and *apartheid* are, like you and me, part of this general text, which is not to say that it can be read the way one reads a book. That is why the text is always a field of forces: heterogeneous, differential, open and so on. That is why deconstructive readings and writings are concerned not only with library books, with discourses, with conceptual and semantic contents. They are not simply analyses of discourse such as, for example the one you propose. They are also effective or active (as one says) interventions, in particular political and institutional interventions, that transform contexts without limiting themselves to theoretical or constative utterances even though they must also produce such utterances. That is why I do not go "beyond the text," in this *new* sense of the word text, by fighting and calling for a fight against *apartheid,* for example. (1968, pp. 167–8)

Like Horkheimer's critical theory, Derrida's deconstruction is "making truth happen, effecting it, forming and forging truth with the fire of justice" (Caputo 1997, p. 116). Each new move introduces new traces and new actors[30] to the play and, as such, changes the tentative arrangement between the present actors, which include words, concepts, institutions, forces, and so on, within the play. Each "movement" of deconstruction changes the *différance*, brings about new relations of difference, new signs and signifiers, which owe their signification to the differential arrangement, and also new signifieds that are inscribed in the play. A deconstructive movement is political in so far as it changes the "mode of production" of concepts and signified/facts (Derrida 1995c, p. 13). Since the reality is cognitive/material, a change in the mode of production of concepts is simultaneously a change in reality.[31]

It is the play that lets deconstruction happen, and it is the happening of deconstruction that changes the play and repeats it differently. Deconstruction is playing the play differently in order to make it more open to the coming of the other. This is why the function and process of deconstruction cannot be limited to literal reinterpretations or semantic transformations of concepts and theories. Deconstruction reshuffles the pattern of distributions and differences in a differential play of forces with sociopolitical, as well as linguistic and theoretical, dimensions. As such, deconstruction transgresses the present effects. It does this all in the name of doing justice to the other.

Deconstruction thus is not destruction. Deconstruction interrupts institutional arrangements, the ongoing processes of the play, not to destroy them but to repeat them differently, to keep them in process more justly. It does so to "keep the *forms* of life from eliminating the *life*-forms they are supposed to house" (Caputo 1989a, p. 60). Accordingly, deconstruction advocates no total break with tradition, even with metaphysical tradition: Deconstruction is self-conscious about its own status as but a move situated within the play.[32]

Deconstruction interrupts the play with the promise of a *different* relationship to the other. Hence, justice implies disadjustment and disjunction in order to open the future to come through rejecting the dominant present. A responsibility and account of justice that is limited to the present (new) coherent reality is always inadequate and deconstructible. It is only in relation to the always-already coming of the other that justice becomes possible and assumes its significance. In the language of political epistemology, it is the voice of the other, the precondition of new happenings of meaning and truth, that we desire. We can hope for its coming and act for it. We affirm it, have faith in its coming without yet "knowing" it (Caputo and Derrida 1997, p. 23). Thus, the messianic of justice does not belong to the future as the telos of the Enlightener's progress of history (Lowy 2001, p. 185). It happens—it should happen—right now (Derrida 1996, p. 38), and there is an epistemological relevance to this urgency.

Therefore, there is a "weak messianic power" that calls us to engage in the deconstructive act of interruption in order to give voice to the other, the wronged differend, and to his or her truth. As Walter Benjamin says,

> There is a secret agreement between past generations and the present one. Our coming was expected on earth. Like every generation that preceded us, we have been endowed with a *weak* messianic power, a power to which the past has a claim. That claim cannot be settled cheaply. Historical materialists are aware of that. (1969, p. 254)

According to Benjamin, we are the ones that the dead expected to come and "redeem" them. Present justice thus is urgently called for by the past. We are called to engage in the present to make the future with infinite responsibility to the past and the dead. We should hear the cries of the dead and do what we can, lest their death be in vain. For pure injustice happens when we forget the dead, the future, and their link in the present.

For the project of political epistemology, seeking the unheard voice of the other is inspired by this inherited promise we never made—a promise that is not only to the past but to the always-to-come other, to the movement toward justice in the future with a memory of the past. The weak messianic power solicits us to bring the messianic time to the present and make the production of truth meaningful, ethically valuable, and politically emancipatory here and now. Otherwise, the storm of "progress" with its eschatological, universal, and telic Truth would "irresistibly propel" the *Angelus Novos* "into the future to which his back is turned, while the pile of debris before him grows skyward" (Benjamin 1969, p. 258).

It is the "feeling" of this promise that makes us say "perhaps" there is still something remaining and waiting to be thought and listened to beyond the present new coherent cognitive/material reality. It is, in other words, this feeling of being expected messianically—as those who were all along expected to come and "redeem" the other/truth—that forms the *ethicity* of political epistemology and *justifies* its faith in hyperrealism. This very faith or feeling also motivates critical theory in general and political epistemology in particular to *decide* that the present cognitive/material reality is a contingent construction that subjects the other.

The promise has a "weak power," since we can simply ignore it, decide to not hear it, and feel happy with the present new coherent cognitive/material reality as just and necessary. This closure, however, is unjust, because justice has to do with "the coming of the other, the absolute and unpredictable singularity of the *arrivant as justice*" (Derrida 1994, p. 28). This is the *promise (see Lucy 2004, p. 74) of emancipation* that the participants in the project of political epistemology keep. Without the messianic spirit that likewise "haunted" Marx in his prophetic moments, deconstruction cannot move. Messianic structure makes it impossible for the present new coherent cognitive/material reality to close and gather around itself, to call and confuse itself as just. The call of the other "haunts" us, like the specter of Marx, who we cannot quite exorcise, bury, or get rid of. Accordingly, being just toward the other-to-come requires a continual active engagement in history as a work of "mourning,"[33] a politics of memory (Benjamin), or, in Derrida's terms, an everlasting enactment of the play of forces differently, while having an "insomniac experience" (Critchley 1995, p. 13) of being captivated by the specter. Let me explain this point through an example.

Marx's philosophy as a political deconstruction in search of truth and justice

For Derrida, *hauntology* is a quasitranscendental condition of possibility of ontology. We should also understand Levinas's idea of the primacy of justice to truth accordingly. Marx thus is a *hauntological* thinker who deconstructs the capitalist mode of sociopolitical life, the capitalist *différance*, in the name of doing justice to capitalism's other, what Enrique Dussel calls the "living labor." Let us use Derridean language in understanding Marxism and its relevance from a political epistemological perspective. From this perspective, Marxism is strategic movements of changing the sedimented capitalist play of differentiation by first denying the fetishized naturalness of this play and then initiating new moves in it. New moves, in their turn, put new concepts, signifiers, institutions, and political forces in effect (e.g., class, the proletariat, alienation, fetishism, ideology, revolution, party, syndicate, international, union, and so on, which, as cognitive/material realities, are traces within the post-Marx play). The linguistic reality, the sociopolitical play of differentiation, repeats itself differently after Marx's strategic moves in the play: After Marx, *différance*, the opening for meaning, "is" *different*. Through Marx's political/epistemic moves, *différance repeats itself differently*, so much so that any movement of meaning making, any truth claim about the nature of the capitalist mode of social, political, economic, and cultural life, is now affected, is now an effect of the post-Marx *différance.*

The mutual constitutiveness of meaning and sociopolitical reality implies that after Marx, the sociopolitical relations of power are different because the play of differentiation among concepts is now altered (and vice versa). Marx altered the play by entering new actors in it, by letting cognitive/material realities like exploitation, alienation, class, and struggle come into the play, enact it differently, and open possibilities for seeing, talking about, and taking political measures against the dark side of capitalism. For the project of political epistemology, the Marxian deconstruction of capitalism is of epistemic value in its giving new nuances to the play of differentiation and opening new horizons for disclosure. In Dussel's account, the practice of the oppressed is an *exteriority*, the other, excluded by the capitalist mode of play. The theoretical articulation of capitalism (liberal individualism and its corollaries), together with the institutional mode of capitalist life, form the historic play of capitalism—a play that claims totalitarian domination. Dussel, however, believes that Marx's *Das Kapital* is not a move toward totality, but a search for the voice of the other, the otherwise. In political epistemology's terms, *Das Kapital* strategically interrupts and transgresses the capitalist play of *différance* in order to change the economy of meaning/power (by initiating and entering new actors, signifiers/ signifieds, into the play).[34]

Accordingly, "living labor" emerges as the unheard, the exteriority, the other of the capitalist cognitive/material play. For Dussel, "living labor" is not "labor competence" or "labor force":

> It is labor "before" being part of capital as an economic system. It is labor but non-capital or, in other words, labor otherwise than capitalism...but once it is transformed into "labor competence," or "labor force," it moves from exteriority to the borders of the system and becomes commodity. (Mignolo 2000, p. 32)

In other words, "living labor" *is* a signifier that aspires to signify the singular other for which there is (prior to Marx) no signifier beyond the dominant play of capitalism. As such, the existence of this singular is easily blurred within the dominant capitalist discourse, since it "lives" in the abyss of nothingness, beyond (the dominant capitalist) language. Upon this singular's coming into language, the capitalist label of "labor force" comprehends, digests, and "domesticizes" it and, in so doing, conceals its great remainder. This is why living labor gets subjugated and prevented from voicing this subjugation. Living labor thus "is" a wronged differend, a "real" entity that is prevented from coming to the scene of language to unconceal its truth.

According to Dussel, Marx demonstrates that this violation of the singular (living labor)—this totalitarian political/theoretical "operation" that subsumes the singular and denies or devalues its otherness to commodity, labor force, and so forth—is the precondition of the conversion of money into capital. The capitalist political/theoretical "operations" (or moves) of the play claim that they grasp the totality of this singular. Hence, they become closed to its remainder. Yet another example of this violence is the appropriation of "land" into "private property."

Like Derrida in *Specters of Marx*, Dussel believes that it is the ethical impulse that makes Marx go after the footprints of exteriority (Mignolo 2000, p. 40). From a normative political epistemological point of view, the post-Marx play of differentiation, the cognitive/material reality, is more truthful because it is less closed to the singular other (living labor). The post-Marxian play is a new coherent cognitive/material reality with more mutual support between its elements: The living labor is now less suppressed; it has been given a voice. Without the strategic move (Marxism as praxis) in *différance*, that is the theoretical/practical contradictions of the capitalist mode of cognitive/material play, the new contradictions that emerge from the exclusion of living labor cannot be solved. This is of course Lukacs in a Derridean voice (see Chapter 3).

Dussel also talks about another wronged differend of capitalism: the colonial world. He deconstructs the construction of modern subjectivity, the Cartesian *cogito*, in the early seventeenth century and shows how Eurocentrism harbors violence toward the other (the African, Latin American, and Asian, the periphery, the old colonial and dependent world: the otherwise than the European self (see Alcoff 2000, pp. 256–7)). Dussel pinpoints the crux of Eurocentrism in Hegel's statement in *Encyclopedia*, where the latter writes:

> [Because] history is the configuration of the Spirit in the form of event, the people which receives the Spirit as its natural principle...is one that dominates in that epoch of world history....Against the absolute right of that people who actually are the carriers of the world Spirit, the spirit of other peoples has no other right (*rechtlos*). (quoted in Dussel 1995, p. 24)

The European self, as the carrier of the Spirit, respects no right of the other. This is what Dussel considers Eurocentrism.

Indeed, the European self–other relationship is a version of the master–slave dialectic, and one can easily see its dramatic distance from Levinas's or Derrida's notion of the self–other encounter (where the self is unconditionally responsible, host, and hostage to the other). In a Derridean language, Eurocentrism is the dominant move and mode of the play of differentiation in the early seventeenth century. (Unfortunately, it still holds its universal and hegemony-seeking claims in the present time.) This mode of the play is closed to the other. Indeed, the sovereign self is an effect of this play, and it is not too difficult to realize the play's other effects throughout everyday political, cultural, and economic behaviors of the Western Selves toward the other. Dussel believes that the "frightful cruelty" and the "unmeasured cynicism" of this violent exclusion of the other "is transformed into the very development of the enlightened reason of the *Aufklarung*" (1995, p. 25). Accordingly, he shows how the construction of the modern Cartesian ego (the sovereign self), a principle of subjectivity "that takes itself to be the center or end of history," has a *historical a priori*, a play of differential forces.

As a consequence, the wrong imposed on the differend other includes a systematic exclusion of this other from accounts of modernity. Where Jurgen Habermas states that "the key historical events for the implantation of the principle of subjectivity are the *Reformation*, the *Enlightenment* and the *French Revolution*" (1987, p. 29), Dussel recognizes in this very statement yet another example of ignoring the victimization of the otherwise as a constitutive part of modernity. Through his deconstructive moves, motivated by his "ethics of liberation" (see Schelkshorn 2000), Dussel interrupts the fetishized Eurocentric play. He affirms the reason, the truth, and the voice of the otherwise than the European self in order to change *différance* and promote a "transmodern" play.

Deconstruction, as the above example demonstrates, is a political act motivated at once by epistemic normativity *and* ethical normativity. Derrida's idea of deconstruction contributes *an* articulation of relationships between epistemic normativity as new coherentism, ethical normativity as radical responsibility to the other, and political activity in the name of justice. As Derrida stresses quite frequently, however, deconstruction is not a method. It is not a thing: It just happens when, haunted by the specter of justice and the call of the other/truth, we encounter the (Derridean) *text*, a sociopolitical reality, a theory, a behavior, an action, and so on. Hence, I do not wish to introduce deconstruction as a fixed methodology of a fixed political epistemology.

While the project of political epistemology and deconstruction are other than fixed sets of principles and rules, we should understand radical ethics and the idea of ethical normativity as compatible with the dialectical flexibility that the project of political epistemology and its criterion of truth, new coherentism, sponsor. Hence, I shall argue that the idea of an ethics without principle helps us realize how ethical and political epistemological norms can coexist: The political epistemological move from a lower level of new coherence toward an upper one is a principleless ethical move, simultaneously. In the following section, I begin with the point that justice-to-come cannot be articulated and fixed in the present; it is undeconstructible. Radical ethics, therefore, is not fixed insofar as its goal is concerned. I shall argue, moreover, that radical ethics is also principleless insofar as its "method" is concerned. These two dynamic characteristics of radical ethics help it comply with political epistemology's endless movements toward upper levels of new coherence.

Undeconstructible justice and new coherence

Deconstruction deconstructs to do justice to the singular. It deconstructs to see whether, and how, a set of moves in the play exclude the other and conceal the truth. Doing justice to the singular is to let its truth be disclosed. In other words, it is the epistemological *responsibility* toward truth, as well as the ethical *responsibility* toward the wholly other, that give the political *right* of deconstructing a theory or a trace *as* socio-politico-juridico-institutional structure, as a new incoherent cognitive/material reality. The call from the other opens a space for deconstruction. It entrusts deconstruction with the anticlosure task of opening a "nonsite" for the yet-to-come other.

Responding to the call of the singular is a singular and idiomatic move,[35] however, which opposes the transhistorical generality of a rule or the universal imperative of law. The idiomatic "nature" of the always to-come singular helps us realize why justice can be neither reduced to law nor thematized. It also explains why deconstruction, as doing justice to the other, has no principle, method, or rule to follow. According to Derrida, justice demands "heteronomic relation[s] to the others, to the faces of otherness that govern me, whose infinity I cannot thematize and whose hostage I remain." Derrida quotes Levinas with approval: "The relation to others—that is justice" (1990, p. 959).

Whereas law is historically constructed and instituted within the play, justice is the undeconstructible that gives incentive to deconstructing the law. In fact, the deconstructibility (contingency) of the law, and the undeconstructibility of justice, are conditions of possibility of deconstruction. Accordingly, as Derrida states, deconstruction takes place in the interval that separates the undeconstructibility of justice from the deconstructibility of *droit* (authority, legitimacy and so on) (p. 945).

Justice is undeconstructible because, as we saw, it is a different and *ethicical* (radical ethical) relationship to the always to-come (the yet-not-constructed) other. Law, truth claims, identities, and other traces of the play as elements of the cognitive/material reality are all contingent and constructed. Accordingly, they are all deconstructible. Deconstruction, therefore, is good news for the betterment of law, truth systems, and other traces of the play. Deconstruction problematizes them, opens them up for the coming of the other as the advent of justice, and makes them flexible and internally responsive.

Law is always violent. It is of a phenomenological order otherwise than justice. Like other universals that want to digest the singular without residue, law's general rules cross the distance of otherness and pay no respect to the singular. Accordingly, law becomes most dangerous when it confuses itself with justice. Deconstruction of law, "which is finally what politics is about" (Laclau 1995, p. 91; also see Caputo 1991b, p. 17), "negotiates" between the undeconstructibility of justice and the deconstructibility of law. Far from destruction, deconstruction reinterprets, reconstructs, and negotiates "between the values, themes, meanings, philosophemes that are deconstructed and a certain maintenance, or survival, of their effects" (Derrida 2002, p. 16).

Therefore, justice should be understood not as a sociopolitical state of affairs but as a moment of just political action—a moment of deconstruction that is to change cognitive/material reality. The present cognitive/material reality is always too disappointing. Neither it nor its constituent, law, should consider itself as just, because there is always a systematic exclusion of the other involved in it. As Horkheimer and Adorno put it, "Justice is swallowed by law" (1988, p. 12). Accordingly, the coherence of a new coherent web of cognitive/material reality is always incomplete. There are always contradictions that signal the suppression of the singular and the concealment of truth. The normativity of the project of political epistemology amounts to taking an epistemic measure toward upper levels of new coherence. This epistemic measure toward upper levels of new coherence is ethical and political in its search for justice.

Following their instinctive hermeneutical suspicion, participants in the project of political epistemology may prescribe deconstructing, or suspending (Derrida 1990, p. 957), the present new coherent cognitive/material reality in order to allow the blossoming of the other. The political epistemological project interrogates the sedimented new coherent reality, its origins, and its limits of conceptual, theoretical, or normative kinds. It does so in the name of another, more encompassing truth that *happens* within a more (new) coherent cognitive/material reality. The normativity of the project of political epistemology amounts to the idea that we should privilege a more democratic, less totalitarian cognitive/material reality: The former is more truthful, and the latter is less unjust.[36] That is, it is more affirmative of the multiplicity of truths to-come.

This conclusion notwithstanding, we shall inquire into the nature of this normativity. What do we mean by the notion of *norm* here? Is there a set of principles that the project of political epistemology offers to be obeyed on the way from the former, less consistent, new coherent cognitive/material reality to the next, more consistent one? Since advancement from the former deconstructed cognitive/material reality to the next reconstructed one is political and ethical, how would political epistemology's normativity attend to, and represent, these political and ethical features and dynamisms?

In other words, can we think of a political (see Critchley 1999, p. 188) as well as epistemic advancement (from the lower level of new coherence to an upper one) that is ethical and simultaneously nonmethodological? Can this advancement not obey preestablished universal rules but dialectically engage with cognitive/material reality? Can an epistemic and political act take place without following universal codes and yet be ethical? Can we think of a principleless ethics, an ethics whose only heuristic—that negates all universal norms and principles—is openness to the other? The answer is positive.

Like Adorno, Levinas and Derrida demonstrate that the "logic of identity," or "logocentrism," suppresses the different other to advance the notion of truth as perfectly self-contained presence[37] (i.e., non-contingent arche; being, not-becoming) and so otherwise than "the social," "the contradictory." The project of political epistemology, however, poses the question of the other to the Cartesian epistemology and asks about the other and the other others in their concrete intersubjective social, political, economic, ethical, and other relationships with the subject/knower. The project of political epistemology *deconstructs* the Cartesian epistemology. The project does not imply that there is no subject/knower, but that the subject is constructed and must be deconstructed in order to become more aware of and appreciative toward the other within the self/subject.

If the self/subject in its relations with the other finds itself already "occupied," claimed, and made hostage, then the subject/knower cannot be the true beginning of knowledge, meaning, and truth. The other who perpetually disturbs the presence and the "sameness" of the subject/knower opens a nonsite from which the Cartesian epistemology feels obligated to look at, and interrogate, itself as other than itself. The project of political epistemology springs out of this interrogation. Therefore, the project of political epistemology as otherwise than the Cartesian epistemology is radically irreducible to the latter. It cannot be defined within the language of Cartesian epistemology.[38] Accordingly, political epistemology's normativity cannot be articulated based on methodological rules and principles. This is why political epistemology promotes normativity without principles.

The present new coherent system is always disappointing, for the voice of the other cannot be heard within it. It is the otherwise of the present cognitive/material reality that political epistemology desires. Therefore, political epistemology demands the openness of the present play to the other by seeking a higher level of mutual support (i.e., a lower level of new incoherence) among the constituents of cognitive/material reality.

Political epistemology's normativity requires us to resolve and lessen the (new) contradictions of the present cognitive/material reality not in favor of universals, but in the interest of the singular. Accordingly, the deconstructive move from the present cognitive/material reality, the present play, toward an upper level of coherence proceeds in dialectical response to, and involvements in, the specific requirements of the situation before us. As such, the incapability of following a general principle is an integral part, or a transcendental precondition, of the *ethicity* of a singular response. The only "general" heuristic is that there is no universal principle to preorient and preestablish our response to the situation. The only "general" heuristic thus is openness toward the other that shatters the universality of principles.

Universals get produced through abstractions of singular, unprecedented, and unrepeatable sociopolitical/cognitive situations. Universal principles are thereby local and restricted to those singular occasions from which they emerge. Concrete engagements in singular occasions precede the production, and knowledge, of the universal. Each specific moment of the praxis of deconstruction confronts with an always different and exceptional "case."[39] The *ethicity* of the passage from a new coherent cognitive/material reality to an upper level of new coherence is interwoven with what Derrida calls the "universality of singularities." There are no guardrails and guidelines when a genuine politico-ethico-epistemological activity, a deconstructive move in which these three dimensions imply one another, moves in response to the call of justice and truth.

Responding to the idiosyncrasy of the situation requires insight, phronesis, and judgment where there are no principles to program our decision making at each moment of the move. Derrida identifies this lack of programming with "undecidability," that is, the precondition of making genuine and resolute decisions (see Derrida, Kearney, and Dooley 1999, pp. 66–7). As Lyotard asserts, Aristotle "recognizes…that a judge worthy of the name has no true model to guide his judgments, and that the true nature of the judge is to pronounce judgments, and, therefore, prescriptions, just so, without criteria." He explains: "This is after all what Aristotle calls prudence. It consists in dispensing justice without models" (Lyotard and Thebaud 1989, p. 25).

The project of political epistemology accordingly encourages prudent deconstructive practices to break through the singularity of the idiosyncratic situation without having access to rules of ethical, political, or epistemological kinds (Caputo 1997, p. 138). Indeed, it is only after the happening of singular decision making that articulations of philosophical, epistemological, political, or ethical principles begin (Hegel 1974a, p. 265). Thus, the project of political epistemology prescribes ethicopolitical acts of deconstruction in response to the urgent and idiomatic demands of the situation, as a move in the play of difference. It also mandates the "repetition" of deconstructive acts according to the changes in new moments of the play. Herein resides an ethics without principle, an *ethicity* without ethics, an ethics that does not use principles as "excuse" but responds by giving, as a "gift" of love, beyond and above "duty" (see Caputo 2003b, p. 179).

The project of political epistemology reminds us that the ethical, political, and epistemological decisions that facilitate a passage from a lower level of new coherence to an upper level are not individualistic decisions. They are all traces within, and enactments of, the play of differential forces. According to political epistemology's idea of the subject/knower, the self is intersubjective. Therefore, decision making under the condition of undecidability cannot be understood as the responsibility and practice of an individual sovereign self. Here, sub-jectivistic autonomy is substituted for by responsibility toward the other.

The project of political epistemology thus indicates normativity without methodological and universal norms. Nevertheless, when the ethicopolitical and epistemological move takes place, when the play of difference alters and new *new coherence* emerges, when the closure of the play is disturbed, we have reasons to believe that, having been polit-ical and ethical all along the way, the emerging cognitive/material real-ity is more truthful. And since the play and the move are endless, we need an endless practice of opening and moving toward upper levels of new coherence. When closure is the source of untruth, the endless prac-tices of opening are normatively preferable. And when the justness and *ethicity* of the move secure epistemic outcomes, epistemic normativity, morality, and political praxis in the name of justice mutually imply one another. If Plato sought the universal and ideal truth through beauty and art (see Gadamer 1987, p. 15), the project of political epistemol-ogy, not so much interested in the idea of transhistorical truth, pursues indexical truths through political practices (praxis/lexis) within the very togetherness of people in the polis.

Conclusion

Political epistemology is a research project about how politics frames the questions of knowledge. It is also a strategic activity to make the production of truth meaningful, ethically valuable, and politically emancipatory here and now. The project of political epistemology poses the question of the other to Cartesian epistemology and asks about the other and the other "others" in their concrete intersubjective social, political, economic, ethical, and other relationships with the subject/knower.

The project of political epistemology does not deny the existence of the subject/knower. It points out, however, that the subject is constructed and must be deconstructed in order to become more appreciative of the other within the self/subject and to become more aware of the embeddedness and involvement of the knower in the known, the reality.

Certainly, the subject–object dichotomy predates the Enlightenment. Nonetheless, the project of political epistemology pays attention to the cognitive/material manner in which this dichotomy is fetishized in the capitalist era. This manner has been politically enslaving, ethically inhumane, and *wrong*. As Horkheimer and Adorno state, "The distance between subject and object, a presupposition of abstraction, is grounded in the distance from the thing itself which the master achieved through the mastered" (1988, p. 13). From a political epistemological perspective, the sociopolitical context of capitalism partially ontologizes the autonomous subject and prioritizes it over the repressed object, the "damaged life" of Adorno, the Other of Derrida. The epistemologically autonomous subject in turn constitutes the autonomous individual, the sovereign self of the capitalist mode of historical reality.

This political epistemological analysis also explains why the project of political epistemology has not been that visible so far—why it has been a suppressed voice since the Enlightenment, while the vociferous Cartesian epistemology has "perfectly" corresponded to the sociopolitical context of liberal capitalism. Cartesian epistemology's autonomous subject was, and still is, the counterpart of liberal capitalism's sovereign self. The autonomous subject is the exclusive source of knowledge, the repository of truth. The sovereign self is the exclusive source of right, political governance, and the social contract. The autonomous subject and the sovereign self are reciprocally constitutive, the project of political epistemology concludes. This "perfect" correspondence, however, simultaneously conceals and subjects the other within the self, and the "more" within the object. And herein lies the untruth of Cartesian epistemology/liberal capitalism, the present cognitive/material reality.

The politically sovereign self, as well as the epistemologically autonomous subject, is so only through an epistemic/political subjection of the other-within-the-self. The project of political epistemology, therefore, amounts to a negation of the epistemologically autonomous subject and, simultaneously, a rejection of the politically sovereign self (since the two are existentially intertwined). The project of political epistemology's point is that we need a new understanding of the political subject, who is neither the autonomous knower nor the sovereign self. The need for this new understanding is indeed a need for truth and justice-to-come. It is a need for what Jacques Derrida calls democracy-to-come.

In addition to being a negation of the sovereign self and the autonomous knower, however, the project of political epistemology is also a reconstructive account. Seeing the political danger of the sovereign self mirrored, among other occasions, in Carl Schmitt's political theology, and feeling "the bare life" under sovereign power (see Agamben 2005, p. 4), the project of political epistemology asks how we may reformulate a democratic political subjectivity that is not sovereign. How can we transgress the present and strive for a politics-without-sovereignty and an epistemology-without-the-autonomous(abstract)-knower? How should we rethink normativity for political subjectivity that involves openness toward the other? How should we change the present cognitive/material reality, enact the possibilities on the horizon, and move toward upper levels of new coherence that are more open to the otherwise and less antagonistic? Certainly, the answers to these questions are strategic, temporal, and praxical. Investigating these answers would further extend this study. Indeed, the fourth chapter suggests an answer that ventures a deconstructive twist to the movement beyond the present cognitive/material reality. This answer is just a sketchy suggestion about how the project of political epistemology might proceed.

Nevertheless, the canonical and common theme throughout this entire study is that the project of political epistemology may offer a normative criterion of truth as new coherence. New coherence is new in two ways. First, it defines *coherence* as the relation of mutual support among the cognitive and the material, the superstructural and the structural elements of reality. Thus, new coherence is new since it transcends the traditional coherence theory of truth that defines truth on the basis of relationship of logical consistency between propositions. Second, the criterion of new coherence is new since it transcends not only the web of propositions but also the present reality. New coherence has to do with openness toward the possibilities of being otherwise, the possibilities of being different than the present. For a new coherentist, truth implies an endless movement toward upper levels of new coherence where the voices of the other and the other "others" can be heard, when sociopolitical antagonisms, new contradictions, or, the locus of subjugation, are less than at present. That moment is coming and remains to-come. It is *the* promise.

Notes

1 The project of political epistemology, its grounds and methods

1. Also see Solomon 1983, pp. 329–37. According to Nietzsche, a word becomes a violent universal concept

   > in so far as it simultaneously has to fit countless more or less similar cases—which means, purely and simply, cases which are never equal and thus altogether unequal. Every concept arises from the equation of unequal things…the concept…is formed by arbitrarily discarding these individual differences and by forgetting the distinguishing aspects. (Nietzsche 1979, p. 83)

2. And vice versa: Hegel rejects the Platonic world of forms. According to Plato, though particulars cannot exist without universals, universals have an independent, genuine, and authentic being. For Hegel, as we shall see, there is only one true world, the world of appearance, in which concepts, ideas, theories, beliefs, culture, superstructure (or in Hegel's terms "the Spirit"), and the object, matter, or *Nature* are dialectically interdependent and reciprocally constitutive.

3. Hegel and Kant are both saying that we contribute the concept of substance in order to constitute, not simply recognize, the particular and establish an underlying unity to host the diversity of properties in their spatiotemporal and causal relations with one another (see Solomon 1983, pp. 337, 346). While Kant believes in an in-itself that *causes*, and gives content to, our categories of understanding, Hegel rejects the notion of an in-itself that is allegedly beyond the reach of understanding.

4. The real world is inverted as well. It is the topsy-turvy world of Plato's inversion, the inversion of the inverted world. Hegel's complex text opens up the possibility of both interpretations, that is, to see the Platonic world as the perverse one and simultaneously consider the real world, the in-itself-for-us, as the inverted world. The verity of these interpretations is discussed in commentaries by Bossart 1982, Flay 1970, Gadamer 1976, and Solomon 1983.

5. The Kantian residual conception of the thing-in-itself is also another "perverse" world, since, according to Hegel's argument, the worlds of phenomenon and noumenon are one and the same. As discussed above, in Hegel's account, Kantian antinomies testify to the fact that the in-itself versus for-us dichotomy is false and, moreover, that the very in-itself-for-us is contradictory and as such harbors antinomies. For the relevance of the world-in-itself to Kant's philosophical system and the importance of Hegel's' criticism, see Findlay 1981. Joseph Flay (1970) reads Hegel's inverted world as ridicule of the notion of in-itself. According to Flay, the idea of the inverted world is an absurd position that Hegel intentionally takes to show the outcome of a Kantian dichotomy of in-itself versus for-us.

6. We may wonder whether Hegel's philosophy is offering a metaphysical *arche* again—though this time, it sounds like an arche of mutation, a structure-as-everlasting-change. Well, yes and no. The structure-as-change is an antinomy

and, as such, signals that perhaps we are moving in the wrong direction: We are asking a question about the ultimate nature, or the in-itself again! Indeed, as Theodor Adorno argues, Hegel's dialectical thought cannot consistently pretend to be a metaphysical system. If a *prima philosophia*, that is, a static ontology of being, it cannot be dynamic as a dialectic. This volume's second chapter explains how Adorno traces this paradox back in Aristotle's thought, where matter's movement, including genuine political action and change, gets suppressed under an invariant higher reality, the form. This observation clarifies why, for the present study, dialectical materialism is a *dynamic device* and a principle of thinking, not a metaphysical position.

7. Unity in difference means each pole of a dialectical involvement can be understood only in relation to the other; each refers us beyond itself to the other and "others." Hegel's *Geist* and its world are dialectically intertwined, and "a system, which expresses the unity in opposition of *Geist* with its world…is called the Idea" (see Taylor 1975, pp. 328–32).

8. Teleological necessity implies that forms of consciousness preserve the truth and negate the inadequacies in their succession. The exclusion of inadequacy, according to Hegel, extends to successive forms of consciousness. Therefore, the unfolding of an essential truth takes place progressively within each stage of consciousness (see Solomon 1983, pp. 350–5).

9. On later scholars' disregard of the dialectic in Hegel and Marx, see Korsch 1970, p. 35.

10. "In the real world…the division of labor and all M. Proudhon's other categories are social relations forming in their entirety what is today known as *property*: outside these relations bourgeois property is nothing but a metaphysical or juristic illusion. The property of a different epoch, feudal property, develops in a series of entirely different social relations" (Marx 1975, pp. 160–1).

11. Although Feuerbach himself considers his criticism a speculative, theoretical act in the world of thought, Marx shows that Feuerbach's "speculative criticism," as a constitutive part of reality, is in dialectical interaction with what Feuerbach calls the "material world." This consideration implies that without paying attention to the practical features and outcomes of this interaction, the "mere" theoretical criticism of Feuerbach's materialism is inadequate. In Marx's view, Feuerbach attempts to make a similar "merely theoretical" criticism of religious ontology. For Marx, "merely" theoretical criticisms (or critiques understood so by the critics) are harmless to the capitalist mode of reality. Such conservative critiques are indeed among the very fetishized products of the capitalist mode of social life that, in the final analysis, reproduce it rather than negate it (see Marx 1972c, p. 113).

12. The mode of human activity, the mode of production—that is, "what" they produce and "how" they produce—form the very changing nature of human beings. According to Marx, "the nature of individuals…depends on the material conditions determining their production" (1972c, p. 114).

13. E. P. Thompson, in his *Making of the English Working Class* (1963), shows that in eighteenth-century England, the market was the main center of struggle. For reasons very specific to the transitory sociopolitical moment, a "free labor" that was not subject to precapitalist and extraeconomic forms of domination was also free from the yet-to-come factory domination. People for a short period of time had control over their modes of work and relations, though "they had very little control over the market for their products or

over the prices of raw material or food." Social struggles thus were mainly centered on the market. Thompson highlights how, through the dynamism of these struggles, the market as a more or less visible institution for guarding the rights of access to the means of life transformed into a more "invisible hand" with practices intended to merely increase profit. Market was becoming a process beyond communal control. Now, to the benefit of the capitalist doctrine of profit, ideas such as the "self-regulating market" and "price mechanisms" were constantly subjugating the voice of communal values. According to Thompson, the state's coercive apparatus helped advance the ideology of private property and the ethics of profit at this period. The court, for example, prioritized the right to profit by increasing productivity above other rights, such as customary use. It is against this sociopolitical background that the concept of "invisible hand" finds its meaning and, in a dialectical reciprocity, partially reproduces the capitalist mode of reality.

14. A metaphysical system that regards reality as a cosmic mind accessible to philosophers is potentially an idealist ideology. Ideologists in this sense believe in the dualism of thought-matter, transcendent-immanent, and so forth, and, according to Marx's critique of Feuerbach, think that progressive social change can be brought about by conversion of people's consciousness. They leave the material condition, the sociopolitical web of relationships, intact. Ideologists of this sort also refuse any material account of their own philosophical ideas.

15. Elizabeth Potter (1994, pp. 27–50) describes how Locke's epistemology, as well as his philosophy, is not politically "innocent." According to Potter's historical study, Locke's epistemology undercut the epistemology and political theory of many women and men engaged in class and gender struggles during the seventeenth century. Locke's epistemology, Potter argues, was, on the one hand, a liberal response to the repressive religious and familial restrictions that were to silence, chasten, and enslave women. This response has potentially liberating results for middle-class women. On the other hand, Potter continues, Locke's epistemology was simultaneously a repressive response to a more radical epistemology of the seventeenth century, the one of Quakers and Levellers that aimed at liberation of lower-class women and men.

    Potter does not simply uncover the historical context (i.e., the context of discovery) of Locke's epistemology. Rather, she demonstrates that Locke's individualistic epistemology (the very foundation of the dichotomy between the context of justification and the context of discovery) obscures the ways in which the political, economic, or gender relations among individuals affect the production of knowledge and, moreover, how this obscurity has performed and is performing politically. Potter concludes that a theory is determined not only by the data and "cognitive virtues" like simplicity, but also by coherence conditions including social constraints.

16. For Jean-Francois Lyotard, philosophy, pretending to be a metanarrative, is also politically functional. It legitimates modern science and the institutions governing the social bond in the modern time. Not only epistemology, Lyotard believes, but also the very idea of justice offered as a grand narrative of truth delivers the same political function to the modern mode of social life (1984, p. xxiv). It is of course not just epistemology that has political function. According to Lyotard, universal narratives like freedom, the people, the nation, progress, and so forth serve the same function: "The State resorts to the narrative of freedom every time it assumes direct control

over the training of the 'people,' under the name of the 'nation,' in order to point them down the path of progress" (p. 32).

17. Contrary to Hegel's essentialist belief in the teleological necessity of the overall movement of dialectic, the nonorthodox dialectical materialism amounts to the idea that the play of opposites, the thesis and the anti-thesis, is contingent through and through. That is, there is no immanent direction for the next contingent dialectical move.

18. For Foucault and Nietzsche, providing a genealogy of the present-day "absolute" truth has a liberating effect in dislodging power and thus freeing our ability to imagine new possibilities (Alcoff 1993a, p. 98).

19. For a thorough study of Marx's "method" of analysis, see Sayer 1979, ch. 4–5.

20. Horkheimer 1974, p. 187. On negation, see Bottomore et al., 1983, p. 352.

2   Critical theory, negative dialectics, and the project of political epistemology

1. For Horkheimer, rationalist idealism amounts to the nondialectic, nonmaterialist elements of Hegel, Kant, Descartes, and Leibnitz. Reductive materialism, including orthodox Marxism, is ultimately compatible with instrumental rationality. It is nondialectic and claims nonhistorical, "scientific" validity. Accordingly, the logical empiricism of the Vienna Circle is a branch of reductive materialism (see Rush 2004).

2. I am aware that the relation of reciprocal constitutiveness between knowledge and reality problematizes both the within–without dichotomy and the use of the term *within* here.

3. For an account of the influence of Lukacs's *History and Class Consciousness* on Horkheimer and Adorno, see Dallmayr 1981, pp. 127–43.

4. For a detailed dialectical criticism of Karl Popper's critical rationalism, see Habermas 1976b, pp. 198–200.

5. On the false whole, see Adorno 1972, pp. 145–6. In a manner reminiscent of Gramsci's idea of Centaur, Adorno and Horkheimer believe that Western societies have become a total system, a whole. It is not the brute coercive force or physical violence but the internalization of them both through cultural conditioning, advertising, and mass media that organically reproduces the modern capitalist society. It is no more the exclusion from society, the physical oppression that raises class conflict. It is, indeed, the very inclusion of individuals and classes into the system, the very penetration of the market system into the conscience of individuals that reproduces modern Western society. For Adorno and Horkheimer, dialectical inquiry into this totality needs a speculative theory, beyond the reach of positivist social sciences. Speculative theory, as Fredric Jameson writes, is a kind of "dialectical pun," a way of thinking about reality while being self-conscious about the dialectical and reciprocal constitutive relationship between this very thinking and its object, the social reality (1972, p. 140). Adorno's and Horkheimer's awareness of the change in capitalist social reality, of the fatal inadequacy of a positivist/reifying understanding of society, and finally, of

the epistemological need to normatively justify any speculative theoretical understanding of society demanded that they think about a new dialectical normative epistemology. The project of political epistemology can greatly benefit from Adorno's and Horkheimer's suggestions for that purpose.

6. And Adorno adds, "in a determinably false society that contradicts the interests both of its members and of the whole, all knowledge which readily subordinates itself to the rules of this society that are congealed in science, participates in its falsity" (1976a, p. 18).

7. "If critical theory consisted essentially in formulations of the feelings and ideas of one class at any given moment, it would not be structurally different from the special branches of science....The relation of being to consciousness is different in different classes of society. If we take seriously the ideas by which the bourgeoisie explains its own order—free exchange, free competition, harmony of interests, and so on—and if we follow them to their logical conclusions, they manifest their inner contradiction and therewith their real opposition to the bourgeois order. The simple description of bourgeoisie self-awareness thus does not give us the truth about this class of men" (Horkheimer 1972d, pp. 214–15). From a political epistemological perspective, Horkheimer's assertion means that "universal concepts" like free exchange and free competition are local to the bourgeois class. They partially constitute the ways in which the bourgeoisie lives and acts. These local "universals," however, aspire to dominate the self-awareness and the way of life of other classes of society—the workers, for example—for whom "the relation of being to consciousness is different." Critical theory traces the social antagonisms and logical inconsistencies that this domination brings about.

8. Like Horkheimer and Adorno, Habermas studies the role of science and technology, the hallmarks of instrumental rationality, in the formation of mass consciousness. According to Habermas (1971, pp. 81–122), it is only in liberal capitalism that the "institutional framework," the superstructure, is coextensive with social relations of production. In other words, it is only in liberal capitalism that the social relations of production are depoliticized. As an explicit social actor, however, the welfare state of late capitalism openly intervenes in economy and "repoliticizes" the social relations of production. Now, it is technology that depoliticizes the public sphere: While the people no more believe in the liberalist fate of formal equality of opportunity, technology and science provide the ground of legitimacy for the capitalist welfare state. Habermas's account indicates the dialectic between the social system and the state on the one hand and the mass consciousness and its legitimacy criterion on the other. It shows the ideological contributions of science and technology to the mechanism of domination in the late capitalist state.

9. In his review of Karl Mannheim's Ideology and Utopia, Horkheimer states that one does not need "any absolute guarantee in order to distinguish meaningfully between truth and error. Rather, what is required is a concept of truth consistent with the dependence of thought on changing social conditions" (McCarthy 1988, p. 79). According to Horkheimer, "Truth is a moment of correct practice" (1993c, p. 200).

10. As a mediating thinker, Aristotle was to find the intermediate position *between* two extremes. His intermediate was "not implicit in the meaning of the extremes," not "accomplished *through* the extremes themselves" (Adorno 2001, p. 47). According to Adorno, Aristotle lacked the idea of dialectic because "the discovery of subjectivity as the constitutive element of knowledge was entirely foreign to antiquity" (p. 48).
11. Horkheimer 1993a, p. 115; see also Adorno 1973. There are philosophical as well as political reasons for rejecting Hegel's teleology. It is philosophically wrong because it is an outdated metaphysics that, as Marx says, glorifies the existing state of things. Accordingly, Horkheimer shares Lenin's critique of Hegel. As Cliff Slaughter states, "Despite Hegel's insistence that the dialectic must take into account the constant state of change of all reality, his own philosophy becomes an adaptation to the existing political set-up in Germany. This came about not because of the dialectical character of his thought, but because he remained an *idealist*" (1963, p. 27). Indeed, Adorno underlines almost the same Aristotelian contradiction in Hegel's metaphysics. Hegel's philosophy is at the same time "dynamic as a dialectic and ontological as a theory of being—is at the same time static and dynamic" (2001, p. 86). Again, the idea/concept as a condition of being neutralizes true concrete change. *Telos* makes the dynamic movement an invariant, something that must happen and can never cease. True change becomes impossible. Adorno's dialectical materialism has no *telos*: It is not a metaphysics insofar as by "metaphysics" one means the first philosophy of eternal universals. It is, rather, a heuristic device or, as mentioned in the introduction, a practice of thinking.
12. Also, according to theoretical arguments, contradictions are never totally resolved. See Tsetung 1971, p. 88.
13. Adorno 1973, p. 295. Teleological essentialism signifies Hegel's "unfeasible practice to arrest dialectics in something solid beyond it" (p. 375).
14. For a Hegelian reading of Adorno's and Horkheimer's dialectic of Enlightenment, see Bernstein 2004, pp. 21–2.
15. In *Negative Dialectics*, Adorno uses this "method" and underscores the "materiality," the sociopolitical situatedness, of subjective reason's universal concepts. Adorno sees this move as an emancipatory act. Adorno's would-be epistemology after Auschwitz must embrace these points.
16. Adorno and Horkheimer trace the commodification of art in Plato's writings: "Art must first prove its utility" (1988, p. 18). The commodification of thought is the crux of Adorno and Horkheimer's criticism of the culture industry.
17. Horkheimer and Adorno 1988, p. 42. According to Adorno, the culture industry and consumerism promote "blind and opaque authority" for the sake of order. (Adorno was one of the first to attend to the role of consumption in binding individuals to the system and its order, thus embougeoisizing the working class. See Kellner 1976; also see Adorno and Rabinbach 1975, p. 17.) For that reason, the individual's self-realization fails to meet the condition of being an end in itself. Individuals, Horkheimer states, become "an agglomeration of instruments without a purpose of their own" (Lohmann 1993, p. 400), and this is "inhuman" (Adorno 1972, p. 147).

18. According to the German idealist tradition, the term *concept* connotes the medium of reasoning and cognition in general (Bernstein 2004, p. 32).
19. For a critical evaluation of this position, see Chambers 2004.
20. Franz Rosenzweig writes that not the self-sufficient subject but "only the single being can die." According to Rosenzweig, metaphysics—its universal concepts, its notion of the totality, and so on—is an artifact made to "swallow up" death and rid mortal men of anxiety (1998, pp. 179–84). Metaphysics, as Rainer Nagele states, "Robs the material life and death in history of its materiality and the reality of its suffering" (1986, p. 96). For a study of Adorno's and Rosenzweig's ideas on metaphysical constructs, see Floyd 1989.
21. "Represented in the inmost cell of thought is that which is unlike thought" (Adorno 1973, p. 408). The "unlike thought" is the sociopolitical context, the "irreconcilable matter" (p. 144) which is "constitutive" (p. 12) of thought.
22. For a detailed investigation of Adorno's critique of German idealism and phenomenology, see Rosen 1982, pp. 153–78.
23. Geuss 2005, p. 6. For Adorno, suffering has a positive epistemic value: It shelters the unhappy consciousness against the consent-manufacturing processes of the modern time.
24. Caputo 1993b, p. 253. Like Adorno, Horkheimer rejects Hegel's identification between history and truth, the idea of history as the subject and the object, since this identification suppresses the suffering individuals who must be heard (Buck-Morss 1979, p. 222). The Jews, Horkheimer and Adorno argue, are the prime targets of the identity principle of the instrumental rationality, because they are the most resolute repository of otherness and difference in the Western world (Horkheimer and Adorno 1988, pp. 186–208).
25. I do not pretend to be offering an articulation of a dialectical realism proper. What is intended is an investigation of how Adorno understands potentiality. This investigation helps me better see Adorno's potential contribution to the project of political epistemology. Howard Engelskirchen (2004) talks about "powers in things" and suggests a reading of scientific realism that, to my understanding, conforms with our sketchy dialectical realism.
26. For Adorno, philosophy must reflect this notion of openness. It must "prove itself the most advanced consciousness—permeated with the potential of what could be different—but also a match for the power of regression, which it can transcend only after having incorporated and comprehended it" (1998, p. 16).
27. "It is the matter, not the organizing derive of thought that brings us to dialectics. Nor is dialectics a simple reality, for contradictoriness is a category of reflection, the cognitive confrontation of concept and thing" (Adorno 1973, p. 144).
28. Adorno's idea of totality is not that of Hegel's metaphysical universal, but rather the Marxian meaning of the total societal reality of structure/superstructure. See Marcuse 1951, p. 314.
29. Adorno and Horkheimer argue that the rationality to which man subjects external nature reveals his internal subjection. As concept objectifies nature, so it does to "I" in objectifying it into the transcendental isolated subject. Adorno thus thinks of individuality instead of subjectivity. Unlike the subject, the individual is not a monad. The individual is "boundlessly

elastic, subjectless subject" (see Love 1987, p. 86). Adorno believes that "only if the I on its part is also not I does it react to the not I. Only then does it 'do' something. Only then would the doing itself be thinking" (1973, p. 201). I will return to this point in the last chapter.

30. Adorno maintains that inconsistency in the web of propositions "indicates the untruth of identity and the fact that the concept does not exhaust the thing conceived" (1973, p. 5). Therefore, to think that reestablishing logical consistency among universal and particular propositions would bring the truth back in the web is a repetition of the reifying logic of identity. Rather, what is needed is a new version of the coherence theory of truth that takes the side of the object and respects the reciprocal mediation between the subject and the object. The project of political epistemology responds to these provisions.

31. Therefore, "epistemology, the quest for the pure realization of identity through seamless reduction to subjective immanence, turns, despite itself, into the medium of non-identity." As Adorno points out, "epistemology is true as long as it accounts for the impossibility of its own beginning and lets itself be driven at every stage by its inadequacy to the things themselves" (2000b, p. 131).

32. Indeed, Adorno's critique of epistemology implies "dynamicization of Kant's a priori forms of thought" by stressing the priority of the object, the nonconceptual, and the sociopolitical constituent of the concept. For Adorno, experience as engagement in sociopolitical reality, Heidegger's being-in-the-world, is not a chaotic mode of nonepistemological discourse. Rather, it is the context of practice and understanding that makes them both possible. In other words, we never assume the role of an epistemological spectator, since "experience lives by consuming the stand-point" (1973, p. 41; see also O'Connor 1994, p. 71; 1998, p. 45).

33. Horkheimer's promotion of an "objective reason" is also a conscious political, epistemological, and ethical program that aspires to inject rationality into the cognitive/material contradictions of the Enlightened era. It seems, however, that Horkheimer's objective reason lacks sufficient sympathy with the singular. Adorno seems more aware of the potential danger of an objective, universality-claiming reason (though this reason, as Horkheimer emphasizes, might not be the abstract instrumental one). For Adorno, the danger lies, more than anything else, in having a universal claim of truth, even if the claim of universal validity comes from an objective reason that denies the fact–value dualism.

34. Experience, for Adorno, is the process of consciousness revising its criterion of truth. It is the very process of rationality that compels us to move beyond contradictory judgments (see O'Connor 2000, p. 12). The cognitive/material nature of contradiction implies that this move should be toward upper levels of new coherence. This point explains why the movement of experience is mediated by, and mediating, the societal totality.

35. See Schmidt 1974, p. 93. According to Adorno's *Minima Moralia*, the possibility that is already opened up is a possibility of a "true, beautiful, and good" life. This possibility, Adorno believes, is also an internal standard for moral evaluation of the present society. As mentioned in the above discussion about Adorno's dialectical realism, this possibility is *within* society

but is not identical to society. It is because of this possibility that society is always nonidentical to, and ahead of, itself. Adorno's articulation of the possibility of moral criticism of the forms of life offers a way out of moral relativism among the allegedly incommensurable forms of life. It simultaneously rejects moral imperialism that takes place when one situated moral standard seeks to dominate all other forms of life (see Jaeggi 2005).

36. It is needless to repeat that, for Adorno, "facts themselves" are cognitive/material, in-themselves-for-us. Facts always emerge in a constellation.

37. In an apparently discouraging tone, Adorno states: "Man must act in order to change the present petrified conditions of existence, but the latter have left their mark so deeply on people, have deprived them of so much of their life and individuation, that they scarcely seem capable of the spontaneity necessary to do so." Adorno is quick to add, however, that "from this, apologists for the existing order draw new power for their argument that humanity is not yet ripe" (1972, p. 153).

38. "We do not face the world in doctrinaire fashion with a new principle, declaring, 'Here is truth, kneel here!' We develop new principles for the world out of the principles of the world" (Marx 1997, p. 214).

39. This point will be further investigated in the following chapter.

40. Chapter 4 suggests a similar dialectical materialist reading of Derrida's *différance* that depicts the play of differentiation as the sociopolitical a priori of meaning. From this political epistemological perspective, I think Derrida's *différance* and Adorno's constellation are comparable.

41. In Antonio Gramsci's language, this understanding of political action establishes "the dialectical position of political activity...as a particular level of superstructure. As a first schematic approximation political action is precisely...the moment in which the superstructure is still in the unmediated phase of mere wishful confirmation, confused and still at an elementary stage" (1972, p. 137). By the "unmediated phase," Gramsci indicates a naïve superstructural moment that does not realize its own dialectical relationship with structure and thus regards the latter as autonomous. For Adorno, identity thinking is the hallmark of such a phase.

42. Both Adorno and Foucault emphasize the "smallest things" and give voice to the subjugated nonconcept. Adorno's political/epistemological project does not stop at this step, however. Adorno also thinks about the social totality and connects the emancipation of the particular/nonconcept to that of the whole. Contrary to Foucault, Adorno remains loyal to the goals of the Enlightenment. Therefore, he parallels emancipation and rationalization, though, of course, the rationality that Adorno—and the Frankfurt School—has in mind is not instrumental reasoning but a critical, and communicative, one. For a comparison between Foucault and the Frankfurt School, see Dews 1987, pp. 150–61.

3　Political epistemology versus sociology of knowledge

1. In addition to Paul Feyerabend (1970), feminist epistemologists also point out the political danger of epistemological objectivity (see Lloyd 1995).

Objectivity and universality are tightly related, and it seems that Adorno's criticisms of universality are also applicable to the notion of objectivity. Yes, there are dangers with epistemological *objectivity*. This does not imply, however, that the only alternative is epistemological *subjectivity*. From a dialectical materialist perspective, the project of political epistemology seeks to overcome the common core that gives meaning to the objectivity versus subjectivity dichotomy, that is, the abstract subject. The project, therefore, offers its own notion of epistemological objectivity that has to do with what Adorno called the primacy of the object, with the fact that the subject and the object are mutually constitutive and that there exists a normative criterion of truth: new coherence.

2. The dialectical notion of mutual constitutiveness between consciousness and social reality demands that *correspondence*, the term that Lukacs usually applies, would not refer to the simplistic idea of representation. It is also a mistake to explain correspondence based on the cause–effect relationship. This point differentiates between Lukacs, Althusser, and Mannheim. Ideology, for Louis Althusser, is an "imaginary distortion that we can observe....It is not the real conditions of existence, their real world that men 'represent to themselves' in ideology, but above all it is their relations to those conditions of existence which is represented to them there. It is this relation which is at the center of every ideological, i.e. imaginary, representation of the real world" (1971, p. 164). In other words, according to Althusser, ideology is an illusion, which distortedly makes allusion to real man–society relations. It does not mirror the real existing relations of production, but the imaginary and necessary relation of individuals to the real relations of production in which they live. Whereas for Lukacs ideology corresponds with reality—that is, ideology and reality are mutually constitutive—for Althusser ideology does not correspond with reality—that is, ideology is a *camera obscura*. Karl Mannheim's concept of ideology will be discussed later in this chapter.

3. While Lukacs's party harbors the totality of truth, or the truth of the totality of sociohistorical reality, Gramsci's organic intellectuals advance local truths. Gramsci's idea of organic intellectuals thus promotes a more democratic notion of truth.

4. Early logical positivists, following Ernest Mach, regarded concepts or perceptions as the subject matter of epistemological analyses and defined the epistemic truth of a concept in its reducibility to a brute single "fact." Karl Popper's subject matter of epistemological analysis was the theory, not the concept. He assigned the "verisimilitude" of theories to their being "corroborated" in experiments. Imre Lakatos's object of epistemological investigation is neither a concept nor a theory but the research program. It is the research program, according to Lakatos, which is epistemologically "progressive" or "stagnating." Finally, Thomas Kuhn's object of investigation is the paradigm. Though Kuhn hardly offers normative epistemological criteria to compare two rival paradigms, his works display more sensitivity to sociopolitical constituents of truth claims. The project of political epistemology, however, takes the reality, the practico-inert, and the cognitive/material as the subject matter of normative epistemological examination.

5. Quoted in Wolding 1986, p. 217. The "relatively impartial intellectuals" have, according to Mannheim, crosscutting attachments and a detachment from political participation that gives them a considerable freedom from practical concerns (see Mannheim 1956b, pp. 105–6). The intelligentsia's solidarity, Mannheim believes, comes solely from its intellectual interests and concerns and not from any preexisting class interests. Its members do not align themselves collectively with any particular class-based party or political program. Historical investigations, however, cast doubt on the validity of Mannheim's account of the intelligentsia's relative freedom (see, for example, Brym 1977). I shall criticize Mannheim's idea from a political epistemological view, according to which the sociopolitical bondedness is the transcendental precondition of understanding.

6. Standpoint epistemology is based on rationalist assumptions and has a tacit commitment to a singularly correct scientific method and to metaphysical realism. This is why I think that a thorough circularity is inimical to it (see Longino 1997, pp. 31–2; 1999, pp. 338–9).

7. Mannheim differentiates "immanent/from within/intrinsic" and "functional" meanings. The latter, according to Mannheim, is a meaning that becomes visible from without when the sociologist/intellectual situates an idea "with respect to a social-existential totality that we conceive of as a context of meaning" (1990, p. 43).

8. For Mannheim, the intellectual's commitment is to the life of the mind and the autonomy of science, rather than to specific praxis: "The relatively impartial intellectual is one who participates in a diverse intellectual community whose members struggle to establish and maintain the *intellectual autonomy* that allows them to compare and to synthesize the perspectives of those who participate in the practical struggles that they study" (Scott 1988, p. 65). In such an intellectual community, Mannheim's free-floating intellectuals engage in "genuine discussions" (Mannheim 1956a, pp. 191–8).

9. Mannheim talks about "the truth of this totality" (1976, pp. 188–99). This truth is reflected in the total vision, the sociological-historical consciousness of synthesizing intellectuals. It is "the only possibility and hence the most nearly *absolute*" (Wolding 1986, p. 232). It is important to remember that Mannheim needs this Hegelian move to defy relativism.

10. Mannheim identifies this overall extrahistorical reality with the "ineffable element at which the mystics aim"—or, perhaps, with the "divine," as Horkheimer puts it.

11. Metaphysics seeks the ultimate transcendentals, the final preconditions that have *caused* the present possible reality. It thus seeks the conditionless conditions at the beginning of the cause–effect chain. Dialectical historicism, however, implies that *anything* might have been otherwise: Though the present reality is contingent upon its preconditions, the latter are not conditionless causes. In other words, there are noncausal reciprocal relationships between the contingents (see Rorty 1996, pp. 50–65).

12. That it depoliticizes the concept of ideology and removes it from the realm of political criticism explains why Mannheim's *Ideology and Utopia* has been regarded as the bourgeois response to Lukacs's *History and Class Consciousness* (see Jay 1974, p. 73).

13. Again, it is evident that according to Lakatos, the meaning and truth of theories are not constituted by sociopolitical contexts. His epistemological and semantic realism is indeed a corollary of what Robert Nola calls *ontological realism*. Ontological realism implies that theoretical kinds (such as electrons, galaxies, or flu viruses) exist in a suitably mind-independent manner. An epistemological realist like Lakatos accordingly believes that "there is good evidence to the effect that theory T is our best tested most comprehensive theory; T tells us that entities E1, E2..., En exist and that there are laws L1, L2..., Lm; therefore it is reasonable to believe (a) that these entities exist and (b) that those laws are approximately true" (Nola 1988, p. 9). The above ontological and epistemological realisms presuppose the Cartesian nondialectical dualism of subject-object, for which the mind-independent existence of something (things, natural kinds, and so forth) is vital. Bloor accepts the ontological realism. His strong sociological program, however, rejects the above version of epistemological realism. In this sense, he is an epistemological relativist. The project of political epistemology, however, transcends the dilemma of choosing among the relativist Bloor or the positivist Lakatos by starting from a non-Cartesian ontology. Moreover, both Bloor and his critic, Larry Laudan, believe that the Lakatosian rationality is *causally* irrelevant to explaining an agent's belief. Because Lakatos's rational reconstruction "judges an agent's rationality by examining the reasons *we* would give for his belief rather than by examining *his own reasons*, then we have disavowed any effort to speak in the causal idiom." This position implies that the sociological/causal explanation of the agent's belief proceeds in the absence of rational/epistemological evaluation of the idea.

14. Barnes' statement amounts to the position that what counts as the evidence for a belief must consist of at least one worldly fact, one sociopolitical or biopsychological cause. This "externalist" conception of the evidence shows that in applying the argument from underdetermination, Bloor and Barnes do not necessarily reduce reasons to causes.

15. Larry Laudan criticizes this argument as the "fallacy of partial description" and objects that "the fact that science is a social phenomenon and that scientists are socially trained does not warrant the claim that all, or most parts, of science are best understood using the tools of sociology." He elaborates, "Only if science were exclusively a social phenomenon would the social character of science support the claim that sociology is the best tool for its study" (1981, p. 194). Some scholars accept Laudan's criticism and offer a modest account of Bloor's and Barnes's argument from underdetermination. According to the modified version, underdetermination "provides a strong *methodological motivation* for searching for sociological determinants" (Okasha 2000, p. 285). Okasha's account is not helpful, however, for Laudan's criticism is not just a pedantic speculation that can be addressed by a modest rearticulation of Bloor's argument. For Laudan, the underdetermination thesis just proves that some extratheoretical factors are involved in scientific theory choices. These extratheoretical factors, however, may still remain noncausal, nonsocial, and instrumentally rational (like simplicity, elegance, parsimony, rigor, or the conventions of scientists). This point, Laudan contends, is fatal to the strong thesis and its symmetry principle, for the symmetry principle requires that the *same* causes be used to explain

both the rational and irrational theory choices. And even if simplicity, parsimony, and so on are regarded as causes of choice, they are definitely different from classes' or social authorities' interests, financial interests, religious prejudices, desires for fame or prestige, desires to uphold the present social order, and the like. I shall discuss Laudan's criticism in what follows. Here, the crucial point is this: Both Bloor and Barnes and their critic, Laudan, believe in extratheoretical factors, though they disagree among themselves on whether all extratheoretical factors are causal/social or whether they might also be values that are instrumentally rational. Laudan frames this disagreement as the battlefield of epistemological realism versus cognitive relativism. Extratheoretical factors for both sides of the argument, however, connote "things" that are not constitutive of the theory, its meaning, and its truth content. Both Bloor and Barnes (who, from time to time and in order to avoid the blame of cognitive relativism, shift the center of their investigations and argumentative claims from normative validity to the social credibility of theories and as such take the position of "epistemological atheists") and Laudan (who remains a faithful analytic epistemologist) share the conviction that theories and extratheoretical factors are two distinguishable things. Their disagreement is only over the empirical cases of extratheoretical causes. The project of political epistemology renounces this *thingification* of theories, meanings, and truth contents. I shall later criticize the strong thesis and its analytic critics accordingly.

16. Those who believe in the "methodological rationality" of scientific theories would find this argument inadequate. In their view, while the truth or falsity of a theory might remain unknown forever, we can justify our conjectures/theories based on the scientific/rational method that precedes them. Therefore, the presence and engagement of social causes in the method does affect the rationality of the method and of the theories.

17. See Feyerabend 1970, pp. 70–1. Interestingly, Thomas Kuhn's historical investigations indicate that scientists understand what they have "discovered" only after they manage to consistently locate an explanatory theory for it within a larger, well-established theoretical framework. A positivist like Popper thinks that the process of justification must happen after the one of discovery, since any justification "necessarily" requires the existence of that which it justifies. Contrary to Popper, Kuhn's study seems to propose that it is the discovery that happens after justification! (Kuhn's historical accounts are about the discovery of "facts" like the existence of oxygen, Uranus, and X-rays. Popper and Kuhn both believe, however, in the theory-ladenness of facts. So the discovery of oxygen and the discovery of the theory of oxygen should not be separated here.) Kuhn concludes: "Discovering a new sort of phenomenon is necessarily a complex process which involves recognizing both *that* something is and *what* it is" (1977, p. 171).

18. For a thorough investigation of the context distinction and its background, see Hoyningen-Heune 1987.

19. Schmaus 1985, p. 191. To secure the symmetry principle, Bloor and Barnes have frequently stated that reasons are indeed akin to causes in their explanatory function. Barnes says: "There is no necessary incompatibility between causes and reasons as explanations of actions, indeed reasons can be listed among the causes of actions" (1974, p. 70). The symmetry thesis of the

strong program implies that the rational and the irrational belief must be given explanations "of the same type." One way of addressing this demand is to believe that reasons and causes are of the same explanatory function and consequently deny the difference between reasons and causes, and between the cognitive and the social. Reducing reasons to causes, however, secures the symmetry principle at the cost of an epistemological relativism. Larry Laudan tends to read the symmetry thesis in this reductionist way (1981, p. 189). The other way is to follow Schmaus and limit the symmetry thesis to a subfield of rational causes (i.e., natural rationality) and so secure a place for "normative rationality," that is, for reasons that are "metaphysically" distinct.

20. The nonevaluative conviction highlights a conservative attitude that the strong thesis shares with Mannheim's sociology of knowledge. As argued above, the strong program does not necessarily reduce reasons to causes, though it aspires to explain the content of beliefs in sociological terms. Dismissing the idea of epistemic validity, however, means that the strong thesis hinders using truth claims for critical purposes in the social, political, or cultural spheres of life. This critique finds more support when the "immodest" version of the strong program emphasizes its relativist character, denies any distinction between the cause and the reason, and rejects the intrinsic power of the latter. This is the political danger of either the nonevaluative or the relativist sociology of knowledge. Peter Farago, for instance, endorses the conservatism of the sociological program and adds that "one cannot be a sociologist of knowledge without being a relativist." He continues: "A so-called value-free attitude may be the most important thesis of the sociology since Max Weber. One stops being a sociologist when one begins to evaluate beliefs instead of explaining and trying to understand their social character" (2002, p. 184). On the contrary, there are philosophical attempts to highlight the critical, nonconservative aspects of the sociology of knowledge. See, for example, Meja and Stehr 1990, p. 294; Meja and Stehr 1988. Both articles contrast the sociology of knowledge's relativism to epistemological absolutism (not to epistemological realism) and consequently assign a critical role to the sociology of knowledge in investigating the indexicality of truth claims. They, indeed, promote a "modest" version of the sociological thesis and hold to the nonevaluative conviction. It seems that this conviction is essential to almost every different interpretation of the sociology of knowledge. We must see whether this conviction sustains the project of political epistemology's criticisms.

21. In their less cautious moments, however, Bloor and Barnes have frequently confirmed the full-blooded relativist nature of the strong thesis. See, for example, Barnes 1974, p. 154; Barnes and Bloor 1982, p. 25; and Bloor 1991, p. 142. Unless they mean two different things by "relativism," there is an inconsistency in their system.

22. The modest version limits the task of sociological investigation to the credibility of beliefs also in order to avoid a "gross" *non sequitur.* For an exploration of the modest version, see Nola 1990, p. 287. Gary Gutting defends the modest version against relativism and asserts that "a fortiori, the fact that a belief is caused tells us nothing about the more specific question of whether the rationality of the belief is absolute or relative; that is whether

    it is rational or irrational only in the particular social context in which it has been produced or would be rational or irrational in any social context." Thus, he concludes, "the strong program's claim that all beliefs can be causally explained does not entail relativism" (1984, p. 106).

23. Larry Laudan, the eminent critic of the strong thesis, states: "I think Bloor is quite right in asserting, with respect to our theoretical beliefs that their truth status is largely if not entirely irrelevant to their explanation. This is an important insight of the strong programme and its rationale needs to be spelled out as clearly as possible. I am not sure my reasons for arguing the causal irrelevance of truth and falsity are the same as Bloor's, but it is possibly worth setting those reasons out briefly since they effectively entail the 'de-epistemologizing' of cognitive sociology" (1981, p. 186).

24. Bloor and Barnes also view the "circularity" of deductive justification as indicating that "our two basic modes of reasoning [i.e., induction and deduction] are in an equally hopeless state with regard to their rational justification" (1982, p. 41).

25. Contextual validity is not very much different from credibility. Here, the relativity of credibility of the modest version and the methodological relativism of the immodest version meet and prove that so far the idea of relativism is concerned, the modest–immodest dichotomy is in fact a pseudo distinction.

26. See Laudan 1988, p. 137. Laudan maintains that Quine's underdetermination brings conventionalism to the positivist and logical empiricist accounts of knowledge. He adds that positivism's fact–value dualism, together with the point that conventionalism operates under the influence of values, leads positivism to relativism (for, on the positivist view, values cannot be rationally adjudicated). Whereas Bloor and Barnes's relativism emphasizes the contextuality of methodological rules, Laudan's account of relativism is based on an ahistorical fact–value distinction. Bloor and Barnes read historicity in Quine's underdetermination (more than Laudan does).

27. On the one hand, Bloor and Barnes's nonevaluative sentiment and their focus on credibility imply their nonrelativism about truth. (Indeed, one can read quite a few sentences in their works accordingly. For an example of such readings, see Nola 1990, p. 289.) On the other hand, Bloor's and Barnes's skeptical view of the absolute validity criteria and reasoning attests to their truth relativism. The modest versus immodest distinction between two versions of the strong thesis might resolve this inconsistency. (The modest version is said to be methodologically relativist, while the immodest one is relativist about truth.) Yet despite this sympathetic reading, the modest version of the strong thesis seems toothless. Though the modest version is not exactly the same as the sociology of error—because it discards, allegedly and contrary to the sociology of error, the epistemic value of its subject matter—it does not say much more than Mannheim's relationism does. It is also not clear what the "metaphysical" distinction between the reason and the cause is good for when, according to the nonevaluative sentiment, the reason and the cause have no different function in preceding sociological explanations. It seems to me that the strong thesis makes truth and epistemology historical through and through.

28. The project of political epistemology holds that a belief in a *new* sociopolitical context is a *new* belief. It is not the same belief with a different epistemic value (as the relativist indicates). Indeed, the very *newness* of the second sociopolitical context is partially due to the *newness* of the belief in it. For the belief and the sociopolitical context are dialectically constitutive. A belief does not carry with it an essential semantic content, a meaning in-itself, from one sociopolitical context to the other. A supposedly context-free belief is no belief at all. It lacks the transcendental preconditions of meaningfulness.

29. Therefore, it is better to talk about multiple traditions instead of a single tradition. The fragmentary nature of traditions restricts the way in which we might apply the concept of continuity to tradition. (In fact, several arguments in defense of Gadamer's hermeneutics and against epistemological relativism use the notion of continuity of tradition.) The continuity of tradition, moreover, implies a "closet essentialism" in Hegel and Gadamer (see Caputo 1989b).

30. Openness is the very I–Thou relationship itself, not an independent precondition of it. Openness thus is a "constitutive" element of Gadamer's "event of understanding," or "the happening of truth." Therefore, the sociopolitical dimension of openness literally—and of course partly—constitutes the truth (which is also an event, for Gadamer).

31. The same analysis also demonstrates the political dimension of happenings like phronesis, the fusion of horizons, dialogue, and the like, which altogether, according to Gadamer, "constitute" what an event of truth is.

32. Gadamer shares this point with Heidegger when he writes, "Understanding is not a resigned ideal of human experience adopted in the old age of the spirit, as with Dilthey; nor is it, as with Husserl, a last methodological ideal of philosophy in contrast to the naïveté of unreflective life; it is, on the contrary, the original form of the realization of Dasein, which is being-in-the-world. Without any differentiation of understanding into the various directions of pragmatic or theoretical interest, understanding is Dasein's mode of being, in so far as it is potentiality-for-being and 'possibility'" (2002, p. 259). In Heidegger's terms, Dasein is "the being-ahead-of-itself" that is "always already in-the-world-with-others-understandingly."

33. For a comparison between Gadamer and Hegel on the idea of dialectics, see Smith 1975.

34. Growing into a linguistic interpretation means "grow[ing] up in the world," the real world. Gadamer does not imply that all reality is literally "just words." He is a realist. He believes that all intelligible realities, the beings we call "entities," the things that are understood as *these things*, owe their intelligibility, their identity, meaning, and truth—their *this thingness*—to language: "the word is that in which knowledge is consummated, i.e., that in which the species is fully thought. Thomas points out that in this respect the word resembles light, which is what makes color visible" (2002, p. 426; also see Wachterhauser 2002, p. 67).

35. There are profound similarities between the ways in which both young Heidegger and young Wittgenstein conceive their ontologies of language. See Rorty 1996.

36. "While whatever comes into language is genuinely different from the spoken word, the word is a word only because of what comes into language in

it. The word, like the perfect mirror, disappears entirely into what appears in it. On the other hand, whatever comes into language and, in the word, comes to be understandable is, like the mirror-image, something which does not exist pregiven apart from language; rather it receives for the first time in the word its own original determination as understandable by being 'thrown back' upon itself and thereby 'intensified' in its being. This intensification of being is its meaning" (Ambrosio 1987b, p. 27).

37. For Gadamer, an engagement in language and being positioned in the web of sociopolitical relationships are two sides of the same coin. The set of social relations and us come together into being within language: The sociopolitical relations are linguistic. Gadamer are both aware of the politics of positioning. Thus, his idea of a successful game (i.e., applying the language of epistemological pragmatism—the one with the maximum disclosure and the minimum concealment of the subject matter "itself") could not wishfully imply the removal of politics from the language games. Gadamer's vouch for a moral-practical phronesis, it seems to me, is to reconcile the ideal of truth disclosure with the power relationships in the praxis of understanding.

38. Therefore, what is said always accompanies (and covers up) what is unsaid, banned, and subjugated. It is not just a matter of falsity or error that would suppress and subjugate coercively. Rather, it is the very truth and meaning of the said that involves violence. As Foucault says, "everything is dangerous," (Foucault 1984b, p. 343) even and especially the truth (see Foucault 1980, pp. 80–1); that is, every presently subjugated truth claim might long for future totalitarian domination. Therefore, inasmuch as a deconstructive movement does not seek totality, we may agree with Laclau (1995) in linking up the "logic of hegemony" (see Laclau, Ernesto, and Chantal Mouffe. 1985) and the "logic of spectrality." For a similar interpretation of Plato's position on truth, see Gadamer 1980, p. 105.

39. Passing from the indeterminacy of the universal question to the determinacy of an answer is itself a contingent path. Lyotard calls the passing like this between two phrases *linkage*. According to him, "the linkage of one sentence onto another is problematic," and this problem is "the problem of politics" (1988, p. 11).

40. Robert Brandom shows that Heidegger's "as-structure" that distinguishes what Dasein assigns to the category of present-at-hand is essentially social. It is within the set of social interactions, which involve appropriation (Gadamer's phronesis), that a thing (ready-to-hand) gets disclosed as *this thing* (present-at-hand). Brandom maintains that for Heidegger even the ready-to-hand is socially constituted. The ready-to-hand, the present-at-hand, and Dasein constitute the three categories of being. And according to Brandom's (1983) reading of Heidegger, they are all social.

41. The notion of context connotes, primarily, the social relations that situate the meaning. It refers only derivatively (and through a reifying separation of superstructure and structure, or the dualistic subject–object distinction) to the whole web of propositions.

42. Gadamer's ontology of understanding implies that the involvement of the interpreter in the process of understanding requires the normative evaluation of (alien) beliefs. This is why, confronted with alien behavior, the interpreter uses the standards of intelligibility or rationality of *his own* context to understand it (see MacIntyre 1977, pp. 62–77).

43. Ironically enough, the "teleological" sociology seems a step ahead of the strong thesis, because it at least does not ignore that the normative evaluation of belief precedes the "sociology of error." Moreover, this observation also indicates that the division of labor between the sociologist of knowledge who concentrates exclusively on explicating the "credibility" of beliefs and the philosopher who engages in epistemic evaluations of the semantic content is a pseudo distinction. In the dialectical view, explication is already evaluation. Therefore, the modest version of the strong thesis is illusory (and the immodest version is simply wrong).

44. Nonetheless, we might still use the cause–reason distinction as a heuristic device (particularly when the cognitive constituent of social reality, the consciousness, is not developed through, and is not subject to, communicative actions). Here, capitalizing only one aspect of social reality—that is, abstracting either the causal or the rational elements of it—might be informative.

45. Georg Lukacs, quoted in Sewart 1978, p. 347. Lukacs nevertheless continues "according to their principle." He applies the "objective teleology of history" and, following Hegel, gives an immanent procedure to the succession of cognitively structured realities. However, as argued in previous chapters, the project of political epistemology's dialectical view of the path-dependency of meaning, truth, and social reality is not teleological (see Ambrosio 1987a, pp. 27–9).

4   *Différance*, deconstruction, and the project of political epistemology

1. Nominalists and realists dispute whether concepts are real or are just signs. This dispute takes place *within* metaphysical inquiry, however: Nominalists do not go beyond metaphysics. Yet a nominalist dialectician is not a nominalist metaphysician. As a dialectician, the former does not believe in metaphysics or first philosophy, and as a nominalist, he or she rejects teleological dialectics. Derrida denies any essence for meaning, any arche for reality, any essence for the appearance.

2. Cartesian epistemologists find the plurality of contingent webs of belief to be a general weakness of the coherence theory of truth. The project of political epistemology, however, indicates that the contingency of a new coherent web of belief/reality is the precondition of its truthfulness, and, moreover, that universality is the sign of untruth. This transcendental argument of the project of political epistemology is not a metaphysical move in search of the necessary, essential, telic, and constitutive of what it is to be a self, a truth-claim, an ethics, or a politics. Metaphysical measures and transcendental arguments are to curb contingency and control chance in the interest of necessity and universal continuity. The project of political epistemology, however, starts with the contingency of language and offers a normative account of truth. Thus, its analysis of the relationship between truth, politics, and ethics is a quasitranscendental argument. The contingency of language indicates that different versions of the metaphysics of presence are in fact linguistic constructa and, as a result, they cease to be

"metaphysical" as such. They are, in other words, local truth claims that pretend universality. The metaphysics of presence thus is untrue, because it closes the window of contingency.

3. Nietzsche's Dionysian woman does not believe in truth, and it is her secret. The secret of woman-truth is a paradox. Jacques Derrida writes: "If woman is truth, she at least knows that there is no truth, that truth has no place here and that no one has a place for truth. And she is woman precisely because she herself does not believe in truth itself, because she does not believe in what she is, in what she is believed to be, in what she thus is not" (Caputo 1984, p. 16).

4. According to liberal democratic theory, within the private sphere, people have the legally sanctioned right to live and act while exempted from giving public justifications for their actions. The idea of truth as a private property implies that since there is no final truth and ultimate justification, the epistemic pluralism of a liberal ironist demands him or her to exempt truth claims from the burden of justification in the public sphere and send them to the private domain.

5. The project of political epistemology is attentive to the phenomenological nature of this obligation. It gives direction and relevance to the ethical and political actions that take place at the passage. This obligation has a crucial epistemological value.

6. The project of political epistemology "links" Lyotard to Derrida in this way. After all, it is Derrida's statement that "there is nothing *beyond* the text" (1968, p. 167).

7. It seems that Rorty and Lyotard both base their antimetaphysics arguments on the notion of the contingency of language (though their articulations of contingency are different).

8. See Lyotard's analysis of this assertion: "I have analyzed thousands of documents....I have tried in vain to find a single former deportee capable of proving to me that he had really seen, with his own eyes, a gas chamber" (1988, pp. 3, 5). The one who has really seen a gas chamber, whose testimony "proves" the existence of the gas chamber, Lyotard says, is the one who is actually a victim of the chamber, the one who is actually dead and as such cannot testify. The wrong is the harm that victimizes the differend twice—as a victim of the chamber and as a victim who lacks the voice to declare his being so. Here, a totalitarian narrative of "proof" does wrong to the differend.

9. Lyotard does not talk about the "ontological status" of the "feeling" that there "are" differends calling us from within the abyss (see Rogozinski 1991, p. 115). The project of political epistemology that shares the same "sentiment," however, believes in a hyperrealism according to which the differend, the other or the singular, has a phenomenological structure of being-beyond-language. As I shall discuss later in this chapter, Derrida names this phenomenon the "structure of call," or "the Perhaps." Also, Levinas talks about this feeling as a sense of "being a hostage to the Other." The feeling is assigned to the "singular."

10. Doing justice to the differend thus has to do with the multiplicity of passages. As Lyotard points out, in the face of Nazism, one calls upon an idea of justice that would also be an idea of pluralism. For Lyotard's idea of justice as plurality, see Lyotard and Thebaud 1989, pp. 66–7.

11. Metaphysics might desire to tell us the "nature" of this *thing* called *différance*. Each articulation of what *différance* is, however, is indeed an effect, a tentative trace, within the play of differentiation. *Différance* withdraws not because it is a secret. It withdraws simply because it "is" the unstable, essenceless difference, the opening, the spacing, the desert-like *Khora*, the receptacle of things, concepts, and words that partially determines what they are and mean. It is not a substance beyond the things, words, and concepts. It "is" the tentative scheme of their arrangement.

12. For an analysis of Derrida's "quasitranscendental" approach in philosophy and to meaning, language, and law, see Caputo 1993a, pp. 157–61.

13. Derrida 1982, p. 7. For overtly political reasons, Derrida, in the 1960s, deliberately *decided* not to produce a discourse against revolution or Marxism, not to deconstruct the Marxist idea of revolution qua a *metaphysical* concept, in order to avoid contributing to the "anti-Marxist concert" of the 1968 period. He decided not to weaken "what Marxism and the proletariat can constitute as a force in France.…he does not want to devalue what [this idea] could contribute…as a force of 're-groupment'." He did not directly attack the Marxism of 1960s while he performed a series of "virtual differences or divergences" from the revolutionary project. Derrida says that this strategy was "a sort of withdrawal or retreat, a silence on Marxism—a blank signifying…that Marxism was not attacked like such and such other theoretical comfort…this blank was not neutral.…It was a perceptible political gesture" (Fraser 1993, p. 57). Political considerations, thus, partially inform, empower, and constitute the way deconstruction moves, the way the play of differentiation goes on, the way *différance* repeats itself differently, and finally the way new meaning and truth emerge within the play. Derrida's *decision* in the 1960s was political, with epistemic implications. Political and ethical practices cannot be seen as strangers to truth-making movements of the play. Therefore, responsibility toward truth cannot be detached from the ethical and political responsibility toward justice. I shall demonstrate this position later in this chapter through further examination of the sociopolitical "nature" of *différance*.

14. He also writes: "Force itself is never present; it is only a play of differences and quantities. There would be no force in general without the difference between forces; and here the difference of quantity counts more than the content of the quantity, more than absolute size itself.…The difference of quantity is the essence of force, the relation of force to force" (1982, p. 17).

15. Here, Derrida uses the term *trace* instead of *sign*, indicating that *différance* is not limited to the play of semiological phonic and graphic signs.

16. Against the backdrop of discussing Derrida's idea of play, I should use the term *dialectics* very cautiously. The play of difference is not a Hegelian dialectical relationship. Hegel's difference penetrates into discourse and takes the shape of a logical difference between ideas—a logical difference that will be resolved, overcome, and integrated in the synthesis. The synthesis thus restores identity in a manner of a closet essentialism by making difference (dialectics, logical difference) internal to the self-presence of the absolute, the essence, the arche. Derrida dislikes this view for its metaphysical logocentrism. Indeed, Derrida's *différance* is a play of forces that does not return to identity. *Différance* repeats itself *differently*. For Derrida, difference

is not contradiction, but difference, period! Derrida does not like teleology (see Dastur 1995, p. 11). For a comparison between Hegel and Derrida on this topic, see Marsh 1990, pp. 148–9.

17. Following Nietzsche, Derrida regards the consciousness as an effect, a locus, of the differential play of forces.

18. According to Hegel, the general context for the reciprocal formation of two or more self-consciousnesses is conflict and opposition. Within this context, the assertion of each self-consciousness is a reaction to the concept of self imposed by another (as the limit of self) through practice. Thus, self-consciousness forms itself through resistance to being self for other. The self and its "freedom" and "autonomy," therefore, have to do with the capacity to resist all attempts at representation. Hegel decontextualizes, dehistoricizes, and universalizes the threat of the other to the self. However, the project of political epistemology demands a material and experimental investigation of exactly *when and how* in a specific sociopolitical context the formation of identity becomes agonistic or rather, moral/*ethichical*. For a critique of the decontextualizing accounts of the self, see Alcoff 2006, ch. 3.

19. As we have seen, this difference is not a Hegelian dialectic. It is a nonantithetical differentiation: a differentiation that harbors love, hospitality, and responsibility—a differentiation in which the exteriority, separation, and distinctness of the other will not be eradicated through a Hegelian synthesis of the self and the other. On the other hand, as Derrida explains, the other is "otherwise than myself." Therefore, the other is not wholly and infinitely other. The exteriority is not absolute: "the Other as *alter-ego,* signifies the Other as another who is irreducible to my ego, precisely because he is himself an ego or has the form of an ego" (1980, p. 125).

20. There is no gap to be leapt over from knowing descriptively that the other is looking at me to the normative obligation that I sense to justify myself. As a phenomenological structure, the descriptive knowing and the normative obligation are simultaneously constitutive of my identity.

21. The term *Being* connotes Heidegger's ontology. From a political epistemological perspective, Levinas's sentence reminds us that this ontology is partially constructed by the way a concrete social individual, Martin Heidegger, lived his sociopolitical life and acted in the play of difference. Let us imagine a Martin Heidegger who left Germany for love of the Jewish Arendt, came to the United States, and found a decent job as a philosophy teacher in a cosmopolitan city like New York; a Heidegger who was more "welcoming" to the people and ideas of non-Greco-Germanic descent, to poets who happened to be otherwise than Holderlin; a Heidegger who played the play of differentiation *differently*—had a different "existent." The project of political epistemology would say that in this case Martin Heidegger's ontology would be different. Derrida and Levinas would also agree. Heidegger's insensitivity and closure toward the concrete, suffering, eating, loving, and dying other is not an accidental issue irrelevant to Heidegger's philosophy. It is, rather, *systematically* interwoven in Heidegger's ontology. His ontology is partially inscribed in the way he acted the play—the way in which he was responsive not to the call of the suffering other but to the "call of Being." Caputo's (1992) reading is an excellent *deconstruction* of Heidegger's philosophy. Deconstruction takes place ethically and uncovers the unjustness

and closure toward the other that informs and gives meaning to Heidegger's ontology. Caputo's deconstruction shows how the *play* in which Heidegger's ontology is inscribed is closed to the other. In here, in this closure, resides the *untruth* of Heidegger's *metaphysics*. Caputo's (1991a) deconstruction demonstrates that there is nothing accidental in Heidegger's call for war and the Nazi domination: *Kampf* is to shape a new epoch of Being, and compared to this disclosure of Being, the suffering of individual victims/others is insignificant.

22. *Ethicity* is older than ethics and ontology. Ethics as a branch of knowledge is derivative and constructed. It can be deconstructed. *Ethicity*, however, is what gives movement to the deconstruction of ethics. It is *undeconstructible*.

23. As mentioned before, *ethicity* is a specific sort of praxis that takes place in the intersubjective sphere of social life. It is not just a "subjective" psychological virtue but a mode of collective social being. It has to do with the way in which social institutions of power are arranged, the way the play "is." A totalitarian mode of social economy of power that stops the fluidity of *différance* lacks ethicity. Hence, ethicity has also to do with politics, and the latter is a key to the happening of understanding. This is how the project of political epistemology extends Levinas's analysis of the ethics of the self–other relationship to a more social level. As Derrida reminds us, Levinas's analysis is half-baked if one forgets that from the very beginning; what we have is the multiplicity of self–other–the other "others" relationships—the society.

24. Derrida 2002, p. 33. According to Derrida, the phenomenological structure of *Perhaps* harbors the same affirmation: *Perhaps* there is still something, the remainder, that is concealed and remains to come. Perhaps resists the closure of totalitarian acts within the play of differentiation (see 2006, p. 38).

25. The hyperreal is "something" beyond the "real" thing that gets produced in language. A hyperrealist *ethicically*—as well as *politically/strategically*—affirms that such a singular referent-without-difference "exists," though he or she does not "know" this matter for an ontological certainty. (Knowledge comes after language.) A hyperrealist has "faith" that there are things that cannot be put into words. For the idea of hyperrealism, see Caputo 2000. The hyperreal is comparable to the potentiality within the object, the "more" that has not come to the concept/language. It seems to me that Adorno's idea of potentiality as reality is not a total stranger to this understanding of hyperrealism.

26. Colonialism, racism, and gender discrimination are familiar examples of metaphysical violence to the other. These metaphysical theories are constitutive of, and constructed by, the sociopolitical and historical reality of suppression, that is, the particular unjust plays of forces (*différances*). "Rituals of power"—strategies of excluding, expelling, silencing the contaminating other—are indeed moves and acts within the play of differentiation. Derrida writes: "There is no racism without a language. The point is not that acts of racial violence are only words but rather that they have to have a word....It [the language of racism, racist *différance*] institutes, declares, writes, inscribes, prescribes a system of marks, it outlines space in order to assign forced residence or to close off borders. It does not discern, it discriminates" (1985, p. 292).

27. It is of course a "feeling," not a metaphysical articulation of the "essence" of the implemented wrong or the wronged differend. However, this feeling is of more humane and, as argued before, epistemic relevance than "ontology." It is, as Lyotard says, a feeling that is not a phrase. It is "outside of" language: It is a feeling of being claimed by an "enigmatic" call from beyond, a call that makes us anxious and awakens an obligation to reach out for "someone" who we do not yet know. It is a feeling that makes us wakeful, astonished, and anguished. Lyotard writes: "The silent feeling that signals a differend remains to be listened to. Responsibility to thought requires it. This is the way in which Marxism has not come to an end, as the feeling of the differend" (1988, p. 171; also see Rogozinski 1991, p. 115). Marx was "haunted" by this enigmatic call (see Derrida 1994, pp. 77–94). Marx cautions us that doing cold and pedantic ontology to "discover" the universal "essence" of the calling in general is but an irresponsible way of evading the obligation of reaching out to the subjugated caller *here and now*. For Marx, metaphysics is an ideology inasmuch as it cools us off and "exorcizes" the specter. Exorcizing the specter is a way of depoliticizing philosophy. For a study of the politics of the depoliticization of philosophy, see McCumber 1996.
28. Richard Bernstein makes this suggestion (1987, p. 108). Following Derrida's "Specters of Marx," we can see Marx's work as a deconstruction of the capitalist mode of cognitive/material reality.
29. This is not a context-free decision, however. It is situated, and, as I shall argue, its morality has a close tie with its situatedness in an ever-changing play. In other words, the decision takes place within a play, on the breakpoints and cracks that a hegemony-seeking play wants to hide. The contextuality of this decision, the fact that deconstruction is a move within the ever-changing play, refutes a voluntarist notion of deconstruction or a solipsist idea of truth. Furthermore, the situatedness of deconstruction makes it clear that deconstruction is not a *method* for understanding the text and interpreting or implementing sociopolitical changes. Deconstruction "happens," Derrida says. There is no method of deconstruction, simply because deconstruction knows no a priori principle to follow. Its lack of principles is exactly what makes deconstruction possible and necessary. The moral and political aspects of deconstruction are indeed contingent upon this lack of principles. Moreover, the unforeseeability of truth as the coming of the wholly other that smashes the present horizon testifies to the fact that *methodology* is always late: It comes after that truth has already arrived. Thus, political epistemology agrees with Thomas Kuhn (and, indeed, with Hegel) that it is only after the explosion of the new truth, the event that blasts the old paradigm, and only within the new "normal science" period, that *methodology* shows up.

    Deconstruction is a practical/strategic/political reshuffling of the play. It is not a method. Nor is it an analysis that presupposes and pursues the reduction of entities to their essentials, for essence is itself an effect of the play. Deconstruction is not a transcendental critique of Kantian kind, for the transcendental *différance*, as discussed above, is a quasitranscendental. Moreover, deconstruction is not an act produced by the subject, for the subject is a trace. To tell the truth, deconstruction does not have an essence. It escapes a priori ontology, for ontology is constructed within the play and can be deconstructed. Deconstruction is not an entity, a thing. "It deconstructs itself whenever something takes place" (see Critchley 1995, p. 22; Derrida 1989, p. 23). "Deconstruction deconstructs"; that is, it takes place when we make a move in the name of justice. The specific nature of the move, its semantic content and political load, and so forth cannot be defined a priori. This much, however, can be said: that the move is to give new bent or twist to the current effects of the play in order to open some space, some nonsites, for certain unforeseeable effects. Deconstruction thus is a transgression beyond the present effects. Deconstruction is a *praxical* and *practical* engagement, it is *doing-really-something,* it is *not-staying-inert* when feeling the fever of *weak messianism.* Deconstruction is not to be grasped from "outside" as a matter for speculation. As demonstrated before, political epistemology promotes deconstruction as the "method" of finding and forging truth. Political epistemology, like deconstruction, is the favorite epistemology of those who feel the *weak messianism.* I shall elaborate on this crucial point later.

30.   For exemplars of new actors, we might think of new words, signs, and concepts, and thus new signifieds. New criticisms; new social, political, cultural, and economic institutions; NGOs; women's studies programs; Research Group for the Teaching of Philosophy; International College of Philosophy (Derrida's own deconstructive moves); new forces; new sites of resistance to power relations, etc.

31.   From a political epistemological perspective, this statement underlines an interesting similarity between Adorno's conceptualization of political activity as alteration of the constellation and Derrida's idea of political activity as strategic intervention/deconstruction of the *différance.*

32.   See Derrida 1978, p. 280. For Derrida, metaphysics establishes ethical-ontological hierarchies that harbor subordination and violence. Thus, Derrida's criticism against metaphysics is primarily political and ethical. Also, as the project of political epistemology shows, metaphysics, as unethical moves within the play, fosters a danger of closure. Hence, metaphysics is untrue, inasmuch as it claims universality and totalitarianism. Metaphysics as archelogy, as a privileged access to an absolutely stable referent-without-difference, is untrue and politicoethically wrong. However, there is a second meaning to metaphysics that has to do with making distinctions (with inclusions and exclusions that usually accompany distinctions). The second meaning of metaphysical thinking is deeply interwoven into the ways we think, argue, and even make ethical evaluations and political criticisms. There is nothing "essentially" contaminating with any distinction, exclusion, and inclusion. (Indeed, to think otherwise is itself a metaphysical move akin to archelogy.) What is humane and just, however, is to always question and problematize the status of what we take as the more principal and more essential among the two sides of each distinction and hierarchy. Deconstruction, for example, does not say that there is no subject/knower, no sovereign, no subject–object dichotomy or no subject of law versus subject of morality distinction. Deconstruction rather highlights the point that these dichotomies and hierarchies are constructed in a play and, as such, they can be deconstructed. (Feminist epistemologies, for example, deconstruct the notion

of subject knower and show its repressive function for the social status of women as nonknowers.) Derrida himself does not think that all metanarratives are illegitimate in an a priori way. As his life and works testify, he is committed to a metanarrative of emancipation (emancipation without totality) or to universals such as human rights. What deconstruction does is it "loosens up" the tongue of philosophy, metaphysics, and the law, to interrupt their rigid dichotomies in order to make them more receptive toward the other—and also to make community "more porous" by staying loyal to idiosyncrasies of the singular and the contingency of the play that together amount to the impossibility of final Truth. In fact, the deconstructibility of the present play is a function of the phenomenological structure of hope and expectation in us—a hope and expectation for the coming of the event. There is nothing within the play that is undeconstructible. Deconstruction is to save the play (philosophy, sociopolitical reality, authority, and the law) from the danger of narcissistic fetishism (see Caputo 1996; Caputo and Raschke 2002).

33. Mourning is remembering the memory and spirit of the dead and, simultaneously, respecting their being different from us at the present time (Derrida 1986, pp. 28–32).

34. The project of political epistemology brings into view that concepts and theories in *Das Kapital* owe their epistemic content and meaning, in part, to Marx's strategic moves. Therefore, an apt evaluation of, for example, the exchange value versus use value dichotomy, or Marx's labor theory of value and ownership, must attend to the political function and context of these concepts as a constitutive part of their meaning and value. For example, it is said that the liberalist John Locke believes in the "same" labor theory of ownership that Marx does. However, while the political relevance of John Locke's theory of property is to enlarge and concentrate landholding in favor of capitalist landlords and farmers and exclude the peasants (Wood 1999, pp. 80–3), Marx's labor theory of property is to empower the workers and address their alienation from their products. While Locke's theory is to exclude the other of the capitalist, Marx's is to open a spot for it.

35. As mentioned before, this move is strategic. In a specific moment of the play, responding to the call might demand from the participants a "universal" theory as guidance to what sociopolitical justice is and what the best course of action looks like. (Needless to say, this "universal" is indexed to the context, and therefore, it is a particular-universal.) Marcuse states: "That man is a rational being, that this being requires freedom, and that happiness is his highest good are all universal propositions whose progressive impetus drives precisely from their universality. Universality gives them an almost revolutionary character.... In a society whose reality gives the lie to all these universals, philosophy cannot make them concrete. Under such conditions, adherence to universality is more important than its philosophical destruction" (1968, pp. 152–3). While justice as care for and responsiveness to the call of the singular is undeconstructible, this latter theory of sociopolitical justice is a specific move in the play. It is, therefore, deconstructible; otherwise, it becomes foreclosed to the other calls of other "others."

36. "Absolute injustice would occur if the pragmatics of obligation, that is, the possibility of continuing to play that game of the just, were excluded. That

is what is unjust. Not the opposite of the just, but that which prohibits that the question of just and the unjust be, and remain, raised. Thus, all terror, annihilation, massacre, etc., or their threat, are, by definition, unjust" (Lyotard and Thebaud 1989, pp. 66–7). The totalitarian game, in Lyotard's terms, is unjust because it rejects the plurality and multiplicity that are associated with the opening for the always to-come other: "Can there be then a plurality of justices? Or is the idea of justice the idea of a plurality? That is not the same question. I truly believe that the question we face now is that of a plurality, the idea of a justice that would at the same time be that of a plurality" (p. 95). Lyotard promotes the idea of justice as multiplicity, as well as the multiplicity of justices.

37. For the notion of "logocentrism" and its violence toward "the alterity that refuses to be totally domesticated," see Derrida 1984, p. 117.

38. As we have seen, political epistemology is not a traditional, but a critical, theory. It denies the normative–descriptive dichotomy. Its unit of analysis is cognitive/material reality. It does not believe in universal truth, but local, situated, and indexical truths. Its "knower" is intersubjective and "essentially" social. Its idea of coherence does not refer to the web of propositions, but to the mutual constitutiveness and support among constituents of material/cognitive reality. It is self-conscious about its political function and ethical responsibility. It is strategic and takes position. In all these features, it is different from Cartesian epistemology.

39. The term *case* itself reflects the particular-universal dialectics: Something becomes a case by being-a-case-of-a-universal. Therefore, I use it cautiously here. In other words, a "case" is calculable by a formula, so the way we respond to it is dictated by principles. Singular is always otherwise than a case.

Works Cited

Adorno, Theodor. 1967. "The Sociology of Knowledge and Its Consciousness." In *Prisms*, trans. Samuel and Shierry Weber. London: Neville Spearman, pp. 35–50.

——. 1968. "Scientific Experiences of a European Scholar in America." In *The Intellectual Migration; Europe and America, 1930–1960*, ed. Donald Fleming and Bernard Bailyn. Cambridge, MA: Belknap, pp. 338–70.

——. 1972. "Society." In *The Legacy of the German Refugee Intellectuals*, ed. Robert Boyers. New York: Schocken Books, pp. 144–53.

——. 1973. *Negative Dialectics*. Trans. E. B. Ashton. New York: Seabury Press.

——. 1974. *Minima Moralia: Reflections from Damaged Life*. Trans. E. F. N. Jephcott. London: Verso.

——. 1976a. "Introduction." In *The Positivist Dispute in German Sociology*, ed. Theodor W. Adorno et al., trans. Glyn Adey and David Frisby. London: Heinemann, pp. 1–67.

——. 1976b. "On the Logic of Social Sciences." In *The Positivist Dispute in German Sociology*, ed. Theodor W. Adorno et al., trans. Glyn Adey and David Frisby. London: Heinemann, pp. 105–22.

——. 1976c. "Sociology and Empirical Research." In *The Positivist Dispute in German Sociology*, ed. Theodor W. Adorno et al., trans. Glyn Adey and David Frisby. London: Heinemann, pp. 68–86.

——. 1998. "Why Still Philosophy." In *Critical Models, Interventions and Catchwords*, trans. Henry W. Pickford. New York: Columbia University Press, pp. 5–19.

——. 2000a. "The Actuality of Philosophy." In *Adorno Reader*, ed. Brian O'Connor. Oxford: Blackwell, pp. 23–39.

——. 2000b. "Metacritique of Epistemology." In *Adorno Reader*, ed. Brian O'Connor. Oxford: Blackwell, pp. 112–36.

——. 2000c. "Subject and Object." In *Adorno Reader*, ed. Brian O'Connor. Oxford: Blackwell, pp. 137–52.

——. 2001. *Metaphysics: Concepts and Problems*. Ed. Rolf Tiedemann, trans. Edmund Jephcott. Stanford, CA: Stanford University Press.

Adorno, Theodor, and Anson Rabinbach. 1975. "Culture Industry Reconsidered." *New German Critique* 6: 12–19.

Agamben, Giorgio. 2005. "The State of Exception as a Paradigm of Government." In *State of Exception*, trans. Kevin Attell. Chicago, IL: University of Chicago Press, pp. 1–31.

Alcoff, Linda. 1993a. "Foucault as Epistemologist." *The Philosophical Forum* 14(2): 95–124.

——. 1993b. "How Is Epistemology Political?" In *Radical Philosophy, Tradition, Counter-Tradition, Politics*, ed. Roger S. Gottlieb. Philadelphia, PA: Temple University Press, pp. 65–85.

——. 1996. *Real Knowing: New Versions of the Coherence Theory*. Ithaca, NY: Cornell University Press.

Alcoff, Linda. 2000. "Power/Knowledge in the Colonial Unconscious: A Dialogue between Dussel and Foucault." In *Thinking from the Underside of History*, ed. Linda M. Alcoff and Eduardo Mendieta. New York: Rowan and Littlefield, pp. 249–68.
——. 2006. *Visible Identities: Race, Gender, and the Self.* Oxford: Oxford University Press.
Althusser, Louis. 1971. "Ideology and Ideological State Apparatuses (Notes towards an Investigation)." In *Lenin and Philosophy and Other Essays*, trans. Ben Brewster. New York: Monthly Review Press, pp. 127–86.
Always, Joan. 1995. *Critical Theory and Political Possibilities: Conceptions of Emancipatory Politics in the Works of Horkheimer, Adorno, Marcuse, and Habermas.* London: Greenwood Press.
Ambrosio, Francis. 1986a. "Dawn and Dusk: Gadamer and Heidegger on Truth." *Man and World* 19: 21–53.
——. 1986b. "Gadamer and the Ontology of Language: What Remains Unsaid." *Journal of the British Society for Phenomenology* 17(2): 124–42.
——. 1987a. "Gadamer: On Making Oneself at Home with Hegel." *The Owl of Minerva: Quarterly Journal of the Hegel Society of America* 19(1): 23–40.
——. 1987b. "Gadamer, Plato, and the Discipline of Dialogue." *International Philosophical Quarterly* 27(1): 17–32.
——. 1988. "Gadamer and Aristotle: Hermeneutics as Participation in Tradition." *Proceedings of the American Catholic Philosophical Association* 62: 174–82.
Ameriks, Karl. 1985. "Hegel's Critique of Kant's Theoretical Philosophy." *Philosophy and Phenomenological Research* 46 (1): 1–35.
Antoni, C. 1972. "Georg Lukacs: The Search for a Revolutionary Subject." In *The Unknown Dimension*, ed. D. Howard and K. Klare. New York: Basic Books.
Arendt, Hannah. 1990. "Philosophy and Politics." *Social Research* 57(1): 73–103.
——. 1998. *The Human Condition*. Introduction by Margaret Canovan. Chicago: University of Chicago Press.
——. 2005. "Introduction into Politics." In *The Promise of Politics*, ed. Jerome Kohn. New York: Schocken, pp. 93–200.
——. 2006a. "Freedom and Politics." In *The Liberty Reader*, ed. David Miller. London: Paradigm Publishers, pp. 58–79.
——. 2006b. *Eichmann in Jerusalem: A Report on the Banality of Evil.* London: Penguin Classics.
Aristotle. 1996. *The Politics and The Constitution of Athens*. Ed. Stephen Everson. Cambridge: Cambridge University Press.
Arndt, Stephen. 1987. "Transcendental Method and Transcendental Arguments." *International Philosophical Quarterly* 27(1): 43–58.
Avineri, Shlomo. 1968. *The Social and Political Thought of Karl Marx.* Cambridge: Cambridge University Press.
Barnes, Barry. 1974. *Scientific Knowledge and Sociological Theory.* London: Routledge and Kegan Paul.
——. 1977. *Interests and the Growth of Knowledge.* London: Routledge and Kegan Paul.
Barnes, Barry, and David Bloor. 1982. "Relativism, Rationalism, and the Sociology of Knowledge." In *Rationality and Relativism*, ed. Martin Hollis and Steven Lukes. Oxford: Blackwell, pp. 21–47.

Barnes, Barry, David Bloor, and John Henry. 1996. *Scientific Knowledge: A Sociological Approach*. Chicago: University of Chicago Press.

Barnes, Barry, and David Edge. 1982. "General Introduction." In *Science in Context: Readings in the Sociology of Science*, ed. Barry Barnes and David Edge. Cambridge, MA: MIT Press, pp. 1–12.

Beiser, Frederick. 1993. "Hegel's Historicism." In *The Cambridge Companion to Hegel*, ed. Frederick C. Beiser. Cambridge: Cambridge University Press, pp. 270–300.

Benhabib, Seyla. 1986. *Critique, Norm, and Utopia: A Study of the Foundations of Critical Theory*. New York: Columbia University Press.

Benjamin, Walter. 1969. "Theses on the Philosophy of History." In *Illuminations*, edited and with an introduction by Hannah Arendt, trans. Harry Zohn. New York: Schocken Books, pp. 253–64.

Berger, Peter, and Thomas Luckmann. 1967. *The Social Construction of Reality: A Treatise in the Sociology of Knowledge*. New York: Anchor Books.

Berlin, Isaiah. 1991. *The Crooked Timber of Humanity: Chapters in the History of Ideas*. Ed. Henry Hardy. New York: Knopf.

Berman, Russell. 2002. "Adorno's Politics." In *Adorno: A Critical Reader*, ed. Nigel C. Gibson and Andrew Rubin. Oxford: Blackwell, pp. 110–31.

Bernstein, J. M. 2001. *Adorno, Disenchantment and Ethics*. Cambridge: Cambridge University Press.

——. 2004. "Negative Dialectic as Fate: Adorno and Hegel." In *The Cambridge Companion to Adorno*, ed. Tom Huhn. Cambridge: Cambridge University Press, pp. 19–50.

Bernstein, Richard. 1982. "From Hermeneutics to Praxis." *Review of Metaphysics* 35: 823–45.

——. 1987. "Serious Play: The Ethico-Political Horizon of Jacque Derrida." *Journal of Speculative Philosophy* 1: 93–117.

——. 1996. *Hannah Arendt and the Jewish Question*. Cambridge, MA: The MIT Press.

Bienenstock, Myriam. 1993. "On Marx's 'Hegelian' Practice of Abstraction." *International Studies in Philosophy* 25(3): 87–91.

Bloor, David. 1973. "Wittgenstein and Mannheim on the Sociology of Mathematics." *Studies in History and Philosophy of Science* 4: 173–91.

——. 1981. "The Strengths of the Strong Programme." *Philosophy of Social Sciences* 11: 199–213.

——. 1991. *Knowledge and Social Imagery*. Chicago, IL: University of Chicago Press.

Bossart, W. H. 1982. "Hegel on the Inverted World." *The Philosophical Forum* 13(4): 326–41.

Bottomore, Tom. 1956. "Some Reflections on the Sociology of Knowledge." *British Journal of Sociology* 7(1): 52–8.

Bottomore, Tom, Laurence Harris, V. G. Kiernan, and Ralph Miliband, eds. 1983. *A Dictionary of Marxist Thought*. Cambridge, MA: Harvard University Press.

Brandom, Robert. 1983. "Heidegger's Categories in Being and Time." *Monist* 66(3): 387–410.

Brym, R. J. 1977. "Democracy and the Intellectuals: A Test of Karl Mannheim's Thesis." *Scottish Journal of Sociology* 1: 173–83.

Buck-Morss, Susan. 1979. *The Origin of Negative Dialectics: Theodor Adorno, Walter Benjamin, and the Frankfurt Institute*. New York: Free Press.

Canguilhem, George. 2005. "The Death of Man, or Exhaustion of the Cogito?" In *Cambridge Companion to Foucault*, ed. Gary Gutting, trans. Catherine Porter. Cambridge: Cambridge University Press, pp. 74–94.

Canovan, Margaret. 1992. *Hannah Arendt: A Reinterpretation of Her Political Thought*. Cambridge: Cambridge University Press.

Caputo, John. 1984. "Supposing Truth to Be a Woman: Heidegger, Nietzsche, Derrida." *Tulane Studies in Philosophy* 32: 15–21.

——. 1987. *Radical Hermeneutics: Repetition, Deconstruction and the Hermeneutic Project*. Bloomington, IN: Indiana University Press.

——. 1988. "Demythologizing Heidegger: Aletheia and the History of Being." *Review of Metaphysics* 41: 519–46.

——. 1989a. "Disseminating Originary Ethics and the Ethics of Dissemination." In *The Question of the Other: Essays in Contemporary Continental Philosophy*, ed. Arleen B. Dallery and Charles E. Scott. Albany, NY: SUNY Press, pp. 55–63.

——. 1989b. "Gadamer's Closet Essentialism: A Derridian Critique." In *Dialogue and Deconstruction: The Gadamer–Derrida Encounter*, ed. Richard Palmer. Albany, NY: SUNY Press, pp. 258–64.

——. 1991a. "Heidegger's Kampf: The Difficulty of Life." *Graduate Faculty Philosophy Journal* 14(2): 61–83.

——. 1991b. "Hyperbolic Justice: Deconstruction, Myth, and Politics." *Research in Phenomenology* 21: 3–20.

——. 1992. "Heidegger's Scandal: Thinking and the Essence of the Victim." In *The Heidegger Case: On Philosophy and Politics*, ed. Tom Rockmore and Joseph Margolis. Philadelphia, PA: Temple University Press, pp. 265–81.

——. 1993a. "On Not Circumventing the Quasi-Transcendental: The Case of Rorty and Derrida." In *Working through Derrida*, ed. Gary B. Madison. Chicago, IL: Northwestern University Press, pp. 147–271.

——. 1993b. "On Not Knowing Who We Are: Madness, Hermeneutics, and the Night of Truth in Foucault." In *Foucault and the Critique of Institutions*, ed. John D. Caputo and Mark Yount. University Park, PA: Pennsylvania State University Press, pp. 117–39.

——. 1996. "A Community without Truth: Derrida and the Impossible Community." *Research in Phenomenology* 26: 25–37.

——. 1997. "A Commentary: Deconstruction in a Nutshell." In *Deconstruction in a Nutshell: A Conversation with Jacques Derrida*, ed. John D. Caputo. New York: Fordham University Press, pp. 33–200.

——. 1997. *The Prayers and Tears of Jacques Derrida: Religion without Religion*. Bloomington, IN: Indiana University Press.

——. 2000. "For the Love of Things Themselves: Derrida's Hyper-Realism." *Journal for Cultural and Religious Theory* 1, no. 3 (August 2000). Available at http://www.jcrt.org/archives/01.3/caputo.shtml (accessed July 3, 2008).

——. 2003a. "After Derrida Comes the Future." *The Journal for Cultural and Religious Theory* 4, no. 2 (April 2003). Available at www.jcrt.org/archives/04.2/caputo.shtml (accessed July 3, 2008).

——. 2003b. "Against Principles: A Sketch of an Ethics without Ethics." In *The Ethical: Blackwell's Reading in Continental Philosophy*, ed. Edith Wyschogrod and Charles McKenny. Oxford: Blackwell, pp. 169–80.

Caputo, John, and Carl Raschke. 2002. "Loosening Philosophy's Tongue: A Conversation with Jack Caputo." *The Journal for Cultural and Religious Theory* 3, no. 2 (April 2002). Available at www.jcrt.org/archives/03.2/caputo_raschke. shtml (accessed July 3, 2008).

Caputo, John, and Jacques Derrida. 1997. *Deconstruction in a Nutshell: A Conversation with Jacques Derrida*, ed. John D. Caputo. New York: Fordham University Press.

Chambers, Simon. 2004. "The Politics of Critical Theory." In *The Cambridge Companion to Critical Theory*, ed. Fred Rush. Cambridge: Cambridge University Press, pp. 219–47.

Chisholm, Roderick. 1978. "What Is a Transcendental Argument?" *Neue Hefte fur Philosophie* 14: 19–22.

Coles, Romand. 1995. "Identity and Difference in the Ethical Positions of Adorno and Habermas." In *The Cambridge Companion to Habermas*, ed. Stephen K. White. Cambridge: Cambridge University Press, pp. 19–45.

Cook, Deborah. 2005. "From the Actual to the Possible: Nonidentity Thinking." *Constellations* 12(1): 21–35.

Critchley, Simon. 1995. "On Derrida's Specters of Marx." *Philosophy and Social Criticism* 21(3):1–30.

——. 1999. *The Ethics of Deconstruction: Derrida and Levinas.* West Lafayette, IN: Purdue University Press.

Dallmayr, Fred. 1981. *Twilight of Subjectivity: Contribution to a Post-Individualist Theory of Politics.* Amherst, MA: University of Massachusetts Press.

Dancy, Jonathan. 1985. *Introduction to Contemporary Epistemology.* Oxford: Blackwell.

Dancy, Jonathan, and Ernest Sosa, eds. 1992. *A Companion to Epistemology.* Oxford: Blackwell.

Dastur, Francoise. 1995. "Heidegger and Derrida: On Play of Difference." *Epoche* 3(1–2): 1–23.

Derrida, Jacques. 1968. "But, beyond…Open Letter to Anne McClintock and Rob Nixon." Trans. Peggy Kamuf. *Critical Inquiry* 13(1): 155–70.

——. 1976. *Of Grammatology.* Trans. Gayatri Spivak. Baltimore, MD: Johns Hopkins University Press.

——. 1978. "Structure, Sign and Play in the Discourse of Human Sciences." In *Writing and Difference*, trans. Alan Bass. Chicago, IL: University of Chicago Press, pp. 278–94.

——. 1980. "Violence and Metaphysics: An Essay on the Thought of Emmanuel Levinas." In *Writing and Difference*, trans. Alan Bass. Chicago, IL: University of Chicago Press, pp. 79–153.

——. 1981. *Positions.* Trans. Alan Bass. Chicago, IL: University of Chicago Press.

——. 1982. *Margins of Philosophy.* Trans. A. Bass. Chicago, IL: University of Chicago Press.

——. 1984. "Deconstruction and the Other." In *Dialogue with Contemporary Thinkers*, ed. Richard Kearney. Manchester, UK: Manchester University Press, pp. 105–26.

——. 1985. "Racism's Last Word." Trans. Peggy Kamuf. *Critical Inquiry* 12: 290–9.

——. 1986. *Memories: For Paul de Man.* Trans. Cecile Lindsay, Jonathan Culler, and Eduardo Cadava. New York: Columbia University Press.

Derrida, Jacques. 1988. *Limited Inc.* Trans. S. Weber. Chicago, IL: Northwestern University Press.

——. 1989. "Psyche: Inventions of the Other." Trans. Catherine Porter. In *Reading DeMan Reading*, ed. Lindsay Waters and Wlad Godzich. Minneapolis, MN: University of Minnesota Press, pp. 25–65.

——. 1990. "Force of Law: The 'Mystical Foundation of Authority'." Trans. Mary Quaintance. *Cardozo Law Review* 11(5–6): 919–1047.

——. 1992. "Mochlos, or, The Conflict of the Faculties." In *Logomachia: The Conflict of the Faculties*, trans. Richard Rand and Amy Wygant. Lincoln, NE: University of Nebraska Press, pp. 3–34.

——. 1994. *Specters of Marx: The State of Debt, the Work of Mourning and the New International*. Trans. Peggy Kamuf. London: Routledge.

——. 1995a. "Khora." In *On the Name*, trans. Ian McLeod and ed. Thomas Dutoit. Stanford, CA: Stanford University Press, pp. 87–127.

——. 1995b. *On the Name*. Ed. Thomas Dutoit. Stanford, CA: Stanford University Press.

——. 1995c. *Points…Interviews, 1974–94*. Ed. Elizabeth Weber and Trans. Peggy Kamuf et al. Stanford, CA: Stanford University Press.

——. 1996. "Remarks on Deconstruction and Pragmatism." In *Deconstruction and Pragmatism*, ed. Chantal Mouffe. New York: Routledge, pp. 77–87.

——. 1999. "A Word of Welcome." In *Adieu to Emmanuel Levinas*, trans. P. Brault and M. Nass. Stanford, CA: Stanford University Press, pp. 15–126.

——. 2002. "Negotiations." In *Negotiations, Interventions and Interviews, 1971–2001*, trans. and ed. Elizabeth Rottenberg. Stanford, CA: Stanford University Press, pp. 11–40.

Derrida, Jacques, Richard Kearney, and Mark Dooley. 1999. "Hospitality, Justice and Responsibility: A Dialogue with Jacques Derrida." In *Questioning Ethics, Contemporary Debates in Philosophy*, ed. Richard Kearney and Mark Dooley. London: Routledge, pp. 65–83.

Derrida, Jacques, and Maurizio Ferraris. 2001. *A Taste for the Secret*. Cambridge, MA: Polity Press.

Dews, Peter. 1987. *Logic of Disintegration: Post-Structuralist Thought and the Claims of Critical Theory*. London: Verso.

Dolan, Frederick. 2000. "Arendt on Philosophy and Politics." In *The Cambridge Companion to Hannah Arendt*, ed. Dana Villa. Cambridge: Cambridge University Press, pp. 261–76.

Dubiel, Helmut. 1985. "The Third Phase: The Critique of Instrumental Reason, 1940–1945." In *Theory and Politics: Studies in the Development of Critical Theory*, trans. Benjamin Gregg. Cambridge, MA: MIT Press, pp. 69–119.

Dussel, Enrique. 1995. *The Invention of the Americas: Eclipse of "the Other" and the Myth of Modernity*. Trans. Michael D. Barber. New York: Continuum.

Engelskirchen, Howard. 2004. "Powers and Particulars: Adorno and Scientific Realism." *Journal of Critical Realism* 3(1): 1–21.

Farago, Peter. 2002. "Relativism in the Sociology of Knowledge." *Periodica Polytechnica Ser. Soc. Man. Sci.* 10(1): 177–88.

Feuerbach, Ludwig. 1855. *The Essence of Christianity*. Trans. Marian Evans. New York: Calvin Blanchard.

Feyerabend, Paul. 1970. "Against Method: Outline of an Anarchistic Theory of Knowledge." In *Analyses of Theories and Methods of Physics and Psychology*, Minnesota Studies in the Philosophy of Science 4, ed. M. Radner and S. Winokur. Minneapolis, MN: University of Minnesota Press, pp. 17–130.

Figal, Gunter. 2002. "The Doing of the Thing Itself: Gadamer's Hermeneutic Ontology of Language." In *The Cambridge Companion to Gadamer*, ed. Robert J. Dostal. Cambridge: Cambridge University Press, pp. 102–25.

Findlay, John. 1981. "The Central Role of the Thing-in-Itself in Kant." *Philosophical Forum* 13(1): 51–65.

Finlayson, James G. 2002. "Adorno on the Ethical and the Ineffable." *European Journal of Philosophy* 10(1): 1–25.

Flay, Joseph. 1970. "Hegel's 'Inverted World'." *The Review of Metaphysics* 23(4): 662–78.

Floyd, Wayne, Jr. 1989. "To Welcome the Other: Totality and Theory in Levinas and Adorno." *Philosophy and Theology* 4(2): 145–70.

Foucault, Michel. 1980. "Two Lectures." In *Power/Knowledge: Selected Interviews and Other Writings, 1972–1977*, trans. C. Gordon et al. New York: Pantheon, pp. 78–106.

——. 1984a. "Nietzsche, Genealogy, History." In *Foucault Reader*, ed. Paul Rabinow. New York: Pantheon, pp. 76–100.

——. 1984b. "On the Genealogy of Ethics: An Overview of Work in Progress." In *Foucault Reader*, ed. Paul Rabinow. New York: Pantheon, pp. 340–72.

——. 1997. "What Is Enlightenment?" In *Michel Foucault: Ethics, Essential Works, Vol. 1*, ed. Paul Rabinow. New York: New Press, pp. 303–20.

Fraser, Nancy. 1993. "The French Derrideans: Politicizing Deconstruction or Deconstructing the Political?" In *Working through Derrida*, ed. Gary B. Madison. Chicago: Northwestern University Press, pp. 51–76.

Frisby, David. 1972. "The Popper-Adorno Controversy: The Methodological Dispute in German Sociology." *Philosophy of Social Science* 2: 105–19.

Gadamer, Hans-Georg. 1975. "Hermeneutics and Social Science." *Cultural Hermeneutics* 2: 307–16.

——. 1976. "Hegel's 'Inverted World'." In *Hegel's Dialectic, Five Hermeneutical Studies*, trans. P. Christopher Smith. New Haven, CT: Yale University Press, pp. 35–53.

——. 1980. *Dialogue and Dialectics: Eight Hermeneutical Studies on Plato*. Trans. P. C. Smith. New Haven, CT: Yale University Press.

——. 1982. *Reason in the Age of Science*. Cambridge, MA: MIT Press.

——. 1987. *The Relevance of the Beautiful and Other Essays*. Trans. Nicholas Walker. Edited with an introduction by Robert Bernasconi. Cambridge: Cambridge University Press.

——. 2002. *Truth and Method*. Trans. Joel Weinsheimer and Donald G. Marshall. New York: Continuum.

Geuss, Raymond. 2005. "Suffering and Knowledge in Adorno." *Constellations* 12(1): 3–20.

Giddens, Anthony. 1976. *New Rules of Sociological Methods: A Positive Critique of Interpretive Sociologies*. London: Basic Books.

Gramsci, Antonio. 1971. *Selections from the Prison Notebooks*. Ed. Q. Hoare and G. Nowell Smith. New York: International Publishers.

Grunwald, Ernest. 1990. "The Sociology of Knowledge and Epistemology." In *Knowledge and Politics: The Sociology of Knowledge Dispute*, ed. Nico Stehr and Volker Meja. London: Routledge, pp. 261–6.

Guignon, Charles. 2002. "Truth in Interpretation: A Hermeneutic Approach." In *Is There a Single Right Interpretation?* ed. Michael Krausz. University Park, PA: Pennsylvania State University Press, pp. 264–84.

Gutting, Gary. 1984. "The Strong Program: A Dialogue." In *Scientific Rationality: The Sociological Turn*, ed. James Robert Brown. Boston, MA: D. Reidel, pp. 95–111.

Guyer, Paul. 1993. "Thought and Being: Hegel's Critique of Kant's Theoretical Philosophy." In *The Cambridge Companion to Hegel*, ed. Frederick C. Beiser. Cambridge: Cambridge University Press, pp. 171–210.

Guyer, Paul, and Allen Wood. 1998. "Introduction." In *Critique of Pure Reason* by Immanuel Kant, trans. and ed. Paul Guyer and Allen Wood. Cambridge: Cambridge University Press, pp. 1–171.

Habermas, Jurgen. 1968. *Knowledge and Human Interests.* Trans. Jeremy J. Shapiro. Boston, MA: Beacon Press.

——. 1971. "Technology and Science as 'Ideology'." In *Towards a Rational Society: Student Protest, Science, and Politics*. Trans. Jeremy J. Shapiro. Boston, MA: Beacon Press, pp. 81–122.

——. 1973. *Theory and Practice.* Trans. John Viertel. Boston, MA: Beacon Press.

——. 1976a. "Analytical Theory of Science and Dialectics." In *The Positivist Dispute in German Sociology*, ed. Theodor W. Adorno et al., trans. Glyn Adey and David Frisby. London: Heinemann, pp. 131–62.

——. 1976b. "A Positivistically Bisected Rationalism." In *The Positivist Dispute in German Sociology*, ed. Theodor W. Adorno et al., trans. Glyn Adey and David Frisby. London: Heinemann, pp. 198–225.

——. 1977. "A Review of Gadamer's Truth and Method." In *Understanding and Social Inquiry*, ed. Fred R. Dallmayr and Thomas McCarthy. Notre Dame, IN: University of Notre Dame Press, pp. 335–63.

——. 1981. *Reason and the Rationalization of Society.* Vol. 1 of *The Theory of Communicative Action*. Trans. Thomas McCarthy. Boston, MA: Beacon Press.

——. 1982. "The Entwinement of Myth and Enlightenment: Re-Reading Dialectic of Enlightenment." Trans. Thomas Y. Levin. *New German Critique* 26: 13–30.

——. 1987. *The Philosophical Discourse of Modernity: Twelve Lectures.* Trans. Frederick Lawrence. Cambridge, MA: MIT Press.

——. 1991. "An Intersubjectivist Concept of Individuality." *Journal of Chinese Philosophy* 18: 133–41.

Haddock, Adrian. 2004. "Rethinking the 'Strong Program' in the Sociology of Knowledge." *Studies in the History and Philosophy of Science* 35: 19–40.

Hall, Stuart. 1983. "The Problem of Ideology: Marxism without Guarantees." In *Marx, a Hundred Years On*, ed. Betty Matthews. Atlantic Highlands, NJ: Humanities Press, pp. 57–86.

Hanson, Russell. 1958. *Patterns of Discovery: An Inquiry into the Conceptual Foundation of Science.* Cambridge, MA: Cambridge University Press.

Harding, Sandra. 1991. *Whose Science? Whose Knowledge? Thinking from Women's Lives.* Ithaca, NY: Cornell University Press.

——. 1993. "Rethinking Standpoint Epistemology: Why Is Strong Objectivity?" In *Feminist Epistemologies*, ed. Linda Martin Alcoff and Elizabeth Potter. London: Routledge, pp. 49–82.

Harvey, David. 1996. "Dialectics." In *Justice, Nature and the Geography of Difference.* Oxford: Blackwell, pp. 46–68.

Hegel, G. W. F. 1974a. *Hegel: The Essential Writings*, edited with an introduction by F. G. Weiss. New York: Harper and Row.

——. 1974b. "Phenomenology of Spirit: Introduction." In *Hegel: The Essential Writings*, edited with an introduction by F. G. Weiss. New York: Harper and Row, pp. 225–52.

——. 1974c. "Understanding and Dialectic in *Science of Logic.*" In *Hegel: The Essential Writings*, edited with an introduction by F. G. Weiss. New York: Harper and Row, pp. 92–101.

——. 1977. *Phenomenology of Spirit.* Trans. A. V. Miller. Oxford: Oxford University Press.

——. 1982. *Reason in History: A General Introduction to the Philosophy of History*, translated with an introduction by Robert S. Hartman. Indianapolis, IN: Bobbs-Merrill.

Heidegger, Martin. 1962. *Being and Time.* Trans. John Macquarrie and Edward Robinson. New York: Harper and Row.

Hesse, Mary. 1980. *Revolution and Reconstruction in the Philosophy of Science.* Bloomington, IN: Indiana University Press.

Honneth, Axel. 1998. "Decentered Autonomy: The Subject after the Fall." In *Reinterpreting the Political: Continental Philosophy and Political Theory*, ed. Lenore Langsdorf and Stephen H. Smith. New York: State University of New York Press, pp. 197–208.

Horkheimer, Max. 1972a. "Materialism and Metaphysics." In *Critical Theory: Selected Essays*, trans. Matthew J. O'Connell et al. New York: Seabury Press, pp. 10–46.

——. 1972b. "Postscript." In *Critical Theory: Selected Essays*, trans. Matthew J. O'Connell et al. New York: Seabury Press, pp. 244–52.

——. 1972c. "The Social Function of Philosophy." In *Critical Theory: Selected Essays*, trans. Matthew J. O'Connell et al. New York: Seabury Press, pp. 253–72.

——. 1972d. "Traditional and Critical Theory." In *Critical Theory, Selected Essays*, trans. Matthew J. O'Connell et al. New York: Seabury Press, pp. 188–243.

——. 1974. *Eclipse of Reason.* New York: Continuum.

——. 1982. "The Authoritarian State." In *The Essential Frankfurt School Reader*, ed. Andrew Arato and Eike Gebhardt. New York: Continuum, pp. 95–118.

——. 1993a. "History and Psychology." In *Between Philosophy and Social Science: Selected Early Writings*, trans. G. Frederick Hunter, Matthew S. Kramer, and John Tropey. Cambridge, MA: MIT Press, pp. 111–28.

——. 1993b. "A New Concept of Ideology?" In *Between Philosophy and Social Science: Selected Early Writings*. Trans. G. Frederick Hunter, Matthew S. Kramer, and John Tropey. Cambridge, MA: MIT Press, pp. 129–50.

——. 1993c. "On the Problem of Truth." In *Between Philosophy and Social Science: Selected Early Writings*, trans. G. Frederick Hunter, Matthew S. Kramer, and John Tropey. Cambridge, MA: The MIT Press, pp. 177–215.

——. 1993d. "The Rationalism Debate in Contemporary Philosophy." In *Between Philosophy and Social Science: Selected Early Writings*, trans. G. Frederick Hunter, Matthew S. Kramer, and John Tropey. Cambridge, MA: MIT Press, pp. 217–64.

Horkheimer, Max, and Theodor Adorno. 1988. *Dialectic of Enlightenment*. Trans. John Cumming. New York: Continuum.

Hoyningen-Heune, Paul. 1987. "Context of Discovery and Context of Justification." In *Studies in History and Philosophy of Science* 18: 501–5.

Jaeggi, Pahel. 2005. "'No Individual Can Resist': *Minima Moralia* as Critique of Forms of Life." *Constellations* 12(1): 65–82.

Jameson, Fredric. 1972. "Introduction to T. W. Adorno." In *The Legacy of the German Refugee Intellectuals*, ed. Robert Boyers. New York: Schocken, pp. 140–3.

Jarvis, Simon. 2004. "Adorno, Marx, Materialism." In *The Cambridge Companion to Adorno*, ed. Tom Huhn. Cambridge: Cambridge University Press, pp. 79–100.

Jay, Martin. 1974. "The Frankfurt School's Critique of Karl Mannheim and the Sociology of Knowledge." *Telos* 20: 72–90.

——. 1977. "The Concept of Totality in Lukacs and Adorno." *Telos* 32: 117–36.

Kellner, Douglas. 1976. "Adorno's Social Theory." *Radical Philosopher's Newsjournal* 76: 31–43.

Kettler, David. 1967. "Sociology of Knowledge and Moral Philosophy: The Place of Traditional Problems in the Formation of Mannheim's Thought." *Political Science Quarterly* 82(3): 399–426.

Kohn, Jerome. 2000. "Freedom: The Priority of the Political." In *The Cambridge Companion to Hannah Arendt*, ed. Dana Villa. Cambridge: Cambridge University Press, pp. 113–29.

Kojeve, Alexander. 1980. *Introduction to the Reading of Hegel: Lectures on the Phenomenology of Spirit*, assembled by R. Queneau, trans. Jams H. Nicholos. Jr. Ithaca, NY: Cornell University Press.

Korsch, Karl. 1970. *Marxism and Philosophy*. Trans. Fred Halliday. New York: Monthly Review.

Kuhn, Thomas. 1977. "The Historical Structure of Scientific Discovery." In *The Essential Tension: Selected Studies in Scientific Tradition and Change*. Chicago, IL: University of Chicago Press, pp. 165–77.

Laclau, Ernesto. 1995. "The Time Is out of Joint." *Diacritics* 25(2): 85–96.

Laclau, Ernesto, and Chantal Mouffe. 1985. *Hegemony and Socialist Strategy: Towards a Radical Democratic Politics*. London: Verso.

Lakatos, Imre. 1970. "History of Science and Its Rational Reconstruction." *PSA: Proceedings of the Biennial Meeting of the Philosophy of Science Association* 70: 91–136.

Latour, Bruno. 2004. "Why Has Critique Run out of Steam? From Matters of Fact to Matters of Concern." *Critical Inquiry* 30(2): 225–48.

Laudan, Larry. 1981. "The Pseudo-Science of Science?" *Philosophy of Social Sciences* 11: 173–98.

——. 1988. "Are All Theories Equally Good? A Dialogue." In *Relativism and Realism in Science*, ed. Robert Nola. Boston, MA: Kluwer Academic Publishers, pp. 117–39.

Levins, Richard, and Richard Lewontin. 1985. *The Dialectical Biologist*. Cambridge, MA: Harvard University Press.

Levinas, Emmanuel. 1969. *Totality and Infinity*. Trans. A. Lingis. Pittsburgh, PA: Duquesne University Press, pp. 47–59.

——. 1981. *Otherwise Than Being or Beyond Essence*. Trans. Alphonso Lingis. Boston, MA: Nijhoff.

——. 1987. "Philosophy and the Idea of Infinite." In *Collected Philosophical Papers*, trans. Alphonso Lingis. Boston, MA: Nijhoff, pp. 47–59.

——. 1996. "Transcendence and Height." In *Emmanuel Levinas: Basic Philosophical Writings*, ed. Adriaan T. Peperzak, Simon Critcheley, and Robert Bernasconi. Bloomington, IN: Indiana University Press, pp. 11–32.

Lloyd, Elizabeth. 1995. "Objectivity and the Double Standard for Feminist Epistemologies." *Syntheses* 104: 351–81.

Lohmann, Georg. 1993. "The Failure of Self-Realization: An Interpretation of Horkheimer's Eclipse of Reason." In *On Max Horkheimer, New Perspectives*, ed. Sheyla Benhabib et al. Cambridge, MA: MIT Press, pp. 387–413.

Longino, Helen. 1997. "Feminist Epistemology as a Local Epistemology." *Proceedings of the Aristotelian Society* 71: 19–35.

——. 1999. "Feminist Epistemology." In *The Blackwell Guide to Epistemology*, ed. J Greco and E. Sosa. Oxford: Blackwell.

——. 2002. *The Fate of Knowledge*. Princeton: Princeton University Press.

Love, Nancy. 1987. "Epistemology and Exchange: Marx, Nietzsche, and Critical Theory." *New German Critique* 41: 71–94.

Lowy, Michael. 2001. "Messianism in the Early Work of Greshom Scholem." *New German Critique* 38: 177–91.

Lucy, Niall. 2004. *A Derrida Dictionary*. Oxford: Blackwell.

Lukacs, Georg. 1971. *History and Class Consciousness*. Trans. Rodney Livingstone. Cambridge, MA: MIT Press.

Lyotard, Jean-Francois. 1984. *The Postmodern Condition: A Report on Knowledge*. Trans. Geoff Bennington and Brian Massumi. Minneapolis: University of Minnesota Press.

——. 1988. *The Differend: Phrases in Dispute*. Trans. Georges Van Den Abbeele. Minneapolis, MN: University of Minnesota Press.

Lyotard, Jean-Francois, and Jean-Loup Thebaud. 1989. *Just Gaming*. Trans. Wlad Godzich. Minneapolis, IN: University of Minnesota Press.

MacIntyre, Alasdair. 1977. "Is Understanding a Religion Compatible with Believing?" In *Rationality: Key Concepts in the Social Sciences*, ed. Bryan R. Wilson. Oxford: Blackwell, pp. 62–77.

——. 1995. "Notes from the Moral Wilderness." In *The MacIntyre Reader*, ed. Kelvin Knight. Indiana: University of Notre Dame Press, pp. 31–52.

Mannheim, Karl. 1952a. "Historicism." In *Essays on the Sociology of Knowledge*, ed. Paul Kecskemeti. London: Routledge and Kegan Paul, pp. 84–133.

——. 1952b. "The Problem of the Sociology of Knowledge." In *Essays on the Sociology of Knowledge*, ed. Paul Kecskemeti. London: Routledge and Kegan Paul, pp. 134–90.

——. 1956a. "The Democratization of Culture." In *Essays on the Sociology of Culture*, with a new preface by Bryan S. Turner. London: Routledge and Kegan Paul, pp. 171–247.

——. 1956b. "The Problem of the Intelligentsia: An Inquiry into Its Past and Present Role." In *Essays on the Sociology of Culture*, with a new preface by Bryan S. Turner. London: Routledge and Kegan Paul, pp. 91–170.

——. 1968. *Ideology and Utopia: An Introduction to the Sociology of Knowledge*. Trans. Louis Wirth and Edward Shils. New York: Harvest.

——. 1976. *Essays on the Sociology of Culture*. Oxford: Oxford University Press.

Mannheim, Karl. 1990. "The Ideological and Sociological Interpretation of Intellectual Phenomena." In *Knowledge and Politics: The Sociology of Knowledge Dispute*, ed. Volker Meja and Nico Stehr. London: Routledge, pp. 37–50.

Marcuse, Herbert. 1951. *Reason and Revolution: Hegel and the Rise of Social Theory.* New York: Humanities Press.

——. 1968. "Philosophy and Critical Theory." In *Negations, Essays in Critical Theory.* Boston, MA: Beacon, pp. 134–58.

——. 1969. *An Essay on Liberation.* Boston, MA: Beacon Press.

——. 1990. "The Sociological Method and the Problem of Truth." In *Knowledge and Politics: The Sociology of Knowledge Dispute*, ed. V. Meja and N. Stehr. London: Routledge, pp. 129–39.

Marsh, James. 1990. "The Play of Difference/Différance in Hegel and Derrida." *The Owl of Minerva: Quarterly Journal of the Hegel Society of America* 21(2): 145–53.

Marx, Karl. 1967. *Capital.* Vol. 1. London: Lawrence and Wishart.

——. 1971. *Theories of Surplus-Value.* Part 3, vol. 4 of *Capital.* Moscow: Progress Publishers.

——. 1972a. "*Capital*: Selections." In *The Marx-Engels Reader*, ed. Robert C. Tucker. New York: Norton, pp. 191–318.

——. 1972b. "The Eighteenth Brumaire of Louis Bonaparte." In *The Marx-Engels Reader*, ed. Robert C. Tucker. New York: Norton, pp. 436–525.

——. 1972c. "The German Ideology: Part 1." In *The Marx-Engels Reader*, ed. Robert C. Tucker. New York: Norton, pp. 110–66.

——. 1972d. "Selections from Economic and Philosophic Manuscripts of 1844." In *The Marx-Engels Reader*, ed. Robert C. Tucker. New York: Norton, pp. 51–103.

——. 1972e. "Theses on Feuerbach." In *The Marx-Engels Reader*, ed. Robert C. Tucker. New York: Norton, pp. 107–9.

——. 1973. "General Introduction." In *Grundrisse.* Harmondsworth, UK: Penguin Books.

——. 1975. "Letter to Annenkov, December 28, 1846." In *Appendices to The Poverty of Philosophy.* Moscow: Progress Publication.

——. 1986. "Letter to Ruge, September 1843." In *Collected Works of Marx and Engels, Vol. 1, 1835–1843.* New York: International Publishers, pp. 398–9.

——. 1997. *Writings of the Young Marx on Philosophy and Society.* Ed. and trans. Loyd David Easton and Kurt H. Guddat. Indianapolis: Hackett.

Marx, Karl, and Frederick Engels. 1972. "Manifesto of the Communist Party." In *The Marx-Engels Reader*, ed. Robert C. Tucker. New York: Norton, pp. 469–500.

McCarthy, Thomas. 1988. "Scientific Rationality and the 'Strong Program' in the Sociology of Knowledge." In *Construction and Constraint: The Shaping of Scientific Rationality*, ed. Ernan McMullin. Indiana: University of Notre Dame Press, pp. 75–95.

McCumber, John. 1996. "Time in the Ditch: American Philosophy and the McCarthy Era." *Diacritics* 26(1): 33–49.

Meja, Volker, and Nico Stehr. 1988. "Social Science, Epistemology and the Problem of Relativism." *Social Epistemology* 2(3): 263–71.

——. 1990. "Relativism and the Sociology of Knowledge." In *Knowledge and Politics: The Sociology of Knowledge Dispute*, ed. Nico Stehr and Volker Meja. London: Routledge, pp. 285–306.

Michelfelder, Diane. 1989. "Derrida and the Ethics of the Ear." In *The Question of the Other: Essays in Contemporary Continental Philosophy*, ed. Arleen B. Dallery and Charles E. Scott. Albany, NY: SUNY Press, pp. 47–54.

Mignolo, Walter. 2000. "Dussel's Philosophy of Liberation: Ethics and the Geopolitics of Knowledge." In *Thinking from the Underside of History: Enrique Dussel's Philosophy of Liberation*, ed. Linda M. Alcoff and Eduardo Mendieta. New York: Rowman and Littlefield, pp. 27–50.

Miliband, Ralph. 1977. *Marxism and Politics*. Oxford: Oxford University Press.

Nagele, Rainer. 1986. "The Scene of the Other: Theodor W. Adorno's Negative Dialectic in the Context of Poststructuralism." In *Postmodernism and Politics*, ed. Jonathan Arac. Minnesota, MN: University of Minnesota Press, pp. 91–111.

Nietzsche, Friedrich. 1979. "On Truth and Lies in a Nonmoral Sense." In *Philosophy and Truth: Selections from Nietzsche's Notebooks of the Early 1870s*. Tran. D. Breazeale. Atlantic Highlands, NJ: Humanities Press, pp. 79–97.

Nola, Robert. 1988. "Introduction: Some Issues Concerning Relativism and Realism in Science." In *Relativism and Realism in Science*, ed. Robert Nola. Boston, MA: Kluwer Academic Publishers, pp. 1–35.

——. 1990. "The Strong Programme for the Sociology of Science: Reflexivity and Relativism." *Inquiry* 33: 273–96.

O'Connor, Brian. 1994. "Adorno's Dialectical Epistemology." *Idealistic Studies* 24(1): 61–76.

——. 1998. "Adorno, Heidegger and the Critique of Epistemology." *Philosophy and Social Criticism* 24(4): 43–62.

——. 2000. Introduction to the *Adorno Reader*, ed. Brian O'Connor. Oxford: Blackwell, pp. 1–20.

Ollman, Bertell. 1971. *Alienation: Marx's Conception of Man in Capitalist Society*. Cambridge: Cambridge University Press.

——. 1990. "Putting Dialectics to Work: The Process of Abstraction in Marx's Method." *Rethinking Marxism* 3(1): 26–47.

——. 1993. *Dialectical Investigations*. New York: Routledge.

Okasha, Samir. 2000. "The Underdetermination of Theory by Data and the Strong Programme in the Sociology of Knowledge." *International Studies in the Philosophy of Science* 14(3): 283–97.

O'Murchadha, Flix. 1992. "Truth as a Problem for Hermeneutics: Towards a Hermeneutical Theory of Truth." *Philosophy Today* 34(2): 122–31.

Peperzak, Adriaan. 1993. *To the Other: An Introduction to the Philosophy of Emmanuel Levinas*. West Lafayette, IN: Purdue University Press.

Pettit, Philip. 1988. "The Strong Sociology of Knowledge without Relativism." In *Relativism and Realism in Science*, ed. Robert Nola. Boston, MA: Kluwer Academic Publishers, pp. 81–91.

Plato. 1994. *Republic*. Loeb Classical Library. Trans. Paul Shorey. Cambridge, MA: Harvard University Press.

Popper, Karl. 1959. *The Logic of Scientific Discovery*. New York: Basic Books.

Potter, Elizabeth. 1994. "Locke's Epistemology and Women's Struggles." In *Modern Engendering: Critical Feminist Readings in Modern Western Philosophy*, ed. Bat-Ami bar On. New York: SUNY Press, pp. 27–50.

Prado, Plinio Walder, Jr. 1991. "The Necessity of Contingency: Remarks on Linkage." *L'esprit createur* 31(1): 90–106.

Quine, Willard Van Orman. 1964. "Two Dogmas of Empiricism." In *From a Logical Point of View*. New York: Harper and Row, pp. 20–46.

Railton, Peter. 2000. "Normative Forces and Normative Freedom: Hume and Kant, but Not Hume *versus* Kant." In *Normativity*, ed. Jonathan Dancy. Oxford: Blackwell, pp. 1–33.

Ricoeur, Paul. 1981. *Hermeneutics and the Human Sciences: Essays on Language, Action and Interpretation*. Trans. and ed. John B. Thompson. Cambridge: Cambridge University Press.

Rehg, William. 2000. "Critical Science as Argumentative Theory: Who is Afraid of SSK?" *Philosophy of social Sciences* 30(1): 33–48.

Rogozinski, Jacob. 1991. "Lyotard, Differend, Presence." *L'esprit createur* 31(1): 107–21.

Rorty, Richard. 1989. *Contingency, Irony and Solidarity*. Cambridge: Cambridge University Press.

——. 1996. "Wittgenstein, Heidegger and the Reification of Language." In *Essays on Heidegger and Others: Volume 2: Philosophical Papers*. Cambridge: Cambridge University Press, pp. 50–65.

Rosen, Michael. 1982. *Hegel's Dialectic and Its Criticism*. Cambridge: Cambridge University Press.

Rosenzweig, Franz. 1998. "The New Thinking: Philosophy and Religion." In *Franz Rosenzweig: His Life and Thought*, ed. Nahum N. Glatzer. Indianapolis, IN: Hackett, pp. 179–213.

Rush, Fred. 2004. "Conceptual Foundations of Early Critical Theory." In *The Cambridge Companion to Critical Theory*, ed. Fred Rush. Cambridge: Cambridge University Press, pp. 6–39.

Sayer, Derek. 1979. *Marx's Method: Ideology, Science and Critique in Capital*. Atlantic Highlands, NJ: Humanities Press.

——. 1987. *The Violence of Abstraction: The Analytic Foundation of Historical Materialism*. Oxford: Blackwell.

Sayer, Derek, and David Frisby. 1986. *Society*. London: Tavistock.

Sayers, Sean. 1985. "The Unity of Appearance and Reality." In *Reality and Reason: Dialectic and the Theory of Knowledge*. Oxford: Blackwell, pp. 32–49.

Schelkshorn, Hans. 2000. "Discourse and Liberation: Towards a Critical Coordination of Discourse Ethics and Dussel's Ethics of Liberation." In *Thinking from the Underside of History: Enrique Dussel's Philosophy of Liberation*, ed. Linda M. Alcoff and Eduardo Mendieta. New York: Rowman and Littlefield, pp. 97–117.

Schmaus, Warren. 1985. "Reasons, Causes, and the 'Strong Programme' in the Sociology of Knowledge." *Philosophy of Social Sciences* 15: 189–96.

Schmidt, Burghart. 1974. "The Political Nature of Epistemological Categories: Introduction to Bloch." *Telos* 21: 87–95.

Schmitt, Richard. 1987. *Introduction to Marx and Engels: A Critical Reconstruction*. London: West View.

Schott, Robin May. 1988. "Morality and Fetishism." In *Cognition and Eros: A Critique of the Kantian Paradigm*. Boston, MA: Beacon Press, pp. 137–48.

Scott, John. 1988. "Relationism, Cubism and the Reality: Beyond Relativism." In *Knowing the Social World*, ed. T. Mary and M. Williams. Buckingham, UK: Open University Press, pp. 103–19.

Sewart, John. 1978. "Verstehen and Dialectic: Epistemology and Methodology in Weber and Lukacs." *Philosophy and Social Criticism* 3–4: 321–66.

Sherratt, Yvonne. 2001. *Adorno's Positive Dialectic.* Cambridge: Cambridge University Press.

Slaughter, Cliff. 1963. *Lenin on Dialectics: An Introduction to the Philosophical Notebooks of Lenin.* London: New Park Publications.

Sluga, Hans. 2008. "The Pluralism of the Political: From Carl Schmitt to Hannah Arendt." *Telos* 142(1): 91–109.

Smith, Christopher. 1975. "Gadamer on Language and Method in Hegel's Dialectics." *Graduate Faculty Philosophy Journal, Philosophy Department, New School* 5: 53–72.

Solomon, Robert. 1983. *In the Spirit of Hegel: A Study of G. W. F. Hegel's Phenomenology of Spirit.* Oxford: Oxford University Press.

Taylor, Charles. 1975. *Hegel.* Cambridge: Cambridge University Press.

——. 1979. "The Validity of Transcendental Argument." *Proceedings of Aristotelian Society* 79: 151–67.

——. 1993. "Engaged Agency and Background in Heidegger." In *The Cambridge Companion to Heidegger*, ed. Charles B. Guignon. Cambridge: Cambridge University Press, pp. 317–36.

——. 1995. "Overcoming Epistemology." In *Philosophical Arguments.* Cambridge, MA: Harvard University Press, pp. 1–19.

Thompson, E. P. 1963. *The Making of the English Working Class.* Harmondsworth, UK: Penguin Books.

Tsetung, Mao. 1971. *Selected Reading from Mao Tsetung.* Peking: Foreign Language Press.

Wachterhauser, Brice. 2002. "Getting It Right: Relativism, Realism and Truth." In *The Cambridge Companion to Gadamer*, ed. Robert J. Dostal. Cambridge: Cambridge University Press, pp. 52–78.

Warnke, Georgia. 2002. "Hermeneutics, Ethics and Politics." In *The Cambridge Companion to Gadamer*, ed. Robert J. Dostal. Cambridge: Cambridge University Press, pp. 79–101.

Weinsheimer, Joel. 1985. *Gadamer's Hermeneutics: A Reading of Truth and Method.* New Haven, CT: Yale University Press.

Weinsheimer, Joel, and Donald Marshall. 2002. "Translators' Preface." In *Truth and Method*, by Hans-Georg Gadamer, trans. Joel Weinsheimer and Donald G. Marshall. New York: Continuum, pp. 11–21.

Wilson, H. T. 1983. "Technology and Late Capitalist Society: Reflections on the Problem of Rationality and Social Organization." In *The State, Class and the Recession*, ed. Stewart Clegg, Geoff Dow, and Paul Boreham. London: Croom Helm, pp. 152–238.

Wittgenstein, Ludwig. 1974. *Tractatus Logico-Philosophicus.* Trans. D. F. Pears and B. F. McGuinness. London: Routledge and Kegan Paul.

Wolding, Henk. 1986. *Karl Mannheim: The Development of His Thought; Philosophy, Sociology and Social Ethics, with a Detailed Biography.* New York: St. Martin's.

Wolf, Kirk. 2000. "Nietzsche's Genealogical Critique." *Philosophy Today* 44(4): 404–14.

Wood, Allen. 1981. *Karl Marx.* London: Routledge and Kegan Paul.

Wood, Ellen Meiksins. 1999. *The Origins of Capitalism.* New York: Monthly Review Press.

Zimmerman, Robert. 1982. "Hegel's 'Inverted World' Revisited." *Philosophical Forum* 13(4): 342–70.

Index